BEHIND
PALACE
DOORS

Nigel Dempster
&
Peter Evans

ORION

First published in Great Britain in 1993
Orion

The Orion Publishing Group Ltd
Orion House,
5 Upper Saint Martin's Lane,
London, WC2 9EA.

Copyright © 1993 Pinebray Ltd and Peter Evans

All rights reserved. No part of this publication may be
reproduced, stored in a retrieval system, or transmitted in
any form or by any means, electronic, mechanical,
photocopying, recording, or otherwise, without the prior
permission of the copyright owner

Nigel Dempster and Peter Evans have asserted their moral
right to be identified as the authors of this work

A catalogue reference is available from the British Library

ISBN 1 857 97254 6

Filmset in Janson by Selwood Systems, Midsomer Norton
Printed in Great Britain by Butler & Tanner Ltd,
Frome and London

Contents

Illustrations appear between pages 152 and 153

Acknowledgements

Acknowledgements in any book about the British royal family must be guarded: the more informed the book, the more circumspect must be the recognition of those who have helped the most. It is not a satisfactory arrangement, it is often hugely frustrating, but these are the only conditions under which a book of this kind can be written. If at times the system seems unfair to the royal family it must be remembered that it is the royal family itself that has laid down the rules, and plays exactly the same game with its unattributable Palace briefings. When 'sources close to Prince Charles,' 'Palace aides,' 'aides' or 'a friend of the Queen Mother' are sometimes members of the royal family itself, or their spokespersons, it becomes a tangled web indeed. Nevertheless, although few can be named, a great number of people went out of their way to assist us.

From Nigel Dempster: My special thanks for their assistance in aiding the accuracy of this book to Lady Caroline Percy, Michael Colborne, the Hon Nicholas Soames, MP, Lord Beaverbrook, Lord Charles Spencer-Churchill, Charles and Carolyn Benson, Rupert Hambro, Simon Parker Bowles, Earl Spencer, Kevin Burke, Sir William Pigott-Brown, the Earl of Lichfield, Frank Lowe, Ronnie Driver, Luis Sosa Basualdo, and John Bryan. Also, thanks to my assistant, Melanie Johnson.

From Peter Evans: To none am I personally more indebted than to John and Lynette Pearson, whose encouragement and affection were above price. Lady Nonnie Campbell, Raymond Hawkey, Bill

Edwards, Christine Walker, William Pratt, John Michel, Yoko Tani, Norma Quine, Leslie Linder, Kate Morris, Brian Wells, Jeanne Hunter, Michael Baumohl, Maureen Conway, Norma Heyman, Joan Cotton, Tania Mallet Radcliff, Andrew Nurnberg and, of course, Ed Victor came through in every way. I certainly have to thank Camilla and Clementine, who were always ready with advice, assistance and occasional hugs. Many of the interviews were taped, involving weeks of transcription. Much of this gruelling work was done as always with dedication and reassuring fascination by my secretary Lisa Jane P. Special thanks as always to my personal assistant Pamela Shuard for her priceless help. Finally, and not for the first time, for watching over me, and this book, from start to finish, I thank my wife, Pamela.

LONDON

MAY, 1993

Introduction

'Whose side are you on, Mummy?' Charles demanded plaintively at one stage of the harrowing and at times acrimonious debate on Sunday, 17 January 1993, at Sandringham, the royal retreat in Norfolk. He probably had cause to wonder. His mother's devotion to the institution of the Crown was consummate. Even as a mother, she found it hard to find any ameliorating words for the harm Charles had clearly done to the monarchy by his now horrifyingly public relationship with Camilla Parker Bowles, whose husband Andrew was one of her own courtiers, her Silver Stick in Waiting. Inevitably, this caused friction and misunderstandings. 'When Charles talked about the future, he was essentially talking about his own future,' says a close friend of the family who had heard accounts of the family summit at Sandringham from both Charles and his father. 'When the Queen talked about the future, she was talking about the monarchy itself.'

If it was impossible to sense at all what the Queen was feeling ('Even when she tells you what she thinks, you never know what she feels,' says a friend), Prince Philip was the opposite. The man who by virtue of his experience should calmly have taken charge simply lost his temper with everybody, his voice becoming more angry and adenoidal with every syllable he uttered. To be fair, the notion that his son's intimate, mildly dirty and decidedly unprincely telephone conversations with a married woman would not only be taped but splashed across newspapers around the world was good reason for ire. Yet perhaps part of that anger, suggests a royal staffer who understands him well, was the realization of just how far both he and the Queen had gone wrong as parents. 'I think they both felt guilty. In that, at least, they shared the same conscience.'

But as a royal father it must have been especially painful. For it meant that his very *raison d'être* had been destroyed. 'When you strip it right down, his prime duty to the family had been to produce a viable male heir to the throne – and at that moment even that achievement seemed to be in the balance.'

Faced with the awesome reserve of his mother and the fury of his father, not to mention the disgusting mix of ridicule and condemnation emanating from the press, the Prince of Wales arrived at Sandringham, according to one source, in a mood of pessimism and despair. According to another source, his desperation was palpable as the family grimly gathered to see what, if anything, could be done. 'A man far more confident of himself than Prince Charles has ever been would have been shaken by the events of that week. He was under attack from so many sides, and for so many reasons,' says one of his friends, putting in yet another interpretation on his mood that weekend. 'But he was resolute, realistic and thoughtful.'

Criticized by his mother, the Prince became angry. Attacked by his father, he found his mood turning to defiance. 'Defiance was something the Queen Mother could build on,' said one of her own aides, who had made a private study of the way she operates.

And so for the first time during that long and difficult Sunday, old Queen Elizabeth spoke up. Perhaps it had taken her time to overcome her own anger and her disappointment in her favourite grandson. Like the Queen, she had not read the excerpts of his outpourings to Mrs Parker Bowles and she said she never would. But it was an article of faith in the British creed, she said, that if a man is born a prince, he must be credited with a kind of moral stature. Charles had made serious mistakes in the conduct of his private life. Women particularly did not like the way he had behaved. But he was fundamentally a good man, and the British people knew that. They knew he was sincere and dedicated. Now, she said, he must prove to the people that he had courage, too. His final problem had been brought out in the open. Now he must work for the people's forgiveness – then he might become more popular than he had ever been.

They were words of consolation, but words of warning too.

BOOK ONE

Chapter One

The crisis that threatened the backbone of the monarchy itself had begun shortly before 6.15 a.m. on Wednesday, 13 January 1993 – 'Black Wednesday', as the royal family came to call it. A junior currency dealer in the City of London, the UK's financial hub, paid twenty-five pounds to a man on the Australian desk for the first unexpurgated transcript of the intimate bedtime conversation between the Prince of Wales and the forty-five-year-old wife of his friend Brigadier Andrew Parker Bowles of the Household Cavalry. By 6.45 a.m., people were lining up to fax their copies to friends and colleagues around the world.

'I knew that, whether the British press had the will to publish them or not, the transcripts had become the biggest *samizdat**
operation outside Russia,' the junior trader would say later. 'I thought, "This is the conversation that will stop Prince Charles becoming king." I knew that all hell was going to break loose.'

Shortly before seven o'clock that morning Sir Robert Fellowes, the Queen's private secretary, her closest adviser – and, married to the former Lady Jane Spencer, also the Princess of Wales's brother-in-law – got the news. He immediately called the Palace press secretary, Charles Anson. Anson said that he was perfectly aware of the situation, and had been fielding media enquiries since midnight.

* Underground publishing

'What are you telling them?' asked Sir Robert.

'We are telling them quite firmly, "No comment,"' Anson, a former diplomat, told him wryly.

Both men knew that it was a delicate and dangerous situation. Only a few months earlier when a similar tape of a conversation between the Princess of Wales and her friend James Gilbey had surfaced, the Palace first of all told journalists privately that it was a fake. Later, when the tape's authenticity became evident, they issued a statement in which they declined to recognize it but refused to dismiss it. Now for the second time in six months they were in the same no-win game they had been in with the Dianagate tape.

'No comment is very wise,' said Sir Robert, smiling grimly.

He next called Commander Richard Aylard, the Prince's private secretary.

The two men walked a fine line between the interests of the Queen and those of the man who would be king. Although disturbed by the news from the City, neither Fellowes nor Aylard was surprised. Indeed, in a sense they were almost relieved. For it had been like a Sword of Damocles hanging over them since Andrew Knight, chief executive of Rupert Murdoch's News International, in an article in the *Spectator* in July 1992, had claimed that the newspaper group had refrained from using highly damaging material about the royal family and that sensational items were locked in a safe in his London office.

Time went by and nothing more was heard of the items ticking away inside Knight's safe; Palace aides, who had feared that Murdoch planned to sit on what they had and leak it piecemeal as part of a sly republican campaign, began to relax. It was not until November, when the *Daily Mirror* revealed that it too possessed a tape of an 'intimate phone call' between the Prince and Mrs Camilla Parker Bowles, that the real scale of the problem became clear.

Although the *Mirror*, showing self-restraint unusual for a British tabloid, drew the line at printing an actual transcript, it implied that the contents were infinitely raunchier and more scandalous than the Dianagate tape published three months earlier, which revealed that the Princess of Wales had an admirer (who called her 'Squidgy') to whom she poured out her most private and romantic thoughts.

Fellowes and Aylard examined the new development that January morning. It was an eventuality they had discussed many times since Andrew Knight's revelation the previous summer. 'As soon as they discovered that the tabloids had the tape, Charles was out on the end of a plank – the only question was how long he would stand there before they made him jump,' said a senior Palace aide. One consolation for the Palace was that publication of the tape would follow, and not precede, the December announcement of the royal couple's separation.

The two courtiers had been informed the previous Friday of the imminent Australian publication of the first full transcript, but they now recognized as perhaps no one in the family would the significance of what was happening in the City of London. As the fax machines and photocopiers worked overtime, things were moving too fast; it was now a problem that could not be contained. Nor could it be kept from British readers, as the story of the Prince of Wales and Mrs Simpson, the last great royal scandal, had been kept from them in the 1930s.

The *Mirror* and Murdoch's *Sun* were unlikely to hold back much longer. And, even as the Palace men talked, Britain's international news agency Reuters, America's AP and France's AFP were releasing extracts to newspapers, to TV and radio stations and to business subscribers around the world; more extensive excerpts were being quoted on Ireland's state-backed radio service RTE, which could be picked up all over Britain.

The private secretaries agreed that they would each inform their 'principals' of the situation that morning, no later than midday. Some time between 8.00 and 8.30 Aylard talked to the Prince, who was visiting the Shetland Islands to commiserate with the islanders over the *Braer* tanker disaster, which had spilled 85,000 tonnes of crude oil on to its shores. He advised the Prince bluntly that the situation in London did not look good and, in his opinion, could become 'extremely tricky'. He told the Prince to be prepared for a national publication of the tape, probably within forty-eight hours.

The tape had also been hanging over Prince Charles since the summer. He had vetoed injunctions banning publication in the UK because of the intense pressure legal action would put on Mrs Parker Bowles, who was already suffering understandable emotional stress. Publication would be an ordeal but also a tremendous release, and he assured Aylard that he was ready for the public response – 'and its judgement'.

But curiously it seems that Mrs Parker Bowles, an obvious media target, was not forewarned of the worrying activity in the City that morning. ('How would you have reached her? By *telephone?*' asked an aide in the Prince's private office.) On hearing the news from a journalist, she cried out, 'I can't believe it, I can't believe it. I must speak to my husband, he is on his way home.'

Fellowes waited until ten o'clock before he contacted the Queen, who was at Sandringham for the long Christmas vacation, and explained as factually and calmly as he could the events taking place in the City of London. She listened quietly, then said, 'And just when we thought things couldn't get any worse, Robert ...'

Nineteen-ninety-two had been her *annus horribilis*: the year of the 'Squidgy' tapes, in which the Princess of Wales engaged in some dirty talk with James Gilbey, described as a man-about-town; the year that had seen publication of Andrew Morton's best-selling book, *Diana, Her True Story*, detailing her depression, her bulimia, her suicide attempts (velvet ropes now kept gawkers off the Sandringham staircase down which she was said to have flung herself) and her estrangement from the Prince; the year when Princess Anne had been divorced; the year of the break-up of the marriage of the Duke and Duchess of York and of the publication of pictures of the Duchess frolicking topless in the South of France with her 'financial adviser', John Bryan of Houston, Texas. And it ended no better than it began, with the Queen herself agreeing to pay income tax. Then Windsor Castle went up in flames.

The Queen felt personally betrayed. People who saw her at Sandringham in those days remember her sense of sorrow. She had succumbed to a despair as if somebody in the family had died. It had been a sad Christmas, a bad New Year. There seemed no end to it. Prince Edward called the atmosphere 'funereal'. The spectre of the absent Princess of Wales, who was with her brother and sisters at the Spencer family home Althorp, still loomed large. The Queen had been accused of selfishly parting her from her sons William and Harry for the holiday. 'It was like an accusation pressed into my mother's heart,' said Prince Charles loyally, although he knew her tactics well, and knew that the indictment was true enough.

The family was split as the royal family had never been split before.

The Duchess of York, the irrepressible Fergie, with Bea and Eugenie, had been given nearby Wood Farm for the holiday so that Prince Andrew could spend some time with his daughters; but she was not invited to the big house, nor had she been asked to attend the traditional Christmas Day church service with the royal family.

Diana had never felt comfortable at Sandringham. She once told Charles that it was a place in which old kings could lie in state in comfort. But, of all the royal family homes, Sandringham was considered to be the Windsors' most 'homely'. With her younger sister, Margaret, the Queen had spent many of her happiest child-hood times there, and perhaps it was the memories of that distant past that made the present so particularly poignant for the Queen, for she was experiencing her irreparable sense of loss in the absence of Princess Margaret.

Oppressed by the unhappy atmosphere, Margaret had made an early exit to celebrate the New Year in Oxfordshire with friends Anouska Hempel and her husband Sir Mark Weinberg, only to col-lapse and be rushed to a London hospital a few days later, suffer-ing from pneumonia. The affection between the sisters was still the affection of two girls (although Margaret Rose had always been jealous of Elizabeth as a child, and even later) and the Queen's anxiety for her little sister must have been filled with nostalgia, too. Once the prettiest, the sexiest and the most romantic member of the royal circus, Margaret had become, at sixty-two, beaten, difficult and bitter, entrenched in her grand apartments at the north end of the royal residence of Kensington Palace, 'doing her best', as one of her younger royal neighbours once put it, 'to make us all feel guilty for enjoying ourselves'. But her life, she had told her friends that New Year's Eve, as she reflected on all the broken royal marriages around her at Sandringham, would have been quite another matter if she had been allowed to marry Peter Townsend, the man she had loved forty years before when divorce was still considered a royal catastrophe.

By the time 'Black Wednesday' arrived with all its horrors, the New Year was already beginning to feel far worse than anything that had happened to the Queen in 1992 or ever before. This scandal, soon to be dubbed Camillagate by the tabloid press, directly involved the Prince of Wales, her son and the heir to the throne.

At that stage, the Queen had no notion of what the tape might contain but she had clearly gathered from Sir Robert's bleak expression that it would not be any more agreeable to her than the content of the embarrassing Squidgy tape, the transcripts of which she still refused to read. She asked whether Commander Aylard knew about the activity in the City and whether he had informed the Prince. When Sir Robert told her that he had discussed the situation with Aylard and that the Prince would be told that morning, she thanked him and said that he was to do nothing more. The matter was not to be referred to until the Prince of Wales chose to bring it up with her personally.

'How can it all have gone so wrong so quickly?' Prince Charles asked again and again after Richard Aylard had broken the news to him on that January day. Although he had been expecting it for months, when it came it proved more shocking than he had ever imagined. 'How can it all have gone so wrong so quickly?' he repeated hopelessly, of no one in particular.

'He had great need of reassurance. Wouldn't anyone in that kind of situation?' asked one of the friends he summoned to the royal retreat in Norfolk, bought by his great-great grandfather King Edward VII while he was Prince of Wales himself in the 1870s.

Charles's nerves were already frayed by the stress and bitterness of his endless battle with his wife – and the haggling which had started since their separation. Now to have this final humiliation of every word of the Camillagate tapes made public was too great for him to bear, although it would not be until the following weeks when he found himself back in his office at St James's Palace that the full reality would strike him and he would actually break down in tears.

At the moment the real damage seemed to be not to his reputation but to his pride. For he genuinely believed that he had dedicated his life to the service of his country – and because of this one random stroke of fate he had been made to seem a laughing stock. His only consolation came, not from his family, but from his private guru, the writer Sir Laurens van der Post, who had told him that 'a private humbling could be good for the soul'. Van der Post added that it was not the end of the world, nor of the monarchy.

But tensions at the most senior level of the Palace were aggravated when it was discovered that the Queen Mother, who had already washed her hands of her own protégée, the Princess of Wales, was now openly and seriously criticizing her favourite grandson's behaviour.

Her anger had been predictable, of course. She had seen it all before: the Windsor men had a dangerous weakness for strong and sensual women. A divorce by Charles and Diana would be the biggest blow to the monarchy since Edward VIII had abdicated in 1930 to marry the American divorcee Wallis Simpson.

The traumatic legacy left by that long-ago event continued to cast its shadow across the whole family. And, even after the outbreak of this new Windsor crisis, the memory of the first retained its hold on the Queen Mother's mind. Her anger, according to one of her own ladies-in-waiting, was 'of a kind she used to keep to express her opinions of the Duchess of Windsor'.

On the next day, Thursday, the nightmare Aylard and Fellowes had been fearing came to pass, and the press around the world picked up the story. By six o'clock, according to the Palace's own count, it had made front page news in fifty-three countries. But far more worrying than the international tally was a report that several British papers were planning to publish the full text on Sunday, 17 January.

It is not clear when the Duke of Edinburgh first learned about the existence of the tape. Although the Queen's private secretary had a cup of tea every morning with the Duke's private secretary, Brian McGrath, a habit that enabled the two courtiers informally to exchange information of interest to their principals, the subject of Mrs Parker Bowles seems to have been diplomatically avoided.

According to one senior staffer in the Duke's eleven-strong private office, this would not have been a simple oversight. 'Charles has always irritated his father,' he said. 'Everybody knows how quickly the Duke can lose his temper with him. The smallest thing can send him into the most fearful rage, and he was especially prickly over Charles's marital problems.' It was no secret in the Palace that the Duke saw his son's difficulties with Diana as 'all part of his inability to stick at anything'.

His father's disapproval could still reduce Charles to tears. It was understandable that the private secretaries, engaged in the most political of professions, should have decided that Mrs Parker Bowles was a subject best steered clear of over their morning cup of tea. And, although his office appraised the Duke in July when the Andrew Knight story appeared in the *Spectator*, it was done 'rather discreetly … he might have missed it'.

It is easy to see now why it was especially necessary to handle the Duke with kid gloves in that summer of '92. And here it is necessary to backtrack a bit.

On 12 June, five days after the first devastating excerpt of the Andrew Morton book appeared in the *Sunday Times* beneath the headline 'Diana driven to five suicide bids by "uncaring" Charles', the Queen and Prince Charles discussed his problems for the first time. Until that moment the Queen had been merely appalled by the indignity of the Morton book. But what Charles told her at that meeting on 12 June – the marriage *was* in deep trouble, he had made a disastrous ill-judged marriage out of duty, and both he and Diana wanted out – truly shocked her.

Exactly how much she was affected by the personal misfortune is hard to gauge, but according to one close family friend, 'most of all she feared that Charles's melancholy [to which he is notoriously prone] and his sense of defeatism would outweigh his sense of duty to the Crown.'

Chapter Two

The Queen is not by nature a passionate woman, but on the subject of monarchy – 'the family business', as Prince Philip called it – she is more than passionate. And now she acted with unregal haste. A second meeting took place three days later in the private apartments at Windsor Castle, in which both the Princess of Wales and the Duke also took part.

'Quite simply, the Queen wanted Philip to knock some sense into the Waleses' heads,' said a member of the Duke's private office. 'She herself continued to take a pretty feeble line, frankly: Charles and Diana should take six months to cool off and reconsider, they should take an official trip together, she suggested the South Korean tour, to demonstrate their togetherness, that sort of thing; all they needed was time, and so on. As usual, Philip was left to crack the whip.'

But the Windsor version of the 'hard cop, soft cop' routine failed.

'The Duke was a great organizer, he could run a tight ship,' said his own staffer. 'But his hand was always far too heavy when it came to family matters. He took a firm line with Diana, which was what he was there to do, but it was totally the wrong line. People need more sympathy, more understanding when a relationship is teetering. ... the Duke isn't capable of that, and neither, alas, is the Queen. She has never been able to reach out.'

Nobody knows exactly what was said during those ninety minutes behind closed doors at Windsor Castle on 15 June 1992, but there have been several informed leaks, and the facts pretty much speak for themselves: Her Majesty was majestic when she should have been warm and wise; the Duke was shouting when he should have been listening.

But Diana was perfectly happy to do most of the listening. 'Don't forget you have the right to remain silent,' a confidant, thought to be James Gilbey, had advised her prior to the meeting, and that is largely what she did.

Nevertheless what little she did say was enough to expose the almost ludicrous yet telling communication breakdown between the generations. 'Diana said she wanted "space",' her puzzled mother-in-law would tell a friend later. 'Kensington Palace isn't *bijou*, is it?'

The Princess of Wales was in a strong position. In her eleven years of marriage, she had become *the* leading player on the royal stage; she could communicate with the people as the Queen, Prince Charles and the Duke could not; she commanded more newsprint than the three of them put together; and she was the mother of Prince William, a future king. She knew it, and they knew it: she had extraordinary power over their lives.

After the failure of the Windsor meeting, and at the instigation of the Queen's private office, the Duke again attempted to bring her back into the Windsor fold. He wrote several letters to her (typed personally on his new laptop word processor) in which he attempted to explain his ideas of the meaning of duty, commitment, loyalty and so on. Unfortunately, the letters were not well received: *lectures*, Diana called them.

'Philip has been much criticized for those letters. I imagine he was blunt, forthright and so on, but I don't think he would have been discourteous to his daughter-in-law. After all, she was still, however tenuously, the future Queen of England,' says a man well placed in the Palace establishment and one who can be trusted not to mislead on these matters. 'He has a highly professional attitude to life. He recognized that there was a communication problem, and he really did spend a great deal of time trying to get through to her.'

And so, thus preoccupied in the summer months of '92 with the immediate problems of Charles and Diana, the Andrew Knight story in the *Spectator* hinting at more troubles ahead was allowed to slip by the Duke. But why he did not react more typically to the *Mirror* story in November is a bigger mystery. 'It would certainly have been brought to his notice,' says a member of his staff. 'Perhaps, when disaster strikes, it always strikes in slow motion.'

Or perhaps Philip, Duke of Edinburgh, Earl of Merioneth, Baron Greenwich and father of the heir to the throne, simply did not care any more.

He was seventy-one years old, nudging old age. His fingers were swollen with painful arthritis, liver spots mottled his high forehead. 'I think he was beginning to recognize that his had been a disappointing life in many ways,' says one of his former senior aides. 'His family was a mess. He was not blameless by a long chalk. He had come to terms with his own powerlessness. Even the Princess of Wales had seen him off. He was indeed, as he had said himself forty years ago, an amoeba.'*

Prince Philip does not appear to have acknowledged or fully appreciated the Mrs Parker Bowles crisis until he saw the headlines on Thursday, 14 January. He then exploded with all his old energy. 'Even diehard *Sun* readers have stopped reading that bloody rag backwards [sports pages first] to find out who's bonking who at the Palace,' he shouted in a familiar Philipian outburst of anger and sarcasm.

Charles was in a pile of trouble with the media, the public and most of all with his own family. No royal marriage in modern times

---

* In 1952 his Mountbatten surname was officially erased from the royal family tree when the Queen proclaimed by an Order in Council that it was her 'Will and Pleasure that She and Her Children shall be styled and known as the House of Windsor ...'. With little to do except act as a handsome clothes-horse for the uniforms he wore so well on ceremonial occasions, he said that he had been reduced to 'an amoeba – a bloody amoeba!'

had been so dramatic in its course or so riveting in its consequence as his to Diana. 'If I had been Charles none of this would have happened,' Princess Anne said, clean forgetting her own recent marital difficulties.

But by Sunday, 17 January, this was not simply a family problem any more. It was, the Queen Mother dared to say, what the others only thought, nothing less than a crisis threatening the existence of the monarchy itself.

Over Sunday morning coffee, surely the whole country was reading the story in the *Sunday Mirror* and the *People*.

Here it was at last. A lovers' conversation, intensely private, embarrassing to read. And the public read all 1,574 words of it. Recorded on the night of 17 December 1989, and purchased by Mirror Group Newspapers for £30,000, the tape removed finally and forever the faded line between movie stars and monarchy: it was clear that the public was at last to be honoured with the same intimate details about the love affairs of the royal family that formerly they read only about rock stars and Hollywood movie queens.

As revealed to the world, the six-minute conversation was full of private jokes, non-sequiturs, intimate remarks. 'I want to feel my way along you, all over you and up and down you, and in and out,' Charles tells her. 'Oh,' she says. 'Particularly in and out,' he says. 'Oh, that's just what I need at the moment,' she tells him. As well as awful schoolboy puns, and the infamous tampon reference (revealing his self-disgust and humiliation, according to the self-taught psychiatry which is practised upon him by the press, and which he resents so much), the conversation makes it clear that an adulterous affair has been going on between the Prince and Mrs Parker Bowles for a considerable while. 'Your great achievement is to love me,' he tells her, perhaps with preposterous vanity, perhaps recognizing that he has not always been deserving of such love. Either way, 'Easier than falling off a chair,' she tells him loyally. They talk about the times he can call when her husband Andrew

('A' they call him throughout the tape, like lovers in a Russian novel) will be away. 'Oh God, when am I going to speak to you?' he asks desperately. 'I can't bear it,' she says. 'Wednesday night?' 'Oh, certainly Wednesday night. I'll be alone.' There is no suggestion of guilt in their words, no suspicion that they might be overheard. They are cuckolding her husband; their only concern is where they can meet to make love again.

'Spontaneous applause and cries of "Good old Charlie" greeted the prince from a crowd of 300 well-wishers as he and the Duke of Edinburgh strode ahead of the royal party on their way to church at Sandringham yesterday in what appeared to be a display of family solidarity,' reported *The Times* the next morning, 18 January. 'Looking cheerful and composed, the prince joined the congregation at the Church of St Mary Magdalene to hear Canon George Hall, rector of Sandringham, pray for the royal family, including the absent Princess of Wales.'

The Prince was not oblivious to the reality that his private actions had consequences for the whole royal family. And his public face – the brave face of the injured party – was not his private face. That weekend, as he considered his position, and agonized over his future, he knew that millions of his future subjects as well as his own family had read or heard part or all of his earthy pillow talk with his mistress.

'It was a terrible moment, the worst moment of his life,' said one of his closest friends who spoke to him several times that weekend. 'He wanted to be taken seriously, to be given respect as a man. He sincerely believed that he had important things to say. He wanted to be thought profound. And in six minutes of private conversation, a conversation that was nobody's business but his and the woman to whom he was speaking, his reputation was ruined. Maybe it was a delusion that he was something of a sage and a philosopher, but it was a fairly harmless delusion. The downfall of a prince holds a terrible fascination, but he really didn't deserve to be destroyed so publicly and so cruelly.'

According to a snap poll on 16 January, the day *before* the publication of the tapes, one-third of the British people thought Camillagate had damaged him 'very badly', another third thought 'fairly badly'. More than two in five thought that the monarchy should skip a generation and Prince William should accede to the throne after the Queen.

Every member of the family was deeply shaken by this wrenching blow to the monarchy. But, for Prince Philip, to have the family mocked and disdained was especially painful, touching a nerve and a source of frustration that lay more in history than in himself. Despite his irascibility, the Duke was a proud man and one still vulnerable to his position as an outsider, a Greek prince brought into the Windsor fold. He understood disdain and he certainly was not pleased to see it heaped upon his son and upon the family. 'One must recognize the sheer unreasonableness of having a wife in such an overwhelmingly superior position to her husband as the Queen is to Philip,' reflects a courtier, who has been close to the strain of that marriage for more than thirty years. 'What other man in the world must swear to be his wife's liegeman, and walk two paces behind her? Ostensibly, he is the head of the family, but when the chips are down his wife is always the Queen.'

In the sorry matter of Camillagate, the Duke was in a particularly difficult position. As a man of the world he understood perfectly the temptations of a prince no longer in love with his wife, whose marriage is a sham, and who becomes sexually obsessed by an older woman. It was a story as old as the monarchy itself. His anger, some thought, was the anger of a father whose son has been found out; it was the discovery and not the deed — it was Charles's failure to cover up the affair — that had aroused his wrath.

But was it also an exercise in deception, the last refuge of the philandering husband? There is no evidence for thinking so, although a great deal of rumour has accumulated through the years. 'Getting away with it is a royal accomplishment, a kingly gift, of course,' says a woman who knew Philip well in the early 1960s, when the rumours were thickest. It didn't matter that Charles had a horny mistress and a dirty mouth. What mattered was that he hadn't been able to hush it up. Philip would never have got into that kind of mess in the first place, but if he had he would have handled the situation with a lot more aplomb. Philip is a genius at keeping his own secrets.'

And even as the crisis meeting was taking place at Sandringham, in London the government was revising the top secret category placed on files relating to the Duke's visit to Argentina in 1962 – extending their secrecy to the year 2063, when he would be safely buried, or aged 141.

Why should a file on the Duke be kept from the scrutiny of historians for a hundred years? It is the kind of question which fuels rumours of philandering, and causes one member of Charles's circle wickedly to suggest that his anger at his son was an expression of relief that it was not himself who had been found out.

The coolest member of the family by far was turning out to be the Queen Mother. She had been a major force in engineering Charles's marriage to Diana, and now she would step forward as the most savvy and sage voice in this maelstrom of woes. It was not the first time that the Queen Mother, almost ninety-three years old, had proved that she was still the best royal to have around in a crisis. Her career indeed had been to an uncommon degree shaped by royal crises of one kind or another. Her voice, gentle but authoritative, seemed to exist for the sole purpose of conveying calm and good sense.

If the ability to show warmth was a missing ingredient in her daughter, it was at the very heart of the Queen Mother's strength. And, when she told her grandson that if he heeded her advice things could only get better, he trusted her. During the following days her opinions – 'orders of battle' she called them – became the basis of what 'informed sources' told the press was the Prince's 'thinking' as he contemplated the future, or life after Camillagate.

The Queen Mother frequently talked to her grandson in the

following weeks, encouraging him, calming him. 'You must show the people that you have a moral courage,' she told him again and again – assuring him, whenever his resolve faltered and he threatened to come apart, that the worst was over. 'You must never belie your name,' she said quietly, reminding him of his destiny, after he had told friends that he was afraid that he was not worthy of what was expected of him. But, even when his depression seemed irrecoverably deep, the Queen Mother always had faith. 'He has to rehabilitate himself – by himself,' she told an old friend. 'And he will. People underrate his strength, just as they underrated Bertie's.'

'Perhaps she was right, but she gave him tremendous encouragement. And Charles listened, he kept his nerve, he did as he was told – just as King George always had,' one of the Queen Mother's friends would say later with amusement and satisfaction. 'She is a wonderful restorer of crumbling backbones.'

But the Prince was not out of the wood yet.

On an engagement in the City of London – where, in effect, his troubles began – a man called out, 'Have you no shame, sir?'

The Prince's face reddened, but he looked straight ahead and continued on his way.

That same week he received a call through his St James's Palace office from Camilla Parker Bowles's father, Major Bruce Shand, demanding a meeting. 'He knew it was going to be the most difficult and embarrassing meeting of the whole Camillagate affair,' said one of his friends. 'But he refused to duck it.'

The meeting lasted almost ninety minutes. According to the Shand family, the Major told the Prince that he had sullied their name and that he was never to see or contact his daughter again until he had 'made his intentions clear'. A doughty figure, and former war hero – he won the Military Cross twice – Shand spelled out the great harm that had already been done, not least to Camilla's children Laura and Tom (Tom had heard boys at Eton calling his mother a 'tart'), and sought an assurance from the Prince that there would be an end to it.

Nobody had ever talked to the Prince in such a forthright manner in his life (except his father) and he was appalled. According to the Shand family the Prince broke down in tears of shame. But whether he did or did not, he promised to 'consider' the Major's pleas.

'The amazing thing is that Charles might have lost a lot of public respect, but he lost none of his friends – even when his behaviour was appalling, even when he had cuckolded one of his best friends. Why? Because he is a prince,' says a former girlfriend sourly.

That is both true and unfair. It is significant that while Camilla's father confronted the Prince with his behaviour, her husband did not. Nor did Andrew Parker Bowles begin the divorce proceedings which the press had so eagerly predicted – and the Palace feared.

The Brigadier's failure to act himself in the matter, it was thought, had to be a sign of remarkable good nature or an inordinate respect for the Prince as a man.

But the explanation was rather more simple and a little sadder than that.

'Andrew and Camilla have always said that they will never divorce, and, while their relationship is rather eccentric, it appears to have worked,' says Parker Bowles's brother, Simon. 'They may not be in love with each other, but they get on well and will stick together. They have had a very open marriage and these sophisticated arrangements can be fine, but they can blow up in your face, my God, as this has done.'

In the immediate aftermath of the publication of the tape, and in the face of the British public's almost unanimous disapproval, Camilla and Andrew retreated to Middlewick House, their eighteenth-century home eighteen miles from the Prince's Highgrove estate in Gloucestershire. It was a bad time for both of them. The joke in White's, Parker Bowles's own club, was that he was a man 'who was prepared to lay down his wife for his country'.

It was cruel and as unamusing as it was unoriginal. 'Whatever happens, their lives will never be the same again and they know it – they were trapped,' said Carolyn Benson (née Gerard Leigh), who, with Kirstie Smallwood, were the Parker Bowles's houseguests that first, troubled weekend.

And if it were true that Charles had lost none of his cronies over the Camillagate affair, the Parker Bowleses were not so lucky. Their friends quickly divided for and against. Lord Charles Spencer-Churchill, who had lunch with Andrew not long after the tape was published, said frankly, 'Sadly, Andrew has got his come-uppance. He got away with so much for so long, but he was digging his own grave. His father was exactly the same – do anything for royalty.'

Meanwhile, the Prince of Wales took delivery of a new portable telephone, built by the official British intercept organization, Government Communications Headquarters at Cheltenham in Gloucestershire, and containing the very latest scrambler technology.

But it was too late, of course.

'He spends a lot of time thinking positively about the future,' says a friend loyally. 'But he would not be human if he didn't reflect on the past dozen years – and wonder where it all started to go so terribly wrong for him.'

BOOK TWO

Chapter Three

Charles Philip Arthur George Mountbatten-Windsor, Prince of Wales, heir to the British throne, and the world's most eligible bachelor, had a problem. He was not in love with the girl he was going to marry.

And nobody would listen to him.

His fiancee, Lady Diana Spencer, was the girl next door. Their families had known each other all their lives, and for generations past. According to popular legend at the time she had been vetted, guaranteed immaculate by the admirable Mr. Pinker, surgeon-gynaecologist to the Queen; and although no such examination ever took place she defined the word 'innocent.' Her face on the cover of a magazine sold out the edition. Exactly as advertised, approved and admired by all, Lady Diana seemed made to order ...

But he barely knew her.

'She is exquisitely pretty, a perfect poppet ... but she is a child,' he told a woman friend plaintively, still brooding less than a month before the nuptials about the wisdom – *the sanity* – of his choice. 'She does not look old enough to be out of school, much less married,' he fretted.

But, for all the angst and the air of irresolution surrounding the Prince in the weeks following the announcement of his engagement to Lady Diana, Palace aides did not sense a crisis or even acknowledge a problem. No code-blue alarms rang in Buck House. The Prince's worries were drowned in the Palace clamour for a marriage that was more than a marriage: it was a massive PR coup for the monarchy itself. Ratings are the name of the game for royalty as well as for television, and The Wedding was to be the essence of triumphalism, the biggest ceremonial event the British monarchy had ever staged: a royal spectacular, a real-life fairy tale shown live on satellite TV around the world. Hundreds of millions of dollars were in play, and the Prince had as much say in the matter as a corporal in the Light Brigade.

There was also another reason why the Prince's Hamlet-like indecision was being ignored by those who knew him well. 'Being beset and vacillating is simply Charles's way,' said a courtier smugly 'Nothing is so sure to me as his uncertainty.'

But for once the Prince's instincts were right. For underlying his familiar philosophical brow-clutching was the human reality: that if Lady Diana did turn out to be 'the wrong bride', it would be not only a disaster for them personally, but also for the monarchy itself. *And still nobody would listen to him.*

The Queen, the mainstay of his life, whose fate he shared and from whom he might have expected understanding and sympathy, showed only stern expectation when he tried to express his doubts to her. ('She wasn't there,' the Prince told an aide who enquired how one particular meeting had gone with the Queen.) He met with his father in an attempt to win him to his side. However ambivalent he may have been about his father (their relationship was volatile; Prince Philip was his meanest critic), the Prince felt that he was always objective and more capable of commitment than the Queen. But the meeting was a disaster and resulted only in a long, inconclusive wrangle which ended with Prince Philip bluntly telling his son that ever since his thirtieth birthday he had been 'living on borrowed time' as a bachelor. Public expectation was at a peak: it was time, Philip growled, 'to get off the pot'.

The Prince left the meeting with his father more depressed and frustrated than ever. 'Why does he always manage to make me feel like the bloody monkey to his organ grinder?' he asked the woman friend in whom he sought solace that evening, and who was one of the several married women in whom he placed a special trust (like his late great-uncle David, the Duke of Windsor, he had a weakness for other men's wives).

Camilla Parker Bowles, the one he trusted most and had loved longest, continued to try to soothe his nerves as the wedding grew closer. She had the most important qualification as a mistress: she was a good listener. She had vetted all his women, the serious ones, as if some fealty were due, as if his future happiness were on her conscience. She knew that Charles fell in love with dangerous ease and she would perceive his conquests through her beady reality rather than his romanticism. Marking them out of ten, none so far had earned more than six on her scorecard. Diana, very different from the others with whom he had been involved, got a nine. 'She's an absolute *mouse*,' Camilla told him in her well-bred Celia Johnson voice. 'She will be fine. She is almost perfect.'

It was heartfelt advice. Only a little older than Charles, she was considerably wiser in the ways of the world, and her strategy as a mistress turned on her sanctioning and taking an early hold on his bride. In Diana, she was convinced that the Prince had found a woman who suited her own book exactly – 'An absolute mouse'.

Short on looks, but a striking woman with a faintly dangerous past, Camilla was married to Lieutenant-Colonel Andrew Parker Bowles, one of the Prince's closer friends. She and Charles had been lovers before her marriage. The emotional bond that attached them went back a long way. Camilla's great-grandmother, Alice Keppel, was a mistress of his great-great-grandfather King Edward VII. Some thought her the most perfect mistress in the history of royal infidelity; others said that she was fortunate in having only the King's beautiful but brainless consort, Alexandra – an absolute mouse, in fact – with whom to compete. Either way, Camilla felt that history was on her side. 'My great-grandmother was your great-great grandfather's-mistress. How about it?' she had boldly propositioned Charles when they first met in the late 1960s, when she was still Camilla Rosemary Shand.

He never recovered from that opening line. From that moment on, wherever Charles was, Camilla was never far away. He was not only attracted to her vivacity and sexual candour – to the idea of her, of them together, as well as the fact – but he also fell deeply in love with her. 'They were always good together,' said a friend who saw much of them at that time, and recognized in them 'the classic chemical fusion' of people in love. 'Camilla was quite a flirt, she liked men,' said Carolyn Benson, who came out with her in '65 and has remained among her closest friends. 'She was a girl's girl as well as being a man's girl. She was funny and bright, not particularly clothes conscious – she's never changed.'

'Charles was able to let down his guard enough with Camilla to say and do things with an ease and a directness that he never seemed able to muster with others,' said a friend who had been a frequent escort when she came out. 'When she was around there was a lightness in him that had been missing in the family for a very long time. It was as if her presence exempted him from the self-consciousness of being the Prince of Wales. You just knew they were having a great time in bed together. She became his ideal, his prototype woman.'

But in 1973, after he had repeatedly refused to commit himself – 'Marriage is a desperate thing,' he would tell his women to amuse them, and to warn them, too: 'The frogs in Aesop were very wise: they wanted some water, but would not leap into the well, because they could not get out again' – Camilla married Parker Bowles. But, in her own fashion, she never gave up on the Prince.

'At Biarritz [where she went with the King every Easter], Alice Keppel was as much the Queen of England as Alexandra herself,' Camilla once told a friend, who got the feeling that she was revealing something about herself, that it was her ambition 'to get at least the same recognition, and nothing less'.

In 1981, it seemed that Camilla was on her way to achieving that goal. All London, her London, knew of her relationship with

Charles; she was welcomed everywhere and treated with respect. Even Andrew Parker Bowles, like George Keppel one hundred years before him, did not question his friend the Prince of Wales's choice of mistress. Like Great-Grandmother Alice, Camilla remained the Prince's La Favorita; her advice listened to above all others'. But she could not persuade him that Diana was 'the right bride'. He had never had anything from her but honesty and caring, so why should he not trust her judgement now? Her feelings were hurt. She was also very angry, and for several weeks refused to take his calls. It was the first sign of discord in their relationship in nearly twelve years.

Eight weeks before the wedding was due to take place, unable to reach Camilla, Charles was in a highly agitated state of mind. Several times he talked to Lady Tryon, another of his trusted women friends, whom he had nicknamed 'Kanga'. An attractive Australian blonde whose accent became broader and conversation more amusing after a glass or two of Krug, Kanga had also been an early and uncompromising supporter of Diana. Did she still think that Diana was the right woman for him? Absolutely, said Kanga. Although not as close to Charles as Camilla undoubtedly was, she had always told him what she thought without regard for proprieties. Most people took endless pains and precautions to tell him what they knew he wanted to hear; the strongest link of her relationship with the Prince she knew was her frankness. Still he remained convinced that his engagement to Diana was 'a bloody awful mistake' that would only be compounded in marriage. But he had failed to convert the Queen or his father; he had been unable to convince anyone at the Palace. His two closest women friends told him that he was worrying unnecessarily.

'He was as frustrated as hell, and he was beginning to suspect that the Court believed in the marriage only to the extent that it served the purpose of the monarchy,' said a close friend of the family. 'Looking back, he was absolutely right, of course. He knew so many things, but nobody at the Palace was prepared to level with him, or help him carry the responsibility of that knowledge.'

In early May he took the unusual step of consulting his sister, Princess Anne.

Their relationship had never been close ('The only time I see much of him is during holidays,' she had once remarked, 'and roughly speaking that's enough'), and their harmony was usually a question of whether the Princess was in a humour to resurrect or forget sibling jealousies. She swam better than he did; she was off a leading rein before him too. But, with its trust in the principle of primogeniture, the royal family showered its attention and concern on Charles, the heir apparent, and with it, many suspected, much of the love of which Anne had felt deprived.

At thirty, she could still be as intimidating and competitive as she had been when they were children, only now he knew her temperament and difficult ways by heart, and could defend himself better. Anne was as much like their father as he was like their mother, 'stubborn and strong-willed where Charles was meek and defensive, petulant and haughty where he was bashful and with-drawn', a recent biographer* had written, not altogether to the Prince's liking (he felt it made him sound like a wimp). Although he recognized that Anne was his complete opposite, (had she not been a princess she would have been what her father still called a go-getter, and one of the few royals who could have made it even without a title), the Prince believed that each admired most in the other the qualities which he or she did not possess, and that at the wire they would always be held together by a common sense of values, a mutual understanding and respect.

The previous June, Anne had indicated a willingness to become closer when she telephoned to tell him that Highgrove, a 353–acre estate less than ten miles from her home in Gloucestershire, was

* Anthony Holden, *Charles, Prince of Wales*, written in 1979 with the Prince's co-operation and generally to his satisfaction. A revised edition in the 1980s displeased the Prince. 'Sources close to HRH' attempted to sully Holden's reputation as a journalist by raising questions about his integrity.

unexpectedly on the market again. She had considered buying it for herself six years earlier, before she found Gatcombe Park, her thousand-acre estate, and she suggested that it would now make a superb country home for Charles. She read him the advertisement in the latest issue of *Country Life*, in which it was described as 'a distinguished Georgian house standing in superb parkland in the Duke of Beaufort's Hunt'. He had been touched by her interest, but surprised that she was proposing that he move so close to her own country home, given her passion for privacy and the pride she took in her independence. (Her mother said that, as a child, if she hadn't been destined for other things, she would have liked to grow up to be a lady living in the country with lots of dogs and horses. In this respect, Anne, who was never happier than when she had mud on her boots, was living out her mother's childhood dream.) When Charles thanked her for suggesting Highgrove to him, she told him with her mordant humour, 'What are little sisters for?'

The following day, Charles's private secretary Edward Adeane telephoned the agents to make an appointment for a viewing. But it was largely because Anne had liked the place so much that the Prince bought Highgrove the following month, shortly before he started to become interested in Diana.

And so finally, after weeks of anguish and frustration, as he felt his early brief euphoria over the engagement continuing to leak away, Charles drove to Gatcombe Park to seek some more sisterly advice.

Anne had been married eight years to Captain Mark Phillips, and was pregnant with their second child ('An occupational hazard if you're a wife,' she had said). Charles admired the way she had broken loose from the stifling protocols of the Court; he respected the way she spoke her mind, fought for what she believed in and was not afraid to say unpopular things. But she could be blunt to a fault, and poll after poll in the 1970s voted her the royal family's least liked member. But Palace directives to her to be kinder and gentler, to de-ice her image, went unheeded. She didn't give a damn. She had made a life and a home of her own, raising her son Peter, the Queen's first grandchild, with a commitment and devotion she felt she had not always received in her own childhood. Although he was not a frequent visitor to Gatcombe Park, a sprawling somewhat untidy upper-class family residence, a house remarkable more for its cheerful comfort than for its beauty, Charles always felt relaxed there.

Aware that his brother-in-law wished to talk to his wife privately, and perhaps sensing the Prince's agitation (the past few months had not been his best, and it showed), Mark Phillips withdrew to his own quarters to watch television, a favourite pastime. Anne and Charles talked in her private sitting-room, where she worked on her speeches and conducted her official and private correspondence.

With her second baby due in ten days, maybe sooner, perhaps she was tired or bored; or maybe she could not take seriously her brother's lugubrious litany of reasons why he feared that Diana would not be a suitable bride for him after all: he barely knew her, she was too young, too naive; he listed all the imaginable situations in which she might not be up to the job. But no sharpened sisterly senses detected the subtext, the really dangerous undercurrent of his concern, that anticipated the biggest crisis the royal family had known since the abdication of Edward VIII. And when he had finished, she dismissed his fears with an almost wilful lack of insight into what he was trying to tell her. 'Footling,' she called them.

He was too stuck in his bachelor ways, she chided, and she told him to grow up. 'You've got to play the hand you are dealt,' she said in her flat, colourless middle-class voice. She added slyly in the tones that had so often angered and motivated him as a child, and now evoked and mocked the Windsor insularity they still shared, 'Just close your eyes and think of England, Charles.'

He returned to London amused and chastened by her gamey bluntness. 'Nothing is more irritating than obtrusive good advice from one's little sister,' he said lightly. But his disappointment was plain to see.

He had gone to Gloucestershire still imagining he might win. Not only had Anne been the one person he was sure who would understand, but she also had the licence and the courage to stand up for him. In her father's admiring words she was 'the mistress of attack'. But she wasn't foolhardy. She knew the score. She knew exactly the way the Court thought and operated in these matters: it would have been fatal to allow the heir apparent to set out by pleasing himself in so important a matter as the choice of his wife, the woman who would be queen. And eight months with child, even if she had supported his cause, Anne did not have the energy, the will or the time to enter the lists against the Court.

Anyway, she also knew – and she knew that Charles knew it too – that he was a trapped man. Royal marriage was an act of obligation, an affair more of prudence than of passion. If the demands of wisdom were satisfied, love, it was held, might one day come. It seldom worked out that way; but that was the most people like them could hope for.

'To get the sharp side of Anne's tongue was no big novelty,' said a London friend, who had dined with the Prince a few days after the Gatcombe meeting. 'But he had bared his soul to her, and she ripped his objections up, down and sideways. She couldn't resist yanking his chain a little bit, too. She told him that the only real problem was his guilty conscience about marrying a virgin, after all those older ladies and married women he'd boffed. But he took her advice. She told him to spend plenty of time with Diana, to make an effort to get to know her, because it was true – he really didn't know her at all. She said that Diana was the best candidate for the job, and Charles had better make the most of it and all that. It wasn't what he wanted to hear, but her frank matter-of-factness seemed to calm his worst fears. Gatcombe helped him to recover his peace of mind.'

But, if the Prince appeared to be resigned to his fate after his visit to Gatcombe Park, it was because he finally had no one else to turn to, and had at last abandoned any expectation that somebody up there would understand his problem. The two people whose wisdom and love he trusted most could not help him this time. His beloved 'Uncle Dickie' – Earl Mountbatten, elder statesman of the royal family and the man Charles called his 'honorary grandfather' – was dead, murdered by the IRA, on a summer's day in 1979.

And cruelly this was the one time when he knew he could not go to his grandmother for help. The Queen Mother was his closest confidante in all the world. It sometimes seemed to him that they were parts of each other. In his parents' long and many absences, she had always been there for him; and it was she, perhaps more than anyone, who had instilled in him a sense of mission to the Crown. In the words of one biographer, she was 'almost a mother confessor when the requirements his parents made of him seemed too great to sustain'. He had discussed affairs of the heart with her many times. But this was different. This time far more than his private feelings were at stake. He knew that his reluctance to abandon his bachelor lifestyle had been seen by his grandmother as the greatest problem for the royal family since the scandal of Mrs Simpson and the Duke of Windsor. She could not always be relied upon to keep her temper when the subject arose. He knew, too, that she was nervous that he would turn out to be Duke of Windsor redux. Yet despite her urgent desire to find him a suitable bride – she regarded it as 'a matter of duty' – her standards were almost unrealistically high, and she had dissected the characters and morals of his previous girlfriends in no very tolerant spirit.

But she did wholly approve of Lady Diana, who was the paternal granddaughter of Countess Spencer, her Lady of the Bedchamber, and the maternal granddaughter of Ruth, Lady Fermoy, one of her Women of the Bedchamber and a dear friend for over sixty years. If she had not conspired to put Lady Diana into his bed, Charles knew that she had done nothing to discourage those who had.

It was a problem. And the prospect of having to go forward with neither the asssurance of Uncle Dickie's firm and worldly guidance nor the friendly warmth of his grandmother's wisdom was not something that he could contemplate with ordinary calmness.

Only the Prince's valet Stephen Barry, to whom he would sometimes unburden himself in private, seemed to recognize the gravity of the situation. He was astonished that nobody at the Palace, nor anybody in the family, seemed to take the Prince's qualms seriously. 'It was perfectly clear to me that the Prince's concern was more than a gentleman's premarital collywobbles,' recalled Barry, an elegant, foppish, rather courtly figure, with the faintest Cockney accent. Valets, like women, acquire information in surprising ways, and it is in the little things that the strongest convictions are often founded.

Shortly before the engagement was announced to the world and the eighteen-carat sapphire in its fourteen-diamond garland appeared on Lady Diana's finger, the Prince asked Barry, who did all his private shopping for him, 'from his socks to his condoms', to acquire some pancake make-up. A former junior footman who had worked his way up the gay network of Palace politics, Barry went to 'the corner shop' (it was Harrods) and after a conversation with a make-up adviser chose 'an unperfumed make-up base tint – a vegetarian product, with a soft natural finish'.

For several months afterwards, the Prince would apply this, or ask Barry to do it for him, usually immediately after his shower, but always before venturing out of his own private apartments on the second floor of the Palace, overlooking the Mall and St James's Park. (Only a very few privileged people are admitted to these apartments, and no one intrudes, not even the Queen, save at his actual invitation.) 'Before then, he had refused to wear any kind of make-up, even when he knew he would be facing television cameras. But I noticed that his cheeks were beginning to develop a high colour, a sort of raspberry flush, which was always a sign that he was stressed or upset,' Barry said.

Despite the popular acclaim and grass-roots enthusiasm that greeted the announcement of the Prince's engagement to the eighteen-year-old Lady Diana – thirteen years younger than

Charles, gauche, quick to blush – it was no secret in his circle, and among London's chattering classes, that he had other dreams; he preferred his women to be worldly, experienced and altogether earthier. He preferred Camilla Parker Bowles, but she was no longer a wifely option. What he needed as a man and what he required as heir to the throne were not the same thing at all. 'It's awfully difficult, because you've got to remember that when you marry, in my position, you are going to marry someone who perhaps is one day going to become queen. You've got to choose somebody very carefully ... People expect quite a lot from somebody like that ... and it has got to be somebody pretty special,' he had stammered out in his first television interview, at the age of twenty, when he was still young enough to relegate marriage to the distant future.

Now, thirteen years later, the distant future had arrived. And although he was not in love with Lady Diana, he knew better than anyone that the monarchy renews its energy through the bodies of beautiful princess brides. The Queen Mother, a woman of matriarchal steel beneath a satiny girdle of grandmotherly charm, had told him that a thousand times. It was simply a fact of the life he knew and loved and – although he was too smart and too much of a gentleman to admit it – basked in. He grew up knowing, accepting, that one day he would probably have to sacrifice feeling for duty and marry not for love but to satisfy the dynastic demands of his family.

Behind Palace doors they called it feeding the beast.

Chapter Four

If there is a kind of metaphysical terror in crossing the chasm that divides ordinary mortals from kings and queens – and in marrying Prince Charles, Diana would become not only a princess, but a future queen and mother of a monarch to come – the bride showed none of it that day. (It seemed merely endearing of her as they exchanged their Anglican vows to jumble the order of her husband's names; Charles blew his lines, too, pledging her 'all thy good' instead of 'all my worldly goods'.) There was little artifice in her unforgettable face. Her make-up was beguilingly light – 'Lady Diana naturally blushes very prettily, and there's no point pretending she doesn't,' said her make-up artist. Barely twenty years old, very much in love, and knowing nothing of her husband's profound reservations, she was indeed a princess of great happiness as well as one of rare beauty and presence.

When the royal family made the ritual balcony appearance at Buckingham Palace after the ceremony, the boisterous crowds swarming around the Palace gates and reaching halfway down the Mall began to chant for the Prince to kiss his bride. '*Kiss her, kiss her.*' Diana looked at him expectantly, detecting something of his nervousness, enjoying his embarrassment.

Charles, thirty-three years old, youngish but no longer young, hesitated, caught off guard by the passion of the crowd, and glanced for the approval of his mother. The Queen – whose footfalls would always be audible behind him – discreetly nodded permission.

And so the royal groom kissed his princess bride full on the lips right there on prime time TV: a shot that rang around the world.

'That's the picture that will seal the romance of the monarchy for twenty years,' said a Palace press aide, watching the balcony scene on TV in a room in another part of the Palace.

But something was said later that afternoon that sent a *frisson* of apprehension if not a sense of portent through at least one of the 120 guests, family and closest friends who had attended the wedding breakfast (quenelles of brill, lobster sauce, chicken breasts stuffed with minced lamb, strawberries and clotted Cornish cream, served with vintage Bollinger champagne) and were now jammed into the inner courtyard of Buckingham Palace to wave goodbye to the bride and groom when they left in an open landau for Waterloo Station on the first leg of their honeymoon.

Standing together in the late-afternoon sunshine, Prince Andrew and Prince Edward, Charles's 'supporters' (royal weddings do not have best men), grinned mischievously when they heard the whooping roar of approval as the honeymooners − flanked by the Sovereign's Escort of the Household Cavalry, twenty-four Life Guards wearing scarlet ceremonial jackets and white-plumed helmets, and twenty-four horsemen of the Blues and Royals in blue jackets with red plumes, commanded by the Prince's old friend and good sport Lieutenant-Colonel Andrew Parker Bowles − entered the Palace forecourt and the crowds saw the hand-lettered 'JUST MARRIED' sign they had tied to the back of the carriage beneath a dozen silver and blue balloons emblazoned with the Prince of Wales feathers.

Edward was a fresh-faced undergraduate at Cambridge University, his neatly parted brown hair already thinning in the male-pattern baldness that had bedevilled both his father, Prince Philip, and Prince Charles (but not Prince Andrew) at an early age. Wearing an outsize white carnation in the buttonhole of his black morning coat, he turned to his elder brother and said, 'And they lived happily ever after, don't you think?'

"Well,' answered Andrew, who is not a profound man but whose way of pondering things yields occasional nuggets of unexpected humour and surprising prescience, 'she's certainly very much in love with Charles. And he's doing his best to fall in love with her. Let's just hope,' he added *sotto voce*, and sounding a great deal less celebratory than he had appeared on the balcony, 'let's just hope he succeeds.'

If it was not entirely a marriage of love, it was a marriage of interest and promise – although there were a few, even at the start, who were less than sanguine about its promise. 'The notion that the Prince must take a virgin bride was dangerously out of touch in the 1980s,' said the valet Stephen Barry, who had overheard the princes' conversation on the wedding day, and was both surprised and pleased that at least Andrew was wise enough to understand how 'bloody delicate' the situation really was. The key issues were purity, pedigree and fertility, and Diana had them all. But the idea that she was a simple, uncomplicated sort of girl – a tractable girl – was a big mistake. The Palace vetters (like Camilla Parker Bowles and so many others) mistook her niceness for weakness, said Barry. 'She was an aristocrat. She had an elemental sense of self-preservation – when the chips are down, that's how those people survive,' he said.

Born the Honourable Diana Frances Spencer on 1 July 1961 in Park House on the Sandringham estate, a few hundred yards from the royal family's Norfolk country home (where they were in residence only in the months of January and February), the third daughter of Edward John Spencer, Viscount Althorp, heir to the seventh Earl Spencer, and his wife Frances, she weighed 7lb 12oz – 'a superb physical specimen', her father, an aristocrat of the old school, commented with a pride that was unmistakably tempered with frustration and disappointment that the new arrival was not a male heir to carry on the Spencer name.

Although Diana would worship her father unconditionally throughout his life, his frustrated expectations entered her soul at an early age. It was an oft-repeated family story that her parents had been so certain that their fourth child (a son was born in 1960, but had died the same day) at last would be a boy that they had not even thought of choosing a girl's name. It was not until it was time to register her birth a week later that they finally decided on the names: Diana Frances. 'Her father really could not have loved her more. She was the apple of his eye. But she was a sensitive little girl, a tidy soul, and I do think she felt terribly miserable about being born a girl when her parents so wanted a son and heir,' said her governess Gertrude Allen (known as 'Ally' to the children), who had also looked after Diana's mother when she was a child.

Although the Althorps got their wish three years later, with the birth of Charles, Gertrude Allen believed that Diana continued to sense 'that she was somehow part of what was at the heart of her parents' unhappiness', and perhaps partly responsible for the eventual break-up of their marriage.

The history of the English aristocracy is first a history of succession, and Viscount 'Johnnie' Althorp's explicit anxiety to beget a son was easy to understand, if difficult for a daughter to accept.

The Spencer line – and its fortune – originated in the fifteenth century with a canny sheep trader who decided there were bigger profits to be made by cutting the local market traders out of the loop and dealing direct with the butchers and wool merchants of London. With the passage of time, the Spencers became one of the wealthiest families in England, and, through a string of pragmatic marriages, allied themselves with some of the most famous families in the land, including the Marlboroughs, the Devonshires and the Abercorns. In the English way of business, as the sheep dealers became chic, the chic became earls and knights, lord chamberlains and ambassadors to the finest royal courts of Europe. They built Althorp House in Northamptonshire; managed farms, stables, parks and gardens; employed armies of servants, grooms, gamekeepers, gardeners and farmworkers; and acquired a family crest and a motto

('God defend the right') and one of the finest private collections of art (Gainsboroughs, Reynolds, Van Dycks) in Europe. They also collected some dazzling and interesting women. Georgiana, daughter of the first Earl Spencer, was sixteen when she wed the Duke of Devonshire; her string of lovers included the Prince of Wales, 'Prinny', who became George IV. At fifty-five, she was still able to write with satisfaction and pride, 'I am courted, followed, flattered and made love to, *en toute les formes,* by four men....'

Passion and audacity, as well as a certain noble respect for bloodlines and other liquid assets, had always been key elements in the Spencer fortunes and it was simply part of the pattern when Johnnie Althorp fell in love with the Honourable Frances Roche, younger daughter of the fourth Baron Fermoy, an Irish peer, Norfolk landowner and crony of George VI. Twelve years Althorp's junior, and one of the most vivacious debutantes of her season (Major Ronald Ferguson, later to become better known as the Duchess of York's father, and the Prince of Wales's priapic polo manager, was an early admirer), Frances was just four months past her eighteenth birthday when they were married in Westminster Abbey on 1 June 1954. It was the society wedding of the year, the list of bridesmaids and attendants glittering with the names of the British upper class: Cholmondeley, Fogg-Elliot, Douglas-Home, Astor and Wake-Walker. Ten members of the royal family, including the Queen and the Queen Mother, were among the 900 guests who attended the reception at St James's Palace.

Educated at Eton and the Royal Military Academy at Sandhurst, godson of Queen Mary and the Duke of Windsor, Viscount Althorp had fought with distinction in the Royal Scots Greys in Europe in the Second World War. After the war, he spent three years as ADC to the governor of South Australia before becoming equerry to George VI. When the King died, Althorp became equerry to Queen Elizabeth, and later her acting Master of the Household. These were prestigious, even glamorous posts, and, in that small charmed circle in which the Althorps and Fermoys moved and danced attendance, considered highly desirable. But they were not posts suitable for a man in a hurry to start a family of his own.

At the age of thirty, Althorp resigned from his royal duties. The couple rented a house in Rodmarten, Gloucestershire, and he spent a year learning estate management at the Royal Agricultural College in nearby Cirencester. In March 1955, exactly nine months and a polite eighteen days after the service in Westminster Abbey, their first daughter was born. She was christened Elizabeth Sarah Lavinia; among her godparents was Queen Elizabeth, the Queen Mother. A second daughter, Cynthia Jane, followed in February 1957 (godfather the Duke of Kent). Three years later, a son, John, was born and died within ten hours.

Convinced that he would never have the son he so desperately desired to carry on the noble Spencer name, Althorp, a man with strong veins of melancholy and fatalism, went into a deep depression. His friends watched apprehensively as pent-up forces of resentment both towards fate and towards Frances's heir-bearing competence were released in the months that followed his son's short life. 'Unfairly,' said a family friend, 'he blamed Frances. He sent her to numberless Harley Street clinics for tests, for some explanation.... It never seemed to occur to him that he might be at fault. It was humiliating and I think a hateful reminder to Frances of Johnnie's reverence for the privileges and sentiments of the old order. I think it was a great shock to her to realize that as a married woman in that milieu she would never have a proper identity of her own.'

Torn with misgiving and torment as she was, Frances nevertheless also understood her husband's anguish and vulnerability.

The following year, Diana was born.

Her father described her as 'sweet-natured' and would later recall her 'remarkable serenity' and fondness for soft toys, which she loved 'almost as much as she loved babies'. She also loved hamsters and gerbils; and a ginger cat called Marmalade. Miss Allen called her 'a conscientious little girl. Not particularly bright ... but she did *try*.'

Diana remained in the nursery at Park House until she was three, when she briefly joined her sisters in their private schoolroom situated next door to the dining-room. But it wasn't long before Sarah and Jane, respectively six and four years older than Diana, and seemingly almost grown up in her eyes, were sewing name tags into their socks and uniforms for boarding school. It was a lonely time for Diana. She belonged to that class in which, according to one American observer of the English social scene, children are taught to 'speak when spoken to, chew with their mouths closed, sit up straight, smile and shake hands when introduced, and disappear silently'. Parents, if they were around at all, arrived shortly before bedtime to say goodnight.

Even by the early 1960s, it was apparent to their friends that the Althorp marriage was far from happy. Many of Frances's friends thought that she had married far too young and that the responsibility of parenthood was putting a strain on her which she was finding hard to handle. 'She was afraid that her life would pass before she had lived it,' said one friend. But, with three children under the age of seven, divorce was a step that nobody wanted to take. And when, in May 1964, the longed-for son was born, it was hoped that the marriage would survive after all.

In all the stories about the relationship between Diana and her parents, and about what she felt as a child about her place in the family, none perhaps reveals her hurt more than a brief exchange she had with a schoolfriend at Riddlesworth Hall, a preparatory school in Norfolk where she became a boarder in 1970. Her father, Diana said, 'simply lit up' when her brother was born. 'He was so proud – so happy at last.' Her brother was christened Charles Edward Maurice in Westminster Abbey, the Queen a godparent. Diana had cracked her head sliding down the stone steps of Park House on a tin tray, and was thought to be either too poorly or too unsightly to attend the service. Her friend enquired where she had been christened. Oh, Diana answered, in a church in Sandringham, 'a far cry from Westminster Abbey, I'm afraid'.

Park House, where Diana spent the first six years of her life, was a rambling ten-bedroomed property, with pool, tennis court, an ancient lawn, staff cottages, stables and garages. In addition to the governess, it needed six servants, a handyman and two gardeners. Generations of Spencers, painted in portrait by artists of varying accomplishments and styles, looked down from nearly every room in the house. Formerly used to house overflow guests and their servants from Sandringham, Park House had been built and rebuilt, restored and added to, till it was impossible to put a date to it or to see where one period ended and another began. Overlooking the royal parklands, and full of dark passages and strangely shaped rooms, it was 'endlessly explorable, and filled with wonderful memories of so many pranks', Diana would later recall with affection. It is still her favourite house. 'I can see myself now,' she has said, 'seated on the nursery floor, playing with my toys – blissfully, totally into my own thing....' Solid, comfortable, full of the character of a bygone age, if Park House did not actually shape Diana's attitudes and values, it was where her father would always 'remember her best'. Although it is now a home for the disabled, she still returns to it, as if it is a book impossible to close.

The agreement was that the Althorps would live at Park House (which was leased to Frances's father, Maurice Fermoy) until Johnnie inherited the title, the ancestral home, the Old Masters, and 8,000 acres of rolling Northamptonshire farmland.

Although he could barely bring himself even to talk to his father, the legendary seventh Earl Spencer – a man of notorious bad temper and eccentric manners, who believed it was neither wise nor estimable to live overmuch in the public eye, and carried a shotgun when he answered the door – Althorp encouraged his children to remain on friendly terms with their paternal grandparents. 'We never looked forward to going there,' says Diana's brother Charles, now the ninth Earl Spencer, whose respect for his grandfather bordered on awe, almost a terror of provoking him to become even more intimidating than he was. 'The place was like a gentlemen's club ... dark, dark, masses of clocks tick-tick-ticking away ... really a nightmarish place for children.'

Nevertheless, there was always the compensation of seeing their beloved grandmother. The Countess Spencer, daughter of the third Duke of Abercorn, Lady of the Bedchamber to the Queen Mother, had been a classic beauty of the 1930s. Before she had married 'Jack' Spencer, she had been wooed by the Prince of Wales – 'long before he met that American woman, Wallis Simpson', she would always add with an elegant shudder, as tremulous as an aspen leaf. Grandmother Spencer liked having children in the house and could always make them laugh with her family stories. It was she who told them the legends of their grandfather's pride in Althorp: how he would follow unreliable guests around with a feather duster, and once snatched a cigar out of Winston Churchill's mouth to save ash from falling on the library floor. He had earned the nickname 'the curator Earl' because he knew the history and the price of every stick of furniture, every plate and picture at Althorp. She told the stories with humour, and a kind of pride, Diana would later recall. 'She was sweet, wonderful, very special ... she was divine,' she said.

Meanwhile, relations between Diana's parents were deteriorating rapidly. After thirteen years of marriage, Frances had grown up and fallen out of love with her Establishment-figure husband and longed for a different life. 'At eighteen she thought she knew what she was getting into, she wasn't a stranger to Johnnie's world and its masculine mores,' said a family friend. 'But in the sixties, the whole world changed and she realized that Johnnie's life wasn't the life she wanted any more.' Deeply dynastic and rooted in Althorp, not a deep thinker, abstemious and somewhat unsusceptible to women, Johnnie was content with his farm and his committees. He had his cricket team, good causes and the annual fireworks display on Guy Fawkes Night to keep him busy. He was as happy as only an English nobleman can be happy with the monotony of waiting for an inheritance.

Although Johnnie Althorp had too much patrician good taste to question the tedium of his existence, or even to show any great awareness of it, 'Poor Frances was bored to distraction'. She liked concerts, she adored the theatre, smart dinner parties, and the company of talented and provocative people. Still only thirty-one, still an attractive woman, she wanted a new start. 'She did not hate Johnnie in the least then, she was only very sad that the marriage had not worked out. They had fallen out of love, they quarrelled, sometimes violently.... I was sorry for both of them, and for the children, of course. It was a family at the breaking point.... Frances simply wanted her freedom,' said one of her oldest friends, who had warned her of the obloquy that quitting Park House would bring down upon her. 'They will call you a "bolter",' she had said prophetically when Frances told her in the summer of 1967 that she and Johnnie had decided on a trial separation. 'It won't be easy for you.'

But it was too late for caution, or to heed the homilies of old friends: Frances had fallen in love with another man. He was Peter Shand Kydd. An heir to a wallpaper business, he had recently returned to England with his wife, a talented artist named Janet Munro Kerr, and their three children, after an ambitious sheep farm venture had failed in Australia. The Althorps and the Shand Kydds had met at a dinner party in London at the beginning of the year. Shortly afterwards, the two couples went on a skiing holiday in Switzerland together. When they returned to London, according to Janet, her husband and Frances became lovers, meeting secretly at an address in South Kensington. Shand Kydd, at forty-two, was everything that Johnnie Althorp was not: a charmer, amusing and comfortable in the company of women – 'He had a talent for bringing out the best in his women. He was an experienced lover,' according to a former girlfriend in Edinburgh, where they had both attended university. He also had a spontaneous almost bohemian streak that Frances fatally could not resist. 'If you had sat down and thought very hard and invented a man to give Frances everything she was looking for at that moment, it would have been

Peter Shand Kydd,' remembered a friend who had watched the drama unfold. 'He reawakened all her old audacity. From the moment she first saw him, she knew that she was playing with fire.'

What happened next happened quickly. 'One day she was just not here any more,' a servant told an inquisitive gossip columnist who had heard rumours and called Park House to check them out. Althorp, instead of attempting to quell the threatened scandal, surprisingly described his wife's departure as 'a thunderbolt, a terrible shock' – and the legend of 'the bolter' was up and running.

It was both inevitable – given the treachery of society gossip, and her husband's misleading reaction to her going – and unfair. Although she was scolded and publicly condemned even by her own mother, Ruth, Lady Fermoy, Frances curiously made no attempt to explain that the separation had been mutually agreed before she moved out of Park House and took a furnished apartment in Cadogan Place, in London's Belgravia. Nor did she reveal that it was also agreed that she should take Diana and Charles with her. In fact, Diana, then aged six, already able to read and write, and certainly sensitive to the change in the relationship between her mother and father (but too dazed to realize the full implications of her altered situation), had already been enrolled at a girls' day school, which she enjoyed enormously after the solitude of the classroom at Park House. Charles, not yet four and too young to know what was happening, was placed at a local kindergarten. Both establishments had been visited and approved by their father. Sarah and Jane were at boarding school at West Heath in Kent. During the school term Diana and Charles spent the weekends with their father at Park House, and he made a point of visiting them on his trips to London.

That Christmas the family was reunited at Park House. An effort was made to bring back a semblance of normality to the holiday. But it was not a happy time. The hope that the season of goodwill would inspire a new understanding, if not a rapprochement, between Frances and her husband was not to be fulfilled. 'It was my last

Christmas there, for by now it had become apparent that the marriage had completely broken down,' Frances would later say, in an attempt to put the record straight in a statement which, in its cold legal formality, emphasized the implacability that had torn the heart out of the whole family.

Friends still hoped that her affair would soon blow over, but for Frances there could be no weakness or turning back, and perhaps it was the realization that she intended to remain with her lover Shand Kydd, who had also moved out of his home, leaving his wife and children, that caused Johnnie to change his mind about the children. For now he insisted that Diana and Charles be sent to school in King's Lynn, five miles from Park House, 'and that they should thenceforth stay at the house' with him. There was an unpleasant scene – 'just awful, awful' – which Diana recalls to this day and which made her realize 'how much misery and anger there is in the world'. There was also behind this, she would later tell a friend, a recognition of her own insignificance – 'a discovery no small child can bear'. That night she cried herself to sleep, unhappy and despairing about the future. Perhaps the only prospect that was more unthinkable than the break-up of her parents' marriage was the end of her life at Park House.

The scene that Diana witnessed was almost certainly the start of the brawling custody battle that Frances knew from the beginning she was bound to lose.

Not only was the whole might of aristocratic opinion on her husband's side, but so was her own mother, the redoubtable Lady Fermoy. Although custody of children involved in a divorce case usually goes to the mother, there is a small wrinkle in British jurisprudence that favours the father – if he is a nobleman. Frances meanwhile had been named as the 'other woman' in the divorce action brought by Janet Shand Kydd against her husband. The action was uncontested and Janet was given custody of her children. It was timing of the greatest cruelty. For it may truly be said that if Johnnie Althorp ever felt hate for anyone it was for Frances after her humiliating public decampment, and his lawyers lost no time exploiting her newly exposed vulnerability as an acknowledged adulteress. Her custody battle was lost. The Althorps' own divorce followed in April 1969: Frances sued on grounds of cruelty; he countersued, branding her an adulteress. Details of the affidavits read in court were spiteful, spicy and highly publicized, and again Frances was on the losing side. A month later, she married Peter Shand Kydd in a quiet civil ceremony, and soon afterwards went to live on the West Sussex coast.

At Park House, Johnnie Althorp prepared for a new life as a single parent. 'I was distressed, even though I got custody of the children, and Diana, being the youngest of my daughters and still very much around, had displaced her mother in my heart,' he said. 'I never thought I'd marry again. I just wanted to bring up my family. We had to learn to live again, it was very hard.' It was worse than that. According to his son Charles, 'He was really … totally shellshocked. No one, absolutely no one, was able to get through to him. He would just sit in his study, alone for hours and hours.'

Au pairs were engaged to look after the two younger children. Their grandmothers, Countess Spencer and Lady Fermoy, became frequent visitors to Park House. With their tenacious vitality and wide interests (from bridge to mah-jong, Charles would later recall wryly) they provided the distraction and emotional comfort after Frances, in Althorp's cutting words, 'became one of those women who achieve some gossip-column recognition because of their bad behaviour'.

But despite the comfort of grandmothers, and her father's well-meaning but awkward efforts to compensate for her mother's absence, it was a bad time for Diana. Her cat Marmalade died; Ally left; new nannies came and went; and she and her brother were the only pupils at Silfield School whose parents were divorced: her world trembled. At night, she would listen to Charles weeping for his mother in his sleep. Diana reacted like so many threatened seven-year-olds, pugnaciously. The staff remember her temper tantrums with a mixture of amusement and awe. 'She could be extremely naughty sometimes,' said butler Ainsley Pendry, who frequently had to remove her from the topmost banister rail for her own protection, and spoke of her in the most tender terms. Another problem, her father felt, was that because she knew that her elder sisters outshone her – 'They always seemed to be leaving me behind,' she would later recall, as if confessing something shameful – she compensated through mischief. 'A favourite prank of hers was to throw the nanny's shoes and clothes out of the window on to the lawn,' remembered a maid. But her father believed it was Charles who kicked a hole in his bedroom door, 'although it was Diana who put her hand up'.

The year following Frances's departure from Park House, Johnnie Althorp noticed many changes in his youngest daughter. Not only was she becoming very protective of her little brother but her timidity was also beginning to give way to a degree of self-confidence. She loved charades and dressing up; she also revealed a talent for mimicry, as well as a neat sense of humour. Trying to find the words to describe to a cousin the sheer goodness of Silfield School, her father overheard her say, 'Well, all I can tell you is, Miss Lowe [headmistress] thinks that "shut up!" is a swear word.'

Mary Clarke, who answered an advertisement for a nanny in the *Lady* magazine in 1970, was interviewed by Viscount Althorp. Nannies had come and gone, put off, he warned her at once, by Diana's 'high spirits'. Introduced to Diana – 'I can see her now, this child with fair hair down to her shoulders, rosy cheeks and downcast eyes' – Mary, twenty-one years old, and half expecting to be yet another nanny who came and went, accepted the challenge. Besides, she liked the Viscount. He was forty-six then, but not a young forty-six. He had, she thought, an aura of sympathy and loneliness that made her want to help him.

A few days after she had been engaged, Miss Clarke collected Diana from school. Diana, who had a charming sense of the fitness of things when she was on her best behaviour, shook her nanny's hand formally as she got into the car. What happened next was so surprising that Mary Clarke would never forget it. 'I don't know why, but suddenly and very quickly, this little girl of nine was talking about love and marriage. I remember her saying, "I shall only get married when I am sure I am in love so that we will never be divorced."' This became a regular theme for Diana. 'The abiding ambition of this child was simply to marry happily and have children. Even then, I never doubted her for a moment.'

Two decades later, married and divorced, and a mother herself, Mary Clarke would sum up her former charge with an affection that is not without some critical insight, too: 'Beautiful, obsessive, every bit an actress, astute, devious, strong-charactered, nonetheless sympathetic, genuine and sensitive, in tune with ordinary folk'.

'Perhaps I was in danger of spoiling her after the unpleasant nonsense of the divorce,' her father would later muse, although he thought that his mother, Lady Spencer, and his mother-in-law, Lady Fermoy, managed affairs at Park House with 'a wonderfully high hand. They were a little more given to scold. This helped Diana and Charles keep things in perspective, and all that.'

Cynthia Spencer was the firmer of the two grandmothers, and the one whom Diana most closely resembled, both in looks and in personality. Perhaps that is why Cynthia understood her grand-daughter so well. 'It was a terribly difficult time,' she said. 'The children had been hurt by their parents' divorce, how could they not? It was a grim experience, and one felt terribly their pain and confusion.' Diana evenly dedicated all her school drawings to both her parents, and although there were periods when she felt betrayed by her mother, and it was difficult to avoid taking sides, she always kept her photograph by her bed, and continued to visit her regularly at her home in Sussex. 'The whole thing was heartbreaking, but it was not something either Diana or her brother talked about ... but what their eyes said was the truth. Nevertheless, somebody had to be able to say no – especially when Diana's tears flowed,' Lady

Spencer added, showing an exact sense both of her granddaughter's distress and of her wiles. For, although Diana had her mother's spirit, she had also absorbed enough of the Spencer ethos to have a certain will and determination, as well as that peculiar shyness, which Lady Spencer knew better than anyone was the shyness of the strong.

Cynthia Spencer's remarkable understanding of the nature of her granddaughter was the first hint of the woman Diana would become, and even perhaps of the life that was waiting for her.

In 1970, when Diana was nine, her father decided it was time for her to become a boarder at Riddlesworth Hall, an all-girls' preparatory school near Diss in Norfolk. Diana was distraught. She did not want to leave her father, or be parted from Charles. She used tears and then guile to make her father change his mind; she pretended to be ill, felt ill, in fact. She accused her father of not loving her, of sending her away. But nothing worked. Although taken aback by the force of her protest, and aware that her departure would leave an emptiness in his life as large as space itself, her father for the first time stood his ground with her. Boarding school was simply something all well-brought-up girls of her class did at nine. Despite her tears, his conscience was clear.

The day she left Park House for Riddlesworth Hall, with her trunk boldly stencilled 'D. Spencer', her father took a photograph for the family album. It shows a pretty, solemn-smiling girl with shoulder-length auburn hair, dressed in school uniform of dark red jacket, grey pleated skirt and knee-length socks. But it is more than that. For it also shows the vulnerability and shyness and deep feelings of unhappiness and reproach that mingle with the sense of adventure – of starting out – in which all new boarders have their being. 'That was a dreadful day,' her father would later recall, and the pain is there in the picture he took. 'Dreadful losing her.'

If a girl of nine must be sent away to school, Riddlesworth Hall was as good a surrogate home as she is likely to find. Diana's homesickness lasted little more than a month; her mother and father visited alternate weekends; and there were several familiar faces – her cousin Diana Wake-Walker, whose mother Lady Anne was her father's sister; Claire Pratt, the daughter of her godmother; and Alexandra Loyd, whose father was the Queen's land agent at Sandringham – to keep her company.

Diana's three years at Riddlesworth passed in the kind of anonymity that would be mercifully forgotten if she had not become royal and famous and her academic mediocrity made into a kind of legend, her smallest accomplishment (Legatt Cup for 'helpfulness'; non-speaking shepherd in a nativity play) recalled with a frenzy of social inferiority by classmates and teachers.

In the autumn of 1972, the second great blow in Diana's life came when her grandmother, the saintly Lady Spencer, died of a brain tumour. Her father broke the news to Diana gently: 'The time has come to be strong and brave ...' She knew at once what was coming. Grandmother Spencer was her favourite, most loved and cherished above all her grandparents. Never before had she known such unhappiness. 'Who else will say no to me now?' she poignantly asked her father at her grandmother's memorial service attended by the Queen Mother in the Chapel Royal beside St James's Palace. 'The living and the dead are never quite separable,' he told her. This sounded so natural, so certain, Diana accepted it as a fact, and whether he meant it or not, or whether he was struggling after a truth for himself (in 1991 Althorp House was exorcised after the family became convinced that the ghost of the seventh Earl was somehow to blame when the eighth Earl's condition inexplicably began to deteriorate after he had appeared to be recovering splendidly from a stroke), from that day Diana has been convinced that Grandmother Spencer watches over her from the spirit world.

But it was a brief almost unnoticed conversation in the real world that day which suggested that somebody else was also taking a particular interest in the young Diana. 'The Queen Mother was particularly kind to her,' her father would recall. 'She knew how close Diana had been to her grandmother, and how upset she was.

She asked her questions about herself, which Diana answered simply.' He was proud and surprised that when the Queen Mother said goodbye to him that afternoon, she said, 'I can't tell you how very much Diana pleases me. I cannot look at her without a smile of pleasure.'

Whether it was Grandmother Spencer's supernatural intervention or simply down to unprecedented swotting, in 1973 Diana passed her common entrance exam to enable her to follow in the footsteps of her sisters, Sarah and Jane, to West Heath, a small, expensive boarding school near Sevenoaks in Kent. But after her examination triumph, the Riddlesworth pattern emerged all over again: perfunctory classwork; began to learn the piano, but gave it up; wanted to become a ballet dancer, but grew too tall. 'She was in that half of the class that made the top half possible,' her father once observed with a kind of resigned affection. Nevertheless, everyone would remember her 'good humour, her willingness to try, and above all her altruism'. Said headmistress Ruth Rudge, awarding her the Miss Clark Lawrence Prize in 1977 for service to the school, 'She's a girl who notices what needs to be done and then does it willingly and cheerfully.' Once a week, wrote an early biographer, Diana 'used to visit an old lady in Sevenoaks, helping her with shopping and domestic chores; she also visited and assisted at a centre for handicapped children.' She was a girl of genuine tenderness, and these were commendable acts of kindness, but told over and over again in books, magazines and newspaper articles inspired by the Palace spinners, the legend grew that she had much to teach Mother Theresa.

Fortunately, the reality of her own stunning mediocrity did not trouble Diana. She always knew that there was more in her than she had yet revealed. 'I always felt very detached from everyone else,' she would later reflect. 'I knew I was going somewhere different, that I was in the wrong shell.'

It was a useful philosophy for a student whose sisters had made such notable impressions at the school. Jane was a prefect in the sixth form, the smartest girl in her class, and captain of the school lacrosse team when Diana arrived. Sarah had a similar talent; but with rather more social conviviality in her make-up, her record was somewhat blemished when she was caught swigging alcohol in the dorm, and rusticated for one term. 'I drank,' she would later say dismissively of the episode, 'because I was bored.'

Sarah was the sister Diana wanted to be.

But the English aristocracy, like God, works in mysterious ways, and it was beyond the West Heath curriculum that Diana's future was being shaped.

Chapter Five

Diana was a tall, leggy fourteen-year-old when Grandfather Spencer died, aged eighty-three, in 1975, and her father became the eighth Earl, turning Diana and her sisters into ladies, and Charles, aged eleven, into a full-fledged viscount.

If her achievements thus far had been modest, as Lady Diana her potential was limitless. She began developing mannerisms that would later become famous all over the world. She began to walk with her head held down, to minimize her height. 'She hated drawing attention to herself. She never paraded the fact that she was a lady,' said one West Heath friend. 'She had class written all over her even then.'

Her beloved Park House was disposed of and the new Earl Spencer and his family at last moved into the ancestral seat, Althorp. The Earl had never been a talkative man; it was said that an awareness of the weather was often the only reliable basis for conversation. But now his taciturnity, and increasingly portly air of appearing to wish he were somewhere else, was respected as the autocratic reserve of the patriarch.

It was, however, an air that some women found strangely seductive in a wealthy, sober, unattached earl with hunting fields, thousands of acres of Northamptonshire farmland, thousands more in Norfolk, and a formidable collection of priceless paintings on the oak-panelled walls of his stately home. It was almost like sex appeal.

But Johnnie Spencer hated his ex-wife and loved Althorp, and these two passions took up most of his time. Diana and her sisters were surprised when the following year he was named in divorce proceedings against Raine, the Countess of Dartmouth, initiated by her husband, the Earl of Dartmouth. 'Sometimes it takes forever for the glaringly obvious to crystallize in your mind,' Diana would later reflect wryly.

Raine was to the grand manner born. Daughter of romantic novelist Barbara Cartland, she was a minor but meddlesome Tory politician in local government, with her mother's flair for publicity and a similar passion for bouffant hairdos, when she met Johnnie Spencer in the early 1970s and proposed that they work together on a book for the Greater London Council called *What is Our Heritage?* She would write the text; he could take the photographs.

Nobody imagined that their relationship had gone beyond its professional understanding when Raine's husband sued for divorce, citing his old Eton chum. 'She came to me,' said Barbara Cartland, 'and said, "Mummy, I'm madly in love, just like one of your heroines."' Well, not quite like one of her heroines: Raine was forty-five years old, the mother of four children, and had a reputation on which you could sharpen knives.

Lord Dartmouth was awarded a decree on the ground of her adultery and given custody of their children. At this point, despite all the pleasure of watching Raine's come-uppance in court, Diana and her sisters grew uneasy. While they could forgive their father his amourette, however unsuitable they considered it to be, his marriage to this woman would be excessive. 'Sometimes,' said Sarah, 'Daddy seems to make life so difficult for himself.' They had met the enemy and taken her measure. They knew that Raine was smarter, stronger and more ambitious than their father, and that her determination to be the next Countess Spencer wouldn't waver. Their father's efforts to bring them together with his mistress continued to fall on stony ground. They hated her. They hated her bossy manner. They hated the way she called their father 'John-nikins'. And especially they hated the way she acted as if she were already the *chatelaine* of Althorp. Some of this, Charles, aged twelve, told her in a letter; some of it she learned from poison-pen missives Diana more cautiously persuaded a schoolfriend to write. Acid Raine, they called her; but their father would not hear a word said against her.

In July 1977, two years after his elevation to the earldom, Johnnie and Raine were wed at Caxton Hall registry office in London. The family was not told about it until it was a *fait accompli*. Diana wept when she was told. But, aware of her manipulative ways, and remembering the tears she had shed when he had told her that he was sending her to boarding school, her father (who thought the disapproval of his children 'unkind but perhaps understandable') believed that she was punishing him by 'pretending to be more dismayed than she really was'.

But her tears perhaps had another purpose. Twice she had failed her O-level exams at West Heath, and she had no intention of sitting them again. If there existed any doubt about Diana's abilities, there existed no doubt about her aspirations. She wanted to go to the Institut Alpin Videmanette, an elite finishing school for European aristocrats, near Gstaad in Switzerland. Her sister Sarah, whom she imitated and adored, had had such a wonderful time there. Although Lord Spencer wanted her to spend another term at West Heath to retake her O-levels, Diana got her way. But the Institut Alpin Videmanette was a great disappointment to her. She found it irksome having to speak in French all the time, especially to other English girls, like her new friend Sophie Kimball, and she quit after only one term, having taken classes in dressmaking, cooking and skiing. Her abrupt departure from Switzerland surprised nobody. 'She never settled down here, she scarcely made a gesture of studying,' said a teacher.

Diana was now seventeen, and her Englishness was unmistakable. She was tall and blonde and wholesome. She had lost and gained weight in all the right places. 'The insignificant ugly duckling was obviously going to be a swan,' said her brother Charles, who had reached an age when he noticed these things. She completed a cookery course at a cordon bleu school in Wimbledon, learned to drive a car, signed up to become a student ballet teacher at the Vacani School of Dancing in Knightsbridge, run by the redoubtable Betty Vacani, who had taught the princesses Elizabeth and Margaret their first steps in the 1930s. Life had never been more fun or more hectic.

The only cloud on the horizon was the Raine cloud. There was a general feeling among the Spencers that their father's second wife dominated him. Disapproving of Raine's efforts to turn the debt-ridden family home into a paying proposition, Althorp became a symbol of their enmity, a whole thesaurus of hatred between them. It was a doubtful kindness, said Charles, to restore the glories of Althorp at the cost of selling off its heirlooms (including eleven Van Dycks and dozens of the estate cottages). But their father resented the suggestion that he had very little to do with the running of things. Raine was simply much better at dealing with people and getting at the root of problems. 'She loves her clothes and jewellery, and I'm happy for her. I don't mind how she is, as long as we're together,' he said.

In London, Diana tried not to think of Raine, or her clothes and her jewellery. As much as she missed her father, she was enjoying her new freedoms. Her mother had kept a house in Chelsea and for a while Diana stayed there, together with Heath schoolfriend Laura Grieg and, later, Sophie Kimball. The girls got on like a house on fire, although Diana would tape notes to the walls reminding them to turn off the lights, and to lock the door if they were last in at night. Some evenings Diana saw her sister Jane, who was an editorial assistant on *Vogue* magazine; she saw less of Sarah, still her role-model, who was working for an estate agency. She loved to listen to Sarah's glorious bulletins of what it was like to be eighteen, or twenty, or twenty-two, to share skiing holidays in

Switzerland with the Prince of Wales, the world's most eligible bachelor – and their sixteenth cousin once removed – with whom Sarah had had a nine-month close friendship, and who had been her guest at a weekend shooting party at Althorp in 1977.

Diana later described that weekend. It was November, cold and extremely wet. On weekend leave from West Heath, sixteen years old and keen to meet the Prince, she was dressed in a borrowed anorak several sizes too large for her, jeans and green wellington boots. With her own share of royal blood in her veins – all of it flowing from illegitimate liaisons: four of her ancestors were mistresses of English kings – she was wise enough to know that princes are never more engrossed than when killing things, and kept out of his way most of the day. Finally in the deepening twilight they came face to face in a ploughed field near Nobottle Wood. 'What a sad man,' she thought. He was slightly under five foot ten inches tall, and she realized that she would tower above him in heels (she was already conscious of her height). But she liked his eyes. They were blue and deep-set, making him seem reserved and watchful. Later, when asked to ascribe significance to that first meeting, the Prince would gallantly recall thinking, 'What a very jolly and amusing and attractive sixteen-year-old – full of fun.' Diana didn't believe a word of it. 'I suppose it makes a nice little segment of history, but I think he barely noticed me at all.'

Meanwhile Sarah had remained a glamorous and worldly figure in Diana's young life. Witty, clever, queen bee of the social circuit, her face and her name well known to readers of gossip columns and society magazines, she had travelled, dined in the best restaurants and stayed in the finest hotels and she had had a brief romance with Gerald Grosvenor, the fabulously wealthy future Duke of Westminster. Diana was longing to be grown up, to have romances and adventures of her own.

Jane, the middle sister, who kept her own company as compulsively as Sarah did not, was the first to wed. Her husband was Robert Fellowes, whom she had known since their Park House days. His father had been one of the Queen's land agents, and now the thirty-six-year-old former broker was Her Majesty's assistant private secretary, already marked out as a high flyer in the royal Establishment. The wedding at the Guards Chapel in April 1978 was the first major social occasion that Diana as chief bridesmaid had attended in her own right as a young woman. Many of the royals attended the wedding, and guests who had not seen Diana for some time were astonished to discover how grown up and attractive she had become. There was a naturalness in her manner, an elegance as well as a certain shyness in the way she moved. She was English and looked it, aristocratic and looked it. It did not escape the Queen Mother's notice how very much she had changed since she had last seen her at Grandmother Spencer's memorial service six years before; she congratulated her father on the fine job he had done in bringing her up. 'But now you have the most difficult part,' she told him at the reception at St James's Palace. 'You must think about her future settlement in life.'

'Perhaps,' Lord Spencer would later reflect, 'her advice was not as uncomplicated as I had thought.'

Chapter Six

By now the Prince and Lady Diana were on a collision course. Her father 'half suspected it', and some believed that the Queen Mother not only more than half suspected it but was also probably helping to set the course. What is not in doubt is that Diana's sister, Lady Sarah, who many had been convinced would be the future Queen of England, had lost her chance. Still only twenty-three years of age, extraordinarily beautiful, with marmalade hair and olive green eyes, she had had almost everything going for her except perhaps discretion – and a clean bill of health.

A chain-smoker ('Fag-ash Lil', Diana called her), shockingly thin, Sarah had been suffering from the slimming disease anorexia nervosa, which began with the collapse of her romance with the billionaire Gerald Grosvenor, the future Duke of Westminster. It was on the rebound from this unhappy interlude that Sarah began her relationship with the Prince in the summer of 1977. Charles, under particular pressure from Prince Philip at that time to 'think about the future with greater energy and determination', indicated his interest in Sarah. Whether this was a ploy to get his father off his back, or whether he genuinely believed that she was a serious possibility, is a question that still divides people: his friends claim he gave the possibility a long, hard look; hers say he was simply using her. However, he was definitely aware of her weight problems (he had urged her to seek a cure in alternative medicine, one of his favourite subjects at that time), and he certainly knew that the

Palace vetters had an implicit prejudice against nervous disorders in a potential queen, the mother of a future monarch. On these grounds alone he knew that there would be the strongest objections to Lady Sarah.

Sarah knew this, too. 'You have to feel exactly right, you have to be very confident in yourself, to put yourself through that ordeal, and Sarah didn't,' said a friend. Anyway, by the time she gave a magazine interview in which she declared that she was not in love with Charles and that she would not marry anyone she did not love – 'whether he were the dustman or the King of England' – she knew that it was all over for her and was past caring.

According to Stephen Barry, what hurt the Prince far more than the disavowal of her love was that after asserting she was 'a whirlwind sort of person, not a person who goes in for a slow courtship', she claimed that after nine months together, including a much speculated-upon skiing holiday in Switzerland – as well as the customary airings at Royal Ascot and polo at Smith's Lawn, where potential brides were submitted to the scrutiny of the world's press – their relationship had remained 'totally platonic'.

'What are people going to make of *that*?' Charles wearily asked Barry, who knew 'how sensitive he was about the wimp label' some critics were still trying to pin on him.

The sudden departure of Lady Sarah Spencer as a potential bride – 'a runner', in Palace parlance – not only increased speculation but also rearranged the field dramatically. Almost all the visible women in Charles's life had credibility, but the question was: did any of them have princess potential? The idea that it would be her own sister who would overshadow and displace her in the Prince's life never entered Sarah's mind.

After nine months, even if they were nine platonic months (and given the somewhat fragile state of her health during that time it is unthinkable that they were not), Sarah knew Charles well enough to know his taste in women. And Diana was not his type at all. 'The women the Prince liked best ... they were the ones who had experienced most,' Stephen Barry would put it in his own succinct way.

Diana was four years old, and Charles was still a pupil at Gordonstoun, when Camilla Rosemary Shand went to bed with her first lover in 1965, the year she came out.

Camilla was of a world Diana would never know. It was the time of Swinging London. The debutantes were preparing for the Season with an extra special sense of excitement and adventure and that anxiety of the young when taking some new direction. But Camilla, who had spent six months in finishing schools in Switzerland and Paris, showed no fear at all. In her group, which included Fiona McGowan, Kirstie Aitken, Jane Wyndham and Carolyn Gerard Leigh, aristocrats to their polished fingertips, she was very much the leader, with a charisma that girls of eighteen rarely have.

'She was terrific fun, enormously popular, and although she wasn't a beauty like Mary Gaye Curzon, she was attractive and sexy,' said Kevin Burke, who, at the age of nineteen, independently wealthy, and considered one of the catches of the Season, became her first lover. 'She was never tongue-tied or shy, and she always had something amusing to say.'

But as the Season progressed and their friendship deepened, Kevin began to understand things about her that nobody else understood. He was struck by the store she placed in the fact that her great-grandmother had been King Edward VII's mistress. 'She was always mentioning it, as if it were something almost talismanic....'

She had always known how to grab a person's attention with some startling admission, or sometimes simply a look. 'She was a Sloane Ranger before there were Sloane Rangers,' remembers Lynn Ripley, who was in the same class at Queen's Gate, a private girls' school in London's South Kensington, a block away from her family's town apartment. The school was popular with aspiring debutantes; actress Lynn Redgrave, who hated it there, said it was simply an establishment to prepare girls for a good marriage. 'When I arrived Queen's Gate was changing. It had been a place where girls were taught how to write cheques and play bridge,' says Booker Prize author Penelope Fitzgerald, who taught English to the sixth form, and believed standards at the school were improving. 'Our girls were so beautiful. Many of them came from old country families where in each generation the man would have married a beautiful young wife. So, of course, many of ours girls were quite lovely to look at.' Those who were a little less lovely were allowed to wear make-up – 'in a discreet way,' recalls Fitzgerald.

Camilla wore a little make-up. Her mother Rosalind was the daughter of the third Lord Ashcombe, whose ancestor Thomas Cubitt built Belgravia and founded the construction company of that name; her father, Bruce Shand, a partner in a Mayfair wine merchants, had been a major in the 12th Royal Lancers, and twice won the Military Cross in the war.

'We called her Milla,' says Lynn Ripley, who had a brief fame in the 1970s as a pop singer named Twinkle. 'We didn't get on very well, but I must admit she had a magnetism and a confidence I envied like anything. She was one of those people who know what they want and know that they will be a success in life. She was fifteen and a half years old when I knew her, but I knew even then that the world was going to hear a lot more of Milla Shand....'

But first Camilla was determined to make her mark as a debutante. She was never going to be Deb of the Year, but she was going to be noticed. (Sadly, she was first noticed when a deb's delight was killed in a car accident after her ball at Uncle Harry Cubitt's estate in Surrey. 'It had a great effect because after that hostesses became seriously nervous about drinking and driving, and hired buses if the party was out of London,' said Kevin Burke.)

The Season began for Camilla on 25 March 1965, with her cocktail party at 30 Pavilion Road to meet some of the other 150 debs and the eligible young men who would escort them through the hectic four months of parties and dances. There would also be the Derby at Epsom on the first Wednesday of June, the four-day Royal Ascot meeting in the third week of June, Wimbledon for the tennis championships, Henley for the rowing, the four months ending with Glorious Goodwood and the Cowes Week regatta on the Isle of Wight.

Mrs Betty Kenward was the venerable social arbiter of *Queen* magazine, in which she wrote the title-dropping 'Jennifer's Diary'. No party was worth going to unless it had her patronage and was noted in her column ('looking after Betty' was considered a price worth paying by ambitious parents of debs on the make). It was also Mrs Kenward who vetted and approved all the young men before they could become acceptable escorts, 'players in the game.'

Kevin Burke, whose father, aviation pioneer Sir Aubrey Burke, was chairman of Hawker Siddeley, had Mrs Kenward's seal of approval. Fun-loving by nature, he found that parties came naturally to him, and it was Camilla with whom he did the rounds (she had other admirers, but Kevin was the most regular). 'Every night we had two or three cocktail parties to go to, and then there was a dance each night of the week in London, and a couple of dances to chose from at weekends in the country,' he remembered of those heady days. 'All you needed was enough money to put petrol in the car [he had a yellow E-type Jaguar, which Camilla called The Egg] and pay for your cleaning, and the rest was provided. It was the best time, and I had just about the best, most fun partner you could wish for. I remained with Camilla all that year ... I suppose we were in love ... Then she ditched me.'

Camilla had met Andrew Parker Bowles.

Andrew had missed her coming out year. A captain in the Royal Horse Guards, part of the Household Cavalry, he had been serving in New Zealand as ADC to the Governor-General. But his younger brother Simon had dated Camilla several times, and it was he who introduced her to Andrew after he returned to England. Captain Parker Bowles, then aged twenty-seven, was a glamorous and sophisticated figure after Mrs Kenward's diet of debs' delights she had been living on for a year, and she was besotted. He seemed to know everybody. His father, Derek Parker Bowles, was regarded as the closest 'straight' friend the Queen Mother had; she was a frequent visitor to Donnington Castle House, the Parker Bowles family home set in a 1,000–acre estate near the Newbury racecourse, in Berkshire.

In London, Andrew lived in a small bachelor apartment in Portobello Road in Notting Hill, and it was there that he and Camilla began what friends remember as 'a very hot affair, indeed'. Andrew was already an accomplished lover and quickly proved himself to be an unfaithful one too. He had a penchant for beautiful titled women, including Lady Caroline Percy who was already the steady girlfriend of a baronet, and pursued Lady Amabel Lindsay – the fascinating wife of Patrick Lindsay, a dashing director of the auction house, Christie's.

'I certainly knew I wasn't the only person being taken out by Andrew at that time,' recalls Lady Caroline, the eldest daughter of the tenth Duke of Northumberland. 'There were always other girls and older women. I never knew Camilla very well when we came out, but when I was with Andrew she would come up to me at parties and ask me what I was doing with her boyfriend. She was always doing this to girls at parties. But I got fed up with it and said to her, "You can have him back when I've finished with him."'

Parker Bowles's reputation as a ladies' man was well established by the time he met Camilla in 1966. He had been engaged to be married three years earlier to Sue Morley, the daughter of a brigadier. Miss Morley, aged nineteen, had previously been engaged to Sir William Piggot-Brown, the amateur champion National Hunt jockey. The weekend before the wedding was due to take place, Sir William and Sue got cold feet and called the whole thing off. 'Her father got very tricky and I agreed to meet his expenses,' recalls Sir William. 'But there was the question of the presents – all the linen and towels were initialled. I wanted to keep the ones with W.P.B. on them, but the S.P.B. ones were no use at all to me.

A month later, Andrew, who was almost my best pal in those days, rang me and said that *he* was going to marry Sue and was prepared to buy all the S.P.B. stuff off me. He wanted to come round at once and do the deal, but I was riding that afternoon and he was off to Scotland the next day for two weeks. We agreed to meet on his return. But when he came back, it was all off – an even briefer engagement than mine to Sue.'

The greatest gift that Andrew Parker Bowles gave to his women 'was the knowledge that sexuality was healthy – something to be explored', says one grateful recipient of a similar gift from him in the 1960s. And, while Andrew continued to see other women, Camilla dutifully started to explore her own sexuality with banking heir Rupert Hambro.

Rupert knew that their affair was futile because of Camilla's obsession with Andrew, but he liked her and knew that they would always be friends. He still remembers the masochistic glee she took in telling him about the tricky situations Andrew's unfaithfulness sometimes caused. But she often saw the funny side of things afterwards; her girls' talk always had the funniest lines and the best anecdotes. Once, she told Carolyn Gerard Leigh, when she let herself into Andrew's apartment (she had a key), she discovered her lover looking distinctly uncomfortable, and Lady Amabel Lindsay, the Earl of Hardwicke's elder daughter, behind him looking distinctly embarrassed. It was, adds Rupert Hambro (whose sister-in-law Charlotte was also eventually to fall under Parker Bowles's remarkable spell), the end of that particular friendship. It was also the end of the *billets-doux* Lady Amabel illustrated with catty, childlike drawings – "champagne bottles labelled *BabyShand*" – mocking Camilla.

'Andrew behaved abominably to Camilla, but she was desperate to marry him. When I was with him I discovered that he was also having an affair with a married woman,' says Lady Caroline Percy. 'I had my revenge by going over to Paris with Mickey Suffolk [Earl of Suffolk and Berkshire]. When Andrew heard of my little fling, he went straight back to Camilla. So she got him back after I'd finished with him, as I'd promised.'

It was 1970, and Camilla would have to wait another three years before she would finally get Andrew to the altar. 'One should never be despairing about the future, it's seldom anything like what one imagines it will be,' Camilla told a friend shortly before Prince Charles came into her life – and just after Andrew had slipped away again.

This time he was in pursuit of Princess Anne, whom he had known for years but had recently met again at Royal Lodge, the Windsor Great Park home of the Queen Mother. It was apparent to both of them that the attraction was mutual, although the Princess, who was to celebrate her twentieth birthday in August, had been considered for over a year to be the property of former Irish Guards officer Brian Alexander, younger son of British war hero Field Marshal Earl Alexander of Tunis. Inexplicably, Alexander had failed to pounce – 'A dear, lovely man, but too wet,' sighed Princess Margaret, who knew wet – and Andrew seized his chance.

Although they had a great deal in common, including a keen interest in horses – he was a fine amateur jump jockey – they also had much that separated them. 'I don't know whether Andrew truly believed he could win Anne's hand or not – but what did he have to lose?' asked a close friend of his at that time. 'Andrew could never resist a challenge, and nothing is quite so aphrodisiac as the unattainable. He was a Catholic [educated at Ampleforth, the leading British Roman Catholic boys' boarding school], and a royal loses the right of succession by marrying into the Church of Rome. I doubt if the succession thing was ever an issue for Anne, but the Catholic thing would have been a real problem for the Queen. Anyway, the affair was always more carnal than cerebral and finally fizzled out. The fact that Andrew was posted to Germany didn't help matters, of course.'

It was into this louche world, if not into Camilla's lap, that Charles fell. 'He was just down from Cambridge and, if he wasn't precisely a virgin,' remembers the Argentine polo player Luis Basualdo, 'he was certainly still wet behind the ears.'

After a sheltered adolescence, the Prince had engaged in a brief romance at Cambridge with history graduate Lucia Santa Cruz, the vivacious daughter of the then Chilean Ambassador to London. Three years older than the Prince, Lucia was sufficiently practised in the ways of courting (and of avoiding the Trinity College curfew which separates sexes after dark) to have acquired a key to the Master's Lodge for their meetings.

'But for the Prince real life began with Camilla,' insists the well-informed Basualdo, who found the Prince's sexual exploits a subject of deep interest. No one knows how Basualdo, a nonentity by royal standards, got himself so firmly fixed in such a closed strata of society, a society with its own rules and customs, and its own view of things. But Charles had a professional admiration, it was almost a kind of awe, of the Argentine's prowess on a polo pony, and the two strangely disparate men developed a rapport on and off the polo field. 'Prince Charles either met his girls at polo or took them to polo,' Basualdo recalls of those early days. 'A favourite place was the Guards Polo Club. There was a little group of them: Carolyn Gerard Leigh, whose father had commanded the Household Cavalry and had been Silver Stick in Waiting to the Queen; Mary Ann Paravicini, whose husband Nick played at the club; and Camilla Shand. Everybody knew that Camilla was sort of Andrew Parker Bowles' Girl in Waiting, but Andrew was in Germany ... and Charles tended to focus on her, and vice versa.'

Nobody doubted that Camilla was an eye-opener as well as an education for Charles. 'That was the time it first struck him that he could have virtually any young woman he desired,' says Basualdo. But, for the moment, he desired only Camilla, and she shared a small flat with Virginia Carington, daughter of Tory grandee Lord Carrington, on the ground floor of an apartment building in Pimlico. It was not a discreet rendezvous for a prince. The press was on almost constant watch, and the danger of exposure was considerable.

Using the houses of trusted friends, or the 'Master's Lodge solution' as Charles called it, was not always practical, especially at short notice. The problem of where to take Camilla, and the many women who would follow her, was solved by Lord Mountbatten, his beloved Uncle Dickie, in whom he confided matters he could never even begin to discuss with his own father.

A bisexual man of the world, Mountbatten was a self-confessed intriguer. When the Queen called him 'a medieval matchmaker', he wrote in his diary, 'I replied that I was about the only one left, and how did she think kings and crown princes found the right brides ...' He was also, according to his biographer Philip Ziegler, a man who rarely took up any book unless it were one of genealogy, most especially one relating to his own forebears. It seemed almost too good to be true, therefore, when he approved of Camilla so fulsomely. But nothing was ever quite as it seemed with Uncle Dickie, and even then he had other plans for Charles: his granddaughter Lady Amanda Knatchbull was waiting in the wings. But Amanda was still a child, not yet fourteen years old, and Charles would have to be kept fully occupied and amused until Amanda reached a marriageable age. Camilla, he decided, was *exactly* the kind of woman to take the tedium out of waiting; Camilla, he encouraged the Prince with insidious self-interest, was 'a perfect first mistress'.

And, on that urbane and wily note, Mountbatten acted quickly to resolve Charles's dilemma.

'Nothing ever seems beyond his powers,' the Prince liked to say, and within weeks, although far from well (he almost collapsed carrying the Sword of State at the opening of Parliament in July 1970, and his doctors had warned him that the arteries of his heart were in an alarming state – unless he reduced his activities at once he could die at any time), the providential Uncle Dickie had won the Queen's approval for Charles's own separate apartments inside the Palace, where no one was permitted to intrude except at the Prince's personal invitation. 'From now on,' Mountbatten told his friend, the romantic novelist Barbara Cartland, who would become the Prince's stepmother-in-law, 'Charles can invite anyone he wishes for dinner, or a bit of boffing, and not even his own family need know.'

In Camilla, Charles had followed exactly Mountbatten's advice to pick his girlfriends from that tiny circle of the wealthy upper classes in which he also made the male friends with whom he weekended, hunted or played polo, and in whom discretion was *de rigueur*.

But Uncle Dickie was not infallible, alas. And another piece of advice which he always emphasized – and which became enshrined in the Prince's personal rules of engagement in matters of the heart – would have disastrous consequences for Charles long after Mountbatten was dead: Never, said Mountbatten, write compromising letters – the telephone was safer than the pen.

Chapter Seven

Back in England after his two-year posting to Germany, his brief but satisfying affair with Princess Anne emphatically over (Anne was now dating Lieutenant Mark Phillips of the Queen's Dragoon Guards), Andrew Parker Bowles rediscovered a keen interest in Camilla Shand. As a career officer in the Household Cavalry, regarded as the military extension of the Royal Household, he was flattered that Camilla – *his* Camilla – had taken the eye of the future King. 'Basically they were together for seven years before they married, and it was always Camilla who made the running to marry Andrew,' says his younger brother Simon. Only gradually did it dawn on Andrew how indispensable Camilla really was to him.

'Her relationship with the Prince would do Andrew no harm – in his own circle it gave him a kind of kudos – but I can't believe it was as cynical as that,' says one of Andrew's former lovers. 'He didn't need it. His power over women was extraordinary. Women had no hesitation in believing what he said. He seemed to *compel* them into loving him, although he sometimes dropped them so quickly their heads spun. He could be completely ruthless in that sense.'

It was a ruthlessness that Uncle Dickie wished that Charles possessed. 'He falls in love too easily – and does *cling* so,' he nervously told Barbara Cartland, admitting that he was unable to stop the very romance that he himself had encouraged and facilitated. But, with the nubile Miss Knatchbull growing up in the wings, he was becoming anxious to put the Prince into Proteus mode. Miss Cartland counselled patience.

He did not have to wait long. The end of Charles's affair with Camilla, when it came, was swift and seemed almost inevitable. 'It was one of those natural breaks that both sides accept, and one suspects almost longs for,' says a friend. 'It had nothing to do with Andrew coming back on the scene. It wasn't a question of Charles politely handing Camilla back to him.' In the autumn of 1971 Charles had enrolled at Dartmouth Naval College; the following summer he would begin spending long periods at sea, which was all part of the Palace plan to augment his reputation as a man of action. The break-up therefore was perceived to be inevitable by the handful of friends who knew about the affair. Despite Lord Mountbatten's worries, 'There was never any question then of Charles marrying Camilla,' says her long-time friend Carolyn Benson, who knew them both well. 'He was much younger, simply a nice boy ... Camilla was conscious of her select status but she never wanted to be Queen.'

Although the relationship had been important to the Prince, and had given him the confidence to draw back from the smothering contact with the rest of his family, it had been barely noticed by the press at all.

When he heard the news, Uncle Dickie breathed a sigh of relief. Although his affection for Charles was very real and he would quickly pounce on 'any symptoms of turpitude or self-indulgence', his advice could also be puzzling and contradictory, one moment telling him to play the field for all it was worth, and the next amiably reflecting, 'I thought you were beginning on the downward slope which wrecked your Uncle David's life and led to his disgraceful Abdication and his futile life ever after.' And shortly after this he urged him to become 'a moving target' where women were concerned. In 1965, Mountbatten had played his favourite role of Grey Eminence at the informal conference the Queen had called at Buckingham Palace, together with the Prime Minister and the Archbishop of Canterbury, to draw up a plan for the Prince's education and career on leaving Gordonstoun, and his advice had won the day: 'Trinity College, Cambridge, like his grandfather; Dartmouth like his father and his grandfather; and then to sea in the Royal Navy, ending up with a command of his own.' And so in the summer of 1972, leaving the field clear for Andrew Parker Bowles, the Prince embarked on the final stage of Mountbatten's plan – and prepared to follow his 'moving target' advice to the hilt.

He was not the best or the most generous of lovers, but he quickly discovered that few women were able to decline an invitation to an *intimate* candlelit evening at the Palace with the Prince of Wales, and it soon became a game of numbers. They came for supper, and left early in the morning, often discreetly returned in a taxi to their flats in Kensington or Knightsbridge, remembered the valet Stephen Barry, who occasionally retrieved women's undergarments from beneath the Prince's four-poster bed or from between the crevices of the sofa. When he was confident that he knew the correct identity of the owner, Barry had the misplaced item laundered and returned discreetly packaged in an Asprey gift-box, delivered by Palace messenger; when ownership was open to question, he would make a present of the item to a suitable member of the Palace staff. 'Sometimes,' he said, soft eyes gleaming wickedly, 'this would be a gentleman.'

'I'm good, but my brother tries to live up to Warren Beatty's reputation,' Prince Andrew would later tell a girlfriend. For their father Prince Philip it had been an eye for actresses; for Andrew, it would be starlets and models; but Charles on the whole remained faithful to Uncle Dickie's dictum that he should choose his women from among the wealthy upper classes.

(Although there were few among his early girlfriends without a drop of blue blood, he was capable of occasionally straying into less salubrious and dependable company. In late 1973, when Charles was twenty-five ('BACHELOR PRINCE CHARLES ENTERS MARRIAGE ZONE', read one headline that year), Mountbatten set up a slush fund, administered by an august British lawyer through a private bank in Nassau in the Bahamas (Mountbatten had a holiday home there, on Windermere Island, Eleuthera), to ensure that potentially troublesome conquests could be swiftly and handsomely paid for their silence. Certainly two, and possibly three, six-figure dollar contracts were signed between December 1974 and July 1979, the month Mountbatten was killed by the IRA, and they explain the flawless and sometimes paradoxical discretion shown by his lovers, often in the face of substantial tabloid inducements to tell all.)

For the few women who succeeded in becoming something more than one-night stands, there were new levels of privilege: weekends at Sandringham or Balmoral; rides with the Prince in his Aston Martin; invitations to watch him play polo at Cowdray Park or Deauville; trips on the Queen's Flight, and maybe even love-making in the private compartment.

'But the girls' talk was that he wasn't a great lover, not even a very good one,' says a former English model who had shared an apartment in the 1970s with one of his one-night stands, and who herself had occasionally been invited to make up the numbers at his dinner parties. 'He was excruciatingly shy, and could only do it in the missionary position with the lights out.' But maybe there was another reason for the dark. 'I don't think he was happy doing what he was doing. He was using women, and he knew it.'

At that time, the Palace was building him up as some kind of action man. And perhaps he really believed that he was. 'He lives in an isolation ward of flattery,' said one woman friend in London. 'He goes to Hollywood and is told that he's handsome. He swaps jokes with a comic genius such as Peter Sellers or the other Goons, and they fall down laughing. He boffs a woman once and she tells him that he's the greatest lover she's ever had.... It would be remarkable if after all that a man didn't think he could charm the warts off a toad. They say, Oh the royals are immune to flattery, they are educated to ignore it. But the best education in the world can't defend you against sycophancy on that scale.'

Many thought that he'd had the wrong education at the wrong school, and was being pushed in ways he didn't want to go. 'He doesn't need to be toughened any more,' the Queen Mother told Cecil Beaton in 1968, already deeply worried that Prince Philip in insisting on sending his son to his old school, Gordonstoun, with its Spartan emphasis on physical prowess, was brutalizing his natural sensitivities: when Charles complained to the headmaster that his head had been pushed down a lavatory bowl by other students, he was told not to be such a sissy.

Some of his friends really believed that the women Uncle Dickie urged upon him were privileges perhaps he did not crave. 'I wish Uncle Dickie wouldn't try to persuade me to do something I really don't want to do because I hate to say no to him,' he confided to Mountbatten's private secretary John Barratt. 'Well, that's the one thing you must do,' Barratt told him wisely. 'You must say no when you really don't want to do it.'

But saying no to Uncle Dickie wasn't easy. His emotional weakness was apparent to all who got close to him. 'The rules of my life were laid down for me before I was born,' he told one lover, who pitied him because 'he was royal and could never get free of it'. Another woman who knew him well at that time says, 'He was a gentle melancholic soul. There seemed to be such a loneliness, a strange desolation trapped inside him. It seems odd to say it, but he *hungered* for acceptance. I think he wanted to believe in love and marriage and happy-ever-after stuff, but he knew that the Mountbattens had spent all their married lives climbing into other people's beds. He must have known that his own parents' marriage was less than satisfactory. Quite frankly, his home life – the long absences of his parents when he was growing up, their own frequent separations – could not have been a good foretaste of things to come. But there he was, the Crown Prince, heir to the whole bag of tricks, with no way out. So he just did what Uncle

Dickie suggested he did ... gathered his rosebuds while he may.'

A well-known English actress, a friend but not a lover, who had heard a cry from the heart similar to his remark that 'The rules of my life were laid down for me before I was born,' was so moved by 'the genuine anguish' in his voice that she sent him a copy of Shelley's notes on *Queen Mab*, and drew his attention to these lines:

> Every human being is irresistibly impelled to act precisely as he does act: in the eternity which preceded his birth a chain of causes was generated which, operating under the name of motives, makes it impossible that any thought of his mind, or any action of his life, should be otherwise than it is.

'I simply wanted him to know that he wasn't alone.... Every human being, not only princes, is pre-programmed to some degree,' she said. But the book was never acknowledged by the Prince. 'Maybe he thought it was *lèse-majesté* to remind him that he was just like everyone else,' she said.

During the next seven years, he would have some genuine romances as he dutifully but unhurriedly explored the market place for a potential princess bride. He seemed to be in love with Georgiana Russell, daughter of Britain's Ambassador to Spain. She was an exotic creature (her mother Aliki, was a former beauty queen: Miss Greece, Miss Europe) who first excited the Prince's interest by her habit of going braless. 'She was a curvy young woman,' remembered Stephen Barry, 'and the Prince liked curvy young women.' Eighteen months older than the Prince, a contributing editor to *Vogue* magazine, she also satisfied his weakness for older, more sophisticated women. 'But London was her natural habitat, and I think she rather lost the plot when Charles insisted on taking her fishing,' says a former colleague at *Vogue*.

Charles, like his grandmother, was a fanatical angler, especially of salmon and trout. Unfortunately, the hobby had grown up with him, and his idea of a romantic time was a fishing trip to Craigowan, a lodge on the 60,000–acre Balmoral estate in the Scottish Highlands. He would stand happily for hours in thigh-length waders in the freezing waters of the Dee, while his date was expected to admire him from the river bank (dry-fly fishermen consider themselves to be the true aristocracy of angling, and the Prince rated himself very highly indeed among their number). But there was more to it than mere fishing. Becoming the Princess of Wales was known as 'getting the job' to Palace insiders, and an invitation to go fishing with the Prince was called the Craigowan Test. The arrival of a new girlfriend was always greeted with a flutter of expectancy in the servants' hall.

Craigowan was not a happy experience for Georgiana. 'She was freezing cold and eating scraps because the Prince was on one of his economy drives,' recalled Stephen Barry, not hiding his amusement at her discomfort. 'I think she thought the week would be rather glamorous – a romantic interlude in the Highlands with her Prince. Nothing of the kind. He was standing with his feet in icy water all day, while she was bored out of her mind. I thought then that she was not going to last the course and I was right.' She packed her bags and returned to London, grumbling that fishing may be a pastime of considerable antiquity, but as a spectator sport it left a lot to be desired.

The Prince and Georgiana were together for nine months, but appear to have reached no great degree of intimacy. When she married Brooke Boothby, heir to a baronetcy, in 1976 and her photograph appeared in a society magazine, the Prince was astonished. 'Good God!' he exclaimed, when Barry showed him the picture. 'Her hair is *black* – she's not a blonde at all!'

Shortly after Camilla married Andrew Parker Bowles in July 1973 – the ceremony at the Guards Chapel was attended by the Queen Mother, Princess Anne, Princess Margaret, but not Prince Charles, who was serving aboard the frigate HMS *Minerva* in the West Indies – the Prince fell in love again. This time the object of his desire was Lady Jane Wellesley, the only daughter of the eighth Duke of Wellington, whose ancestor, the Iron Duke, defeated Napoleon at the Battle of Waterloo in 1815, and saw off a blackmailer with his famous retort 'Publish and be damned!'

Small, hardly more than five feet four, but with such vitality that few people ever thought of her as small, Jane was an attractive, bright young woman who worked for a public relations company run by a fey well-connected Irishman named Billy Hamilton. Aged twenty-two, she looked self-confident and sexy; her skin was flawless and photogenic. She was 'already more of a princess than some princesses I know', said Hamilton, who was a close friend of Princess Margaret's husband Lord Snowdon and claimed to know a great deal about princesses.

The Prince and Jane had known each other since childhood (she had attended many of his childhood birthday parties at Buckingham Palace) and it looked serious when he flew to Spain to join the Wellingtons – the Iron Duke had also collected the Spanish title of Duke of Cuidad Rodrigo, and the family owned ancestral estates at Molino del Rey, near Granada – to shoot partridges. 'There is no romance,' Jane offered the obligatory denial. 'We are just good friends.' Some felt it lacked conviction as well as originality, and when she was invited back to Sandringham for the New Year's Eve festivities, 10,000 people jammed the roads around the royal estate to catch a glimpse of the woman who they were convinced would be their next Queen. 'I almost feel I should espouse myself at once,' Charles said.

Nevertheless, the Palace dismissed the idea of marriage as pure speculation. But nobody believed the Palace (they had said there was no truth in the rumour of a romance between Princess Anne and Captain Mark Phillips, and a few weeks later they were engaged to be married), and in London photographers and reporters camped for weeks outside Jane's small terrace house in Fulham. She did not like what was happening to her. She was not the first and would not be the last of the Prince's women to feel that her private life had been taken away from her. Press photographs show a grim and anxious woman under pressure. 'I don't want another title – I've already got one, thank you,' she said with Wellingtonian acidity. But the romance lasted eighteen months before she announced, 'My future lies in another direction,' and headed in the direction of a career in television – and the Earl of Lichfield, a successful photographer of beautiful women. Two days later Charles flew to Singapore and reported for duty aboard HMS *Jupiter*.

The Palace spin doctors, working from a broader design, continued to attempt to push his private life to the periphery of things. Although the Prince was not a happy sailor, and worried dreadfully about being seasick (so did Nelson, Uncle Dickie pointed out positively), he was being packaged in the image of his father and all those other staunch seafarers of the nautical families of Windsor and Mountbatten. But while the royal spinners continued to emphasize his Royal Navy activities and release press statements on matters they deemed to be interesting (his appointment to flight deck officer was considered newsworthy: he duly posed waving his ping-pong landing bats for the benefit of photographers), the media kept their own watch on the more private details of his life.

In March 1974, they got lucky. When the *Jupiter* paid a courtesy call to San Diego, home of the US Pacific Fleet, reporters turned up a real live admiral's daughter for the Prince. She was blonde out-of-this-world pretty Laura Jo Watkins. She gave good quotes, too: 'At the party [to welcome the Prince, held at the Coronado Island Yacht Club] he loaded up a double hamburger with every kind of sauce on the table and ate it without spilling a drop,' she said. 'There's one thing you can't be delicate with – and that's an American hamburger. Only a man with the most delicate manners could have gotten away with it.'

She was American, Catholic and, in her father Admiral James Watkins's own words, 'a free spirit'. Charles was besotted. He had never met a girl quite like her. Uninhibited and amusing ('She called him sir, but in a teasing American way that let him know that she didn't take any of that royal hooey seriously,' says a friend) she was the first of his tall blondes. Uncle Dickie, who had had some worrying moments over Jane Wellesley, considered Laura Jo to be quite a different matter; she was not remotely a viable candidate. 'Queen *Laura Jo?* I don't think so,' he was heard to murmur, confident that nothing could come of her. His granddaughter Amanda Knatchbull, now aged nineteen, remained his secret choice; but it was he who had advised Charles not to contemplate marriage until he was thirty, and he was still biding his time.

In 1974, shortly after he had set up the slush fund, he felt confident enough to write further amorous encouragement to the Prince: 'I believe, in a case like yours, the man should sow his wild oats and have as many affairs as he can before settling down but for a wife he should choose a suitable, attractive and sweet-charactered girl before she met anyone else she might fall for. After all Mummy [the Queen] never seriously thought of anyone else after the Dartmouth encounter [with Prince Philip] when she was 13!* I think it is disturbing for women to have experiences if they have to remain on a pedestal after marriage.'

Although Mountbatten had not met Laura Jo, he knew and liked her father, whom he had met in Malta when the American was in the Mediterranean with the US Sixth Fleet. Confident therefore that she would be a popular choice (and no threat to the attractive and sweet-charactered Amanda), the great Palace puppeteer suggested that Charles invite Laura Jo to London to accompany him to Walter Annenburg's farewell party after five years as the American Ambassador to the Court of St James. A publishing billionaire always willing to encourage anything that would enhance the

---

* The meeting of Elizabeth and Philip at Dartmouth on a rainy July day in 1939 was engineered by Philip's uncle Lord Louis Mountbatten, King George IV's personal ADC. Governess Marion Crawford (Crawfie) recalled his entrance: 'A fair-haired boy, rather like a Viking, with a sharp face, and piercing blue eyes.' In Sir John Wheeler-Bennett's biography of George VI, personally approved by the Queen, he wrote of Philip: 'This was the man with whom Princess Elizabeth had been in love from their first meeting.'

'special relationship' between the two countries, and also quite keen for his party to be the social event of the year, Annenberg immediately offered to fly Laura Jo to London at his own expense.*

Although the Ambassador knew it was the kind of offer the Palace couldn't refuse ('They pay no more than they have to,' he said, aware that women were often expected to make their own way to any rendezvous with the Prince), he must have been disappointed when they asked for her presence in London to be treated discreetly. Unfortunately, or fortunately, depending on which side of the 'special relationship' you stand, Charles invited her to hear him deliver his maiden speech in the House of Lords (a big occasion: the last time an heir to the throne had addressed the Lords the speaker was his great uncle David, Prince of Wales), and she was spotted sitting with the Annenbergs in the Strangers' Gallery by an eagle-eyed reporter. Charles spoke earnestly for sixteen minutes on the need for better co-ordination of leisure facilities to meet the challenge of 'removing the dead hand of boredom and frustration from mankind'. It was a speech he had personally worked on for months, and the Palace spinners were not happy when the presence of Laura Jo in the gallery got rather more attention in the press the following morning than the Prince's worthy call. They were especially unhappy that several papers were describing her as 'an unmarried Wallis Simpson', a reference to a woman the mere mention of whose name still caused deep anguish at the Palace. Nowhere was the anguish more deeply felt than in the breast of the Queen Mother, who blamed the 'meddling' Mountbatten for encouraging Charles to invite Laura Jo, *an American*, in the first place. 'What can he have been thinking?' she asked,

---

* Mountbatten later learned that Admiral Watkins had paid his daughter's fare to England for her date with Charles. He informed the Prince. Stephen Barry heard Charles say that he would recompense the Admiral. But he never did. 'I remember the conversation very well because it was the only time I ever heard Charles discuss money on a personal basis. Air fares, hotel bills, his store accounts were something other people took care of,' said Barry.

although she probably knew, for there was very little in the Palace that she did not know.

Nevertheless, it was not royal pique but Court mourning that prevented the Prince from accompanying Laura Jo to the Ambassador's party on 13 June after all. His great uncle the Duke of Gloucester had died, and the funeral was to take place on the morning after the party. He was, however, sufficiently over his grief to entertain Laura Jo that night in his suite at Buckingham Palace. She returned before midnight to Winfield House, the Regent's Park official residence of the Ambassador. But now the press was on to her and a weekend at Balmoral with the Queen and Prince Philip had to be cancelled because of the amount of publicity she was generating. Two weeks later she returned to the States, where she fell in love with an actor and got married.

'I've fallen in love with all sorts of girls and I fully intend to go on doing so, but I've made sure I haven't married the first person I've fallen in love with. I think one's got to be aware of the fact that falling madly in love with someone is not necessarily the starting point of getting married,' he said in an interview shortly after Laura Jo had gone out of his life. 'By the age of thirty you've seen a great deal of life, met a number of girls, been able to see what types there are, fallen in love every now and then, and you know what it's all about. I would never recommend getting married too young. You miss so much. You get tied down.'

It was not long before he was falling in love again. This time the woman he couldn't get out of his mind was Davina Sheffield. She was not a titled lady, but she was the cousin of Lord McGowan, and that was close enough. Anyway, he didn't want another girl who could throw in his face the fact that she had a title and didn't want another. (He could be inordinately sensitive to imagined slights; although he would remain friends with the daughter of the eighth Duke of Wellington, her remark hurt.)

Born on St David's Day 1951, Davina was a five feet ten drop-dead blonde, with the most beautiful mouth in England.

Photographed by Lord Lichfield, who seldom wasted his time photographing girls who were less than gorgeous, she had even impressed Stephen Barry, who was not easily impressed by women. 'She had the sweetest smile,' he said, and for a time romantically believed that since she was descended from the Buckinghams of Buckingham House, now Palace, she was 'predestined to return'.

Although Davina was deeply involved with James Beard, a powerboat racer and designer (they were said to be unofficially engaged), Charles felt sufficiently encouraged by her smile when they first met to invite her to Balmoral for the Bank Holiday weekend. Cancelling a holiday in Cap Ferrat on the French Riviera with the unfortunate Mr Beard, she accepted. But, like Andrew Parker Bowles before him, James was almost flattered that his beloved should have become the apple of the Prince's eye. 'I'm not annoyed,' he said in valedictory tones when the press caught up with him. 'As far as I am concerned, there is nobody that could match her... But I am delighted that she should have the opportunity to be with him.'

Professionally and privately, 1974 had been a good year for the Prince. He completed his helicopter flying course at the Fleet Air Arm base at Yeovilton (throughout his solo flying time his Wessex v helicopter had been shadowed by aircraft with medics, fire-fighting and other emergency equipment aboard), taking the top-gun Double Diamond Trophy and leading a celebratory fly-past, his personal standard flying from the winch wire beneath his craft. And, still basking in his new love, he heard that his old never-to-be-forgotten love Camilla Parker Bowles had given birth to her first child on 18 December. He accepted her invitation to become godfather to the infant, who was christened Thomas Henry Charles.

But in January 1975, when Davina heard that the Prince had been posted to 845 Naval Air Squadron aboard the aircraft carrier *Hermes*, bound for NATO exercises in the Atlantic, *en route* for Western Australia, the Caribbean and Canada, she decided it was time to make plans of her own. 'She wanted to get out of England for a while and I was a good friend and visiting the Far East on business and took her with me,' recalls Kevin Burke, who had done so much to make a woman of Camilla. In Thailand, Davina split from Kevin and flew to Vietnam, where she worked in an orphanage during the last days of the war. 'I feel a real sense of purpose here and I don't want to leave,' she said, shortly before she was forced by the Viet Cong advance to flee to Bangkok, and eventually in 1976 to return to England to a more personal tragedy: the murder of her mother by raiders at their Oxfordshire home.

She turned to the Prince for solace, and in June was back in the Aston Martin's passenger seat when he drove to the Royal Windsor Horse Show to compete in a carriage driving event. Davina was beginning to look promising again. She was beautiful, intelligent and clearly a woman of some courage and compassion. 'She and Charles were wonderful together,' said a friend. She had passed the fishing test at Craigowan and been driven to a polo match in a royal carriage. She had lunched with the Queen at Windsor and been entertained at Balmoral; she even seemed to have the approval of the Queen Mother (but not, of course, of Uncle Dickie).

But within a few months she would fall prey to the hypocritical criterion and double standards by which a future queen of England must be judged. On a surfing trip to a remote beach on the Devon coast which Charles had discovered during his time at Dartmouth Naval College, she was discovered pleasantly naked by a lifeguard in the men's changing room. 'She didn't bat an eyelid,' he said, and described the experience as 'memorable'. The *coup de grâce* followed when her former boyfriend James Beard revealed in a Sunday newspaper that he and Davina had once lived together in an eighteenth-century thatched cottage near Winchester.

It was no doubt a very nice thatched cottage, and Winchester is a very admirable city, and they were no doubt respectably intentioned lovers, but Davina could never be queen – so Uncle Dickie informed his 'honorary grandson' at a luncheon that, he would later tell his friend Barbara Cartland, was 'not a very festive function – the young man [Charles] was quite keen on her, I'm afraid, and minded greatly for her sake, too'.

And Davina was out of his life forever.

Chapter Eight

At the close of 1976, the Prince bid farewell to his service career. In the navy he was a commander; in the Royal Air Force he held the rank of wing commander. But there were more private satisfactions than the three gold rings on his commander's sleeve, and the wings he wore as a pilot: at twenty-seven, he had been given a command of his own – the minehunter HMS *Bronington*, with a complement of four officers and thirty-three ratings – and that was two years younger than his father had been when given command of the frigate *Magpie* in 1950. 'What a great relief it is when you find that you've actually brought up a reasonable and civilized human being,' his father would say when he heard the news. If it wasn't exactly a crowning compliment, it was probably as close as Prince Philip would ever get to one in the often crotchety relationship he had with his eldest son.

On 15 December, the crew of the *Bronington* ritually 'pushed' the Prince back into Civvy Street seated in a wheelchair, a lavatory seat for a laurel wreath around his neck. The duty to feign cheerfulness was probably easier to perform than to contemplate the life he was being pushed back into. Already the press – and some believed the Queen and Prince Philip, too – had their eye on yet another bride for him. This time it was Princess Marie-Astrid of Luxembourg, popularly known as 'Asty', who was in the frame. Already he must have felt that he had been doing nothing different from this all his life.

In 1977 Queen Elizabeth would celebrate her Silver Jubilee, commemorating the twenty-fifth year of her reign, and he would play an important role in that, as chairman of the Jubilee Appeal. But, that apart, life would go on and he would go on, obeying the rules of a life that had been laid down for him before he was born. Now that he had lost Davina, and it was a loss he felt deeply, he was restive and querulous. Stephen Barry complained of his nit-picking. Even the prospect of the coming-out ball the Duke of Marlborough was giving in June for his daughter Lady Henrietta Spencer-Churchill at Blenheim Palace could not restore his spirits.

He was chafing, too, at rumours in the press that Prince Philip had held secret talks in Belgium with Marie-Astrid's parents, Grand Duke Jean and Grand Duchess Josephine Charlotte, together with Cardinal Joseph Suenens, the Belgian Primate, and a representative of the Church of England, to discuss the religious problems (Marie-Astrid was a Catholic) that would have to be overcome before a marriage could be contemplated.

Although he knew that such rumours were inescapable, a strange distrust had grown between him and his father that made some rumours more difficult to withstand. And the Astrid story rankled. He barely knew her. She had attended his Investiture as Prince of Wales in 1969. He had seen her briefly at Cambridge. 'That does not constitute a romance,' he said.

But it was hard to separate his anger at the rumour from the anger caused by his general disgruntlement with life. The Marie-Astrid stories smacked of media hype. For reasons he could not understand their very publication made him look ahead with a kind of despair for himself that he had never felt before.

It all came to a head when the *Daily Express*, claiming a Cabinet source, ran a front page story in June headlined 'CHARLES TO MARRY ASTRID — OFFICIAL'. The Queen's press secretary issued a denial. The Prince didn't think it was strong enough, and with none of his usual trepidation (astonishing Stephen Barry, who knew 'how much pride he took in his cautious nature'), he picked up the telephone and dictated his own statement to his own press secretary, John Dauth: 'They are not getting engaged this Monday, next Monday or the Monday after, or any other Monday, Tuesday, Wednesday or Thursday. They do not know each other, and people who do not know each other do not get engaged. The Royal Family do not go in for arranged marriages.'

As Palace press statements go, it was a humdinger. It also served notice on his father: if Prince Philip was talking to anyone about his son's future, *he could stop it right now*.

The reason for the Prince's wrath is easy to understand. The enormity of his situation was finally coming home to him: the royal family *did* go in for arranged marriages. His parents' own marriage was proof of that; the ruthless removal of Davina from his life was proof of that. He could have as many women as he liked, and probably any woman in the land he wanted, but he would never be able to please himself about the girl he married.

But what could he do? Sacrifice is the essence of commitment, his beloved grandmother Elizabeth, the Queen Mother, had told him just as firmly as she had told his mother that her work was 'the rent for the room you occupy on earth'. They were more than tracts she expected to be honoured, it was the faith she shed: it was the imprescriptible resin that held the royal family together. But along with Uncle Dickie, she was still the person the Prince increasingly turned to for counsel and advice. And although she was now in her seventy-seventh year (she was as old as the century and had reigned in a world of kings and queens that no longer existed), she always had the time and patience to listen to his problems. She was never irritable with him, like his father; she was never remote and uncomfortably regal like his mother. Her governing emotion was love, not simply allegiance. She was full of shrewdness and understanding; she always knew what to do.

Or to put it another way: the Queen Mother was smart, experienced and tough as nails. Her grandmotherly charm was a convenient mask: it concealed both her professional ruthlessness in matters concerning the royal family and, although she would never betray the bond of trust between them, her determination to see that Charles married the woman of *her* choice, and *not* Uncle Dickie's, a man whose personal ambitions, and influence over Charles, she viewed with suspicion and occasional alarm. (She knew all about his plans for his granddaughter, Amanda Knatchbull; and she disagreed vehemently, but she was sending the tough messages privately, not publicly.) Charles had always been her favourite grandchild, perhaps because she detected in the sensitive Prince many of the traits that she remembered from her husband, George VI. Charles, like him, was nervous and rather shy, and as a boy had been tyrannized by Prince Philip, as poor George had been tyrannized by George v. And, as she had given her strength to George, so she would now give it to the grandson he had barely lived to see, yet in whom he lived on so wonderfully for her.

It was no accident that since the palmy days of Queen Victoria the British monarchy had been a matriarchy, its menfolk ruled by a succession of strong and influential women with the will to make things happen. During the sixty years she reigned, Victoria became the mother of the nation. Her grandson, sailor George v, was overshadowed by the former German princess he had married: ramrod backed, impregnable Queen Mary, who would speak English with a Teutonic accent all her life. But the most popular – and most sweetly ruthless of them all – was undoubtedly Queen Mary's successor, King George vi's consort Queen Elizabeth.*

For nearly forty years this daughter of a Scottish earl had been the lynchpin of the House of Windsor. She had married George – 'Bertie' to his intimates – in 1923, while he was Duke of York, and his elder brother, the future Edward viii, was Prince of Wales. She had serious doubts about marrying the shy, stammering, intensely nervous Bertie – 'as royalty, never, never again to be free to think or speak or act as I feel I ought to think or speak or act', she

---

* At George's death in 1952, she assumed the title of Elizabeth, the Queen Mother.

reflected. But the match was made anyway, and there is little evidence that anyone ever stopped her acting or speaking exactly as she felt she ought.

But her true grit was revealed at the end of 1936, when King Edward in one of the great romantic climaxes of all time abdicated to marry the American divorcee Mrs Wallis Simpson ('... I have found it impossible to carry the heavy burden of responsibility and discharge my duties as king as I would wish to do without the help and support of the woman I love'), and Bertie was enthroned as George VI. Probably no English monarch since Henry VIII had had to play a hand as difficult as the one George was dealt by his abdicating brother. But it was his Queen who acted to save the day with a forceful combination of sweetness and steel. The steel showed in the merciless way she turned the former King, now simply Edward, the Duke of Windsor, into a royal non-person – an outcast who could pose no threat to her beloved, weak Bertie. No Siberian banishment was ever more unsparing. On her command, the Duke's telephone calls to his brother were turned away by the Palace switchboard; even his name could not be mentioned in the family. On her orders, there would be no royal status for his wife, no bows, no bobs for her. Apart from a brief visit to England when his mother Queen Mary died in 1953, the Duke was permitted to return to Windsor only in his coffin, his unroyal and unforgiven widow by his side.

The Queen Mother was a destroyer of people – as primitive as a psalm – to protect her own.

But it was only the gentler, sweeter side of her that the nation saw. Her royal parents-in-law had been disasters as parents: of their four sons, Kent took drugs and was probably bisexual; Gloucester drank and was undoubtedly half-witted; Bertie was Bertie and came sixty-eighth out of sixty-eighth in his year at naval college; and the Duke of Windsor all but wrecked the monarchy. Queen Elizabeth, with an innate genius for the public relations of monarchy, created a whole new image for the House of Windsor – the image of a simple, kind and loving family – on which much of the remarkable success of the post-war British monarchy would rest, and would rest, she was convinced of it, for the rest of time.

As the years rolled on, and she became first the Queen Mother, and then the nation's favourite grandmother, the role seemed made for her. And in June 1977, when this shrewd and strong and beautiful old lady listened to her grandson's apprehensions, and heard the hurt and the anger in his voice, it reminded her of Bertie a long time ago, and it was nothing that she had not heard and dealt with many times before. Her voice, always kind and gentle, was reassuring. In her own understated, worldly way, and for her own reasons, she told him what Uncle Dickie had told him: be patient, play the field. This was not what his father was saying, of course, but the Queen Mother had more influence over the Queen than anyone else in the royal family, and, even at seventy-seven, was not intimidated by the prospect of a fight with Philip. The right girl would come along all in good time, she insisted. Her reasons for counselling delay remained obscure, but her sincerity was unquestionable.

Reassured, the Prince began seeing Lady Sarah Spencer. But it was a romance that was going nowhere and he had time for dalliances, too. Dalliances were also his friend Luis Sosa Basualdo's speciality, and the handsome Argentine polo player became a familiar and provocative figure at the Prince's side at this time. The Prince was a regular member of Basualdo's successful polo team, the Golden Eagles, which won the Silver Jubilee Cup at Cirencester that year. (Now married to the former Lucy Pearson, the daughter of Lord Cowdray, Basualdo was living in a style in keeping with his wife's £8 million fortune.)

At the end of July, the Golden Eagles played at Cowdray and the Prince and Basualdo attended the Cowdray Park Polo Ball. There the Argentine introduced Charles to Cristabel Barria-Borsage, a beautiful South American socialite. 'Christabel came from Colombia, her family were the best there, landowners and coffee growers, and *very* rich,' says Luis, to whom such things are important and must always be stressed. Although Sarah Spencer was Charles's date that evening, it was clear that he fancied Miss Barria-Borsage tremendously and had no hesitation in exercising his princely rights. 'They danced together for hours, and Sarah wasn't very happy,' says Basualdo. Later Charles insisted on driving Miss Barria-Borsage back to London in his Aston Martin. She sat beside him in the front; Sarah and his detective were jammed in the back.

But whatever reservations Sarah may have had about the Prince's ungallant behaviour towards her at the Polo Ball, and the exigent travel arrangements afterwards, she was sufficiently appeased a few days later to accompany him to a party given by Robert de Pass at his Petworth home. But again Cristabel was a guest, and this time Charles's attention was more blatant. During the evening he asked Basualdo to loan him his car. 'He said that Cristabel was feeling tired and he wanted to drive her back to my house, which was about two miles away, without his detective knowing,' recalls Basualdo.

The following morning, Cristabel was blissfully frank about their encounter. 'As they got into bed,' Basualdo repeats her story, 'she asked the Prince: "What shall I call you – Sir, or Charles?" And as he started making love to her, he replied, "Call me Arthur."'

Chapter Nine

In November 1978, the Queen Mother made her first tentative move when she suggested to Charles that he invite Lady Diana, as well as her sisters, to his thirtieth birthday party to be held at Buckingham Palace in November. (It would so please Diana's grandmother, her own dear friend, and one of her Women of the Bedchamber, Lady Fermoy, she had told the Prince in order to explain her unusual interest in the matter.)

If the timing was not exactly to the Queen Mother's liking – Diana was still only seventeen, 'with mousy hair and a lot of puppy fat,' recalls Luis Basualdo, who sat next to her during the cabaret which followed the birthday dance – it was forced on her by the news that Uncle Dickie was finally poised to make *his* move.

Plans were afoot for a visit to India the following year by the Prince of Wales. And the Queen Mother had learned that Uncle Dickie was to accompany him – with his granddaughter and protégée Amanda Knatchbull, who was now a ripe twenty-one. She knew that Mountbatten had always insisted that Charles should not contemplate marriage until he was thirty years old – and his timing, she acknowledged as one professional to another, was perfect.

Although bountifully blessed with the charm that the gods bestow on old ladies, it was twice as lethal in her case because she had lost none of her joyous native cunning, none of her Scottish far-sightedness and indomitable zest for Court intrigue. She would not be outmanoeuvred by this man. She had never trusted him; she could never forget or forgive the fact that he had once been the closest friend of the Duke of Windsor (with whom he had first visited India in 1922). 'Next to American widows bearing gifts,' one of her oldest friends once said, 'she distrusts no one so much as Dickie Mountbatten baring his charm.' And as the years passed, far from mellowing her attitude towards Mountbatten, she increasingly perceived a threat in his views that the monarchy should be modernized, made more relevant: she feared that his salon socialist ideas, the brash manner in which he violated all the accepted rules of the monarchical hype, would destroy the mystique and traditions on which the royal family rested. 'I think what stirs the queen mother's ire most is talk of demythologizing the royal family,' one of her friends says. But this time it was more than that. Mountbatten had placed one relation beside the throne, and she was determined that it would not happen again.

But her profound suspicions of Amanda's grandfather, the undeclared war between them, blinded her to the fact that Amanda herself, apart from being supremely aristocratic (her mother Patricia was Mountbatten's elder daughter; her father was the film producer John Brabourne, a.k.a. John Ulick Knatchbull, the seventh Baron Brabourne), was precisely the kind of woman (brunette, small bosomed, rather serious) who fascinated the Prince barely at all.

And while she continued to think up new ways of outsmarting the smart Uncle Dickie ('It was what put her on her mettle – she was always looking for new ways to rain on Mountbatten's parade,' said a close woman friend, reiterating what she claimed she had once said to the Queen Mother personally), the Palace went into festive mode.

The Prince's thirtieth birthday party was to be the biggest and most glamorous private party the royal family had thrown since the old Prince of Wales was in his partying prime in the 1930s. Five hundred embossed invitations went out bidding guests to

Buckingham Palace on the evening of 15 November. Dancing would begin at 10:30 p.m. Before that, guests would be entertained at fifty dinner parties around London. At the Palace the Queen and Prince Philip and Charles dined with the most important guests, their own ilk, the people with whom they were always most comfortable: Crown Princess Beatrix of the Netherlands and her husband Prince Claus, ex-King Constantine of Greece and Queen Anne-Marie, Prince and Princess George of Hanover, and Princess Elizabeth of Yugoslavia.

'It was one of the great London parties. An extraordinarily mixed bunch of people – from the crowned heads of Europe to the crowned teeth of movie stars,' observed one guest afterwards. But there were some old friends too: Andrew and Camilla Parker Bowles (who had given birth in the spring to a daughter, Laura Rose); Lord Tryon and Kanga; Jane Wellesley; Luis Basualdo, who got a little drunk and, despite his reduced circumstances following his divorce from Lucy (with a final pay-off from the Cowdray family of a mere £220,000), rashly offered the Prince a polo pony for his birthday. (A week later, Charles's polo manager, Major Ronald Ferguson, called Basualdo in New York, reminded him of his generous offer, and asked him to confirm it in writing!)

But just about the youngest person at the party was Lady Diana and, far from making any impression on the Prince, she appeared to be positively overwhelmed by the occasion. The Prince danced with Camilla and Kanga, and with Leonora Lichfield (who, as Leonora Grosvenor, had been an early protégée of the Queen Mother); he danced with Jane Wellesley, and also with the actress Susan George, with whom he had also had a loving relationship. But he did not dance with Diana. 'She was very shy, very naive but rather nice,' recalls the ubiquitous Basualdo, who accompanied her into the Picture Gallery to watch Charles' favourite American group, the Three Degrees, perform a cabaret.

Although the night was far from being a personal triumph for Diana – 'Nobody could have guessed that evening that she would soon be the most famous woman in the world,' says Basualdo – it did not deter the Queen Mother one bit. Indeed, the more she thought about it, the more ideal Diana seemed to be. The dear child, after all, was 'one of us', and not at all unlike what she herself had been when she married Bertie ... pretty, virginal and the daughter of an earl. She was also maternal and apparently good with children. True, she seemed something of a goose, but geese can always be made into swans, and sometimes even into icons. No, pretty young Diana was suitable in every way. Indeed, just as Charles appeared the member of the family closest to departed Bertie, so it was not fanciful to see her friend Elizabeth Fermoy's granddaughter entering the family as her own ultimate replacement. With a little schooling and advice, which the royal dowager was all too ready to provide, Diana was her perfect successor.

But first there was the problem of Mountbatten and *his* protégée, Amanda. It would have been the culmination of a lifetime lived so tantalizingly close to the throne, to end up knowing that his own descendant would one day reach that throne himself (or herself). The Queen Mother *knew* that the proposed trip to India with Amanda and the Prince was to be the start of Uncle Dickie's grand design to bring them romantically together.

'This was more than mere surmise or instinctiveness on her part,' one of her friends said. 'She was, and still is, the best-informed person in the whole royal family.'

It is no secret in Palace circles why this is so. The Palace staff not only like her, they come near to worshipping her: they trust her. Also, since her widowhood, she has had several highly sympathetic male confidants and friends – Malcolm Bullock, Osbert Sitwell, Harold Nicolson, Noel Coward and Anthony Blunt – who were closely tuned to the powerful gay intelligence network at the Palace: 'the single most invaluable source of information on everything that happens inside the royal family,' a senior courtier admits.

(It is a fact that gay men make ideal courtiers. Suffering no wifely competition for their time or loyalty, they can give their full attention to their duties. Devoted, tasteful, loving gossip and the minutiae of Court dress and royal ceremonial, they are comfortable in the milieu of the monarchy. And the Queen Mother, unlike the Queen, was sensibly relaxed about it. Once, discovering her private line crossed by two Clarence House courtiers engaged in a deeply personal conversation, she finally butted in: 'Excuse me, but there's another old Queen here who'd like to use the telephone.')

But now it was Christmas 1978 and time was running out. If the Queen Mother was to stop the Mountbatten–Charles–Amanda passage to India in the New Year she knew she would have to act swiftly. 'Exactly what she said, and to whom she said it, whether she used the network or did it openly herself, I haven't the faintest idea,' one of her oldest friends would say later. 'But it was bloody effective because suddenly, for reasons that still remain unexplained, the Duke of Edinburgh became deeply involved, and was furiously set against the whole notion....'

The Duke argued that Charles 'should not pay his first visit to India in the shadow of this legendary figure, who would inevitably claim the limelight,' Mountbatten's biographer Philip Ziegler would later write. Mountbatten, the last Viceroy of India, when it was the Jewel in the Crown of the British Empire, was stunned by his nephew's objections and by the sense of rebuke in his tone. (Was Philip jealous because his own glamour had long since dimmed in the minds of the people, while Mountbatten's had remained so bright?)

Mountbatten pleaded with the Palace to let him accompany the Prince. He professed shock, amazement, incomprehension. He insisted that he would be able to help the Prince. He would guide, brief, disillusion. He would be the destroyer to protect the flagship, he said to Philip, as one old salt to another. 'It was rather sad to listen to the man who had never prided himself on his modesty, solemnly swearing that he would remain silently unobtrusive,' says one of Mountbatten's former aides.

But Prince Philip was adamant. On 27 January 1979, in frustration and melancholy, Uncle Dickie wrote to his great-nephew:

From a purely selfish point of view I must confess I would be very, very sad to have to forgo the great happiness of being with two young people I love so much and showing them the country which means so much to me, but if the price of my selfishness were to spoil the visit for you, then that would be a price I could not even contemplate.*

It would be the Queen Mother's last victory over her old enemy, but no less sweet for that. 'And it was valid,' says a friend. 'Her *motives* may have been suspect but her *argument* was absolutely valid. Nobody understands the dynamics of royal public relations better than she does. Mountbatten *would* have hogged the whole show. He would not have been able to stop himself. He was a terrible scene-stealer – just like the Queen Mother herself. They were two of a kind.'

Mountbatten's murder that August (by a bomb which also caused the senseless deaths of his grandson, Nicholas Knatchbull, aged fourteen, and a young friend, as well as terrible injuries to other members of his family) was shocking on a global scale, but on a deeper personal level it put new pressures on the Prince's already complex and troubled state of mind. 'Now I have experienced the worst, personally and professionally,' he told Stephen Barry, the day his 'honorary uncle' was buried with all the drums and pageantry the old royal showman could have planned for his own farewell. But long after the headlines had faded he continued to grieve.

'It was ironic that in his sorrow he was drawn even closer to his grandmother,' says a friend. 'In the whole of that family, she was

---

*A compromise was finally reached: Mountbatten and Amanda would travel to India with the Prince but then split up, reuniting only for the final couple of days. Mountbatten was killed by the IRA shortly before the visit was to begin.

the only one – *the only one* – who could feel the weight of his pain....'

The Prince tried to rid himself of grief in activity, and, as if he were still obeying Uncle Dickie's dictum, in a string of calculated, meaningless liaisons: pretty Jane Ward, assistant manager at the Guards Polo Club ('We are very fond of each other ... sometimes I think things could have been different had I never married'); heiress Sabrina Guinness, as cool and sexy as you can possibly imagine ('I love being with him, but please don't try to marry us off'); and Camilla Parker Bowles, never far away ... and saying nothing at all.

Frankly, the Prince's attitude towards women was hardly admirable. Some even said he was a shit. 'He is shy, he is sensitive, he is even sometimes desolatingly lonely, but he is also a shit,' one of his polo friends says pleasantly, pointing out that the words are not mutually exclusive. But the women knew the rules of the game, or they would not come to play. 'An awful lot of women who went to bed with him would never have gone to bed with him if he had not been HRH,' readily admitted one woman who had. 'However badly Sir may treat you afterwards – it's a kind of pact: you know that the royal psychology is based on the notion of rule, right? – you only get what you deserve.'

Even Jane Ward, who lived in a grace-and-favour cottage close to the Guards Polo Club, appeared to take it in her stride when, a few days after giving a mildly indiscreet interview to a British newspaper – admitting her friendship with the Prince, acknowledging the Queen's 'concern' and calmly accepting the overriding impasse – she found herself out of a job and out of the Prince's life.

The Palace was a smoothly functioning machine geared to the protection, promotion and merchandizing of the royal family. But it had been Uncle Dickie who had taken care of the details of Charles's private life, and guided him in his sexual relations and affairs of the heart. Had Uncle Dickie still been alive he certainly would, in the words of one courtier, 'never, never have allowed a person such as Mrs Ward to have happened'.

Jane Ward was a strikingly attractive blonde, intelligent and even mildly well connected in ways that should count for something in Palace circles (her brother, David Herring, was the Joint Master of the Middleton Hunt in Yorkshire, for example). But she was not *quite* from that exclusive charmed circle of extremely wealthy upper-class women from which Mountbatten had insisted the Prince choose his mistresses (and how well this strategy had worked). But infinitely more troubling was the fact that she was considered to be a *career woman*. Moreover, and this was truly alarming, she was separated from her husband, a captain in the Royal Hussars.

The revelation of the close friendship sent shockwaves through the Palace, and even the Queen Mother might have begun to regret the loss of Mountbatten's sophisticated, cynical influence. Almost eighty now, she tired more easily but the pother of the Jane Ward episode, or 'adventure' as she called it, although swiftly and even brutally dealt with by the Palace, convinced her more than ever that she was right about Lady Diana, and about the need to work quickly.

The difficulties of finding a suitable bride were becoming larger every day, given the age factor – the older Charles got, the more difficult it was going to be to find a convincing and tasteful virgin – and given the press attention that by now was building up around the issue.

In November, the Prince began what would be his last great love affair before Diana. Her name was Anna Wallace, daughter of a Scottish laird, whose fearless horsemanship had gained her the interesting nickname 'Whipper'. She was fun, intelligent, feisty, twenty-five years old and even more beautiful than Davina Sheffield. By the time the polo season began in the spring, she was firmly at his side.

In June, when the Prince, as Colonel of the Welsh Guards, was to take the salute at the final rehearsal of the Trooping the Colour parade, Anna was invited to Buckingham Palace to watch from the first floor windows as he rode off. Being invited to watch the Prince play polo was considered a privilege; this was an honour. Stephen Barry, who had seen so many women come and go in the decade he had been the Prince's valet, and usually had such good judgement, suspected that she was destined for 'the job'. When the Prince told him to show Anna around the Palace while he took the salute at the other end of the Mall, he was convinced of it.

He said, 'She had already seen his private rooms, of course. But I showed her the State Apartments. I took her all round. She was fascinated, she wanted to know everything. There was an intensity in the way she looked at things. I think we both had the same idea in our minds: this was the place in which she would one day live.'

According to some of Anna's friends, and to Homayoun Mazandi, whose personal assistant she had been before Homayoun married Lord Renwick, Charles actually did propose to her.

But finally she had too much past – she was twenty-five, not a child, there had been lovers – for the royal family to absolve.

'Once it was revealed that there had been a couple of other men in her life ['the Wallace Collection',* Princess Anne gleefully but unjustly dubbed them], it was all over for Anna. Nevertheless, she definitely walked out on the Prince,' says Barry, who liked her and thought that she had too much class to put up with the Prince's displays of arrogance and chauvinism. 'She walked out on him, there is no question of that. He never spoke of the end of the friendship, but he was subdued for a long time afterwards. She'd been important to him....'

Fittingly, perhaps, the beginning of the end of their affair came at the party the Queen and Prince Philip gave to celebrate the

* She had recently ended an affair with Bahamian-based banker Alan Morris, who was twice her age and whose ex-wife, Johanna, was living with Brian Alexander, Princess Anne's former escort. Previously, Anna had lived briefly with London stockbroker David Coaten; her first love was commodity broker Jonathan 'Jake' Morley, who would shortly marry Davina Sheffield.

Queen Mother's eightieth birthday. It was the end of Royal Ascot week and over 400 guests had been invited to Windsor Castle. Many of them were close friends of the Prince and were there at his personal invitation. 'Naturally, he felt obliged to make them welcome, to circulate, to dance with a few of the women,' says a friend who was a guest that evening.

Abandoned at their table, perhaps aware of how he had similarly treated Sarah Spencer – and remembering *her* fate – Anna fumed. And when eventually the Prince returned, she told him in an emotional voice, 'Don't ever, ever ignore me like that again! No one treats me like that, not even you!'

But it seems the Prince wasn't listening. Or, if he was, he was controlled by a stronger force – Camilla Parker Bowles.

Anyway, a few weeks later at a polo ball at Stowell Park, the Gloucester estate of Lord Vestey, he treated Anna in exactly the same way. But this time he added salt to the wound by dancing almost the whole evening with one partner – Camilla.

It was too much for Anna to bear. She swept out of the party and out of his life.

Why did Charles behave so badly if he loved Anna so much?

'In retrospect,' says one man who knew Anna Wallace well at that time, and remembers that summer, 'HRH was in a corner and looking for a way out. Anna had levelled with him about her previous romances. She had been absolutely honest with him. But he had been slow to tell the Palace, and even more sluggish to reveal the fact that he had actually asked her to marry him. He knew that there was no way the Palace could approve of Anna after her past was out in the open, and he dreaded the trauma of a trial of strength with Prince Philip and fighting the whole Palace Establishment. What was the point? He couldn't win. In the end he simply gave up, he simply abandoned all thoughts of marrying Anna.

'Dancing with Camilla Parker Bowles at Stowell Park that night – I mean, *Camilla Parker Bowles*. Anna wasn't stupid, she knew how

Camilla vetted all his women: Camilla dangled him like a trout – HRH knew that Anna would never put up with that,' Anna's friend remembered. 'And she didn't ... it was all over, she was out of there, and out of his life.'*

Anna's departure could not have been a nicer gift to the Queen Mother on her eightieth birthday.

* Within two weeks of the Stowell Park exit, Anna Wallace became involved with Johnny Hesketh, younger brother of Lord Hesketh. Married in December 1980, they were divorced thirty months later.   ·

Chapter Ten

In the summer of 1980, Lady Diana Spencer was nineteen years old, and it would be her last fallow summer before she became engulfed by the fame of the years ahead, when her smile would become as famous as Mona Lisa's. But already her reputation was being raised and her name discussed in some of the finest, most informed and influential houses in England.

And now she had been invited to a weekend house party at New Grove, the Sussex home of Commander Robert de Pass, a polo playing friend of Prince Philip, whose wife Philippa was a lady-in-waiting to the Queen. Ostensibly, Diana was the guest of their son Philip. 'You're a young blood,' he had said, telling her that the Prince would be a fellow guest, 'you might like him.'

But, drawing on a variety of highly reputable Palace sources, it is clear that Diana's invitation to New Grove on the weekend the Prince would be present was not a coincidence, nor was it simply a matter of fate, as the Palace has always claimed (possibly to combat any suggestion of an arranged marriage: anathema to the Prince), but the result of the Queen Mother's adroit campaign of gentle persuasion to convince Charles to consider Diana's merits.

But precisely who politically engineered the invitation is still a mystery.

According to one of his close women friends, Charles took his grandmother's advice as his cue for a move he was already contemplating. 'The Queen Mother was surprised and delighted at the speed with which he picked up on her suggestion, but he mapped his own strategy,' she said. Yet a senior Clarence House aide says that the Queen Mother fixed the whole thing, most likely through Philippa de Pass, adding proudly, 'She could give a few lessons in statecraft to Machiavelli. People think she is simply a charming and adorable old lady, but when it's a question of the royal family she is a tiger.'

Either way, Diana's presence at New Grove that weekend was the first explicit recognition by the Prince that there was a problem that had to be tackled without any more delay.

Diana knew none of this (and, if she did, she did not go dressed for seduction: most of the weekend she wore jeans and T-shirt, described by one guest as 'your typical early rummage-sale look'). But she did know that New Grove, part of Lord Egremont's historic Petworth estate, was one of Charles's 'safe houses' – the string of apartments and country houses of rich friends on whose discretion he could utterly depend, and in which he spent those times which do not appear in the Court Circular.

She was fascinated. Three years is a long time when you are so young, and she had grown up considerably since that rainy day at Althorp when she first met the Prince; the meeting then had been far too brief to judge him by, and she was curious to meet him again. Although his friends took endless pains and precautions to preserve his privacy, she knew that he was sexually promiscuous and successful with women, and she was at an age when rakish behaviour had a powerful fascination.

'Like most of us girls then, Diana *read* Barbara Cartland, but she *thought* Jackie Collins,' says one of Diana's girlfriends ('*circa* Coleherne Court days') who is something of a connoisseur of the beginnings of her romance with Charles. 'And I imagine that her sister Sarah must have told her some stories out of school. I remember she was going to meet HRH at New Grove the weekend of the Cowdray Gold Cup, which is Britain's premier polo competition, and she was very excited. Here was this famous man, the future King of England, who had had all these women, this thoroughly fulfilling sex life.... Of course she was curious. When you are eighteen, you speculate a lot about those things.'

It is also a matter of speculation what Diana made of her future husband that weekend. After the Saturday polo game at Cowdray Park (the Prince played for his team Les Diables Bleus), the house party returned to Petworth for a barbecue. A fellow guest who noticed her and Charles in deep conversation on a bale of hay considered the thought that she might make a suitable bride for the Prince ('She was Protestant, aristocratic, probably virginal, why not?') but eventually dismissed the idea as too implausible.

If Charles had set up the New Grove meeting, he would certainly have had a Palace intelligence briefing paper on Diana, and have known far more about her life than she could ever have dreamed. Perhaps he even knew that according to the legend on her bedroom door she was the chief in the three-bedroom £63,000 apartment in Coleherne Court, a Kensington mansion block between Earl's Court and more fashionable South Kensington. (The flat had been her eighteenth-birthday present from her parents; but to buy it she had to persuade her father to break two family trusts due to mature when she was twenty-one.) The other resident girls (paying landlady Diana £72 a month, telephone calls extra) were her old schoolfriend Carolyn Pride, who was now a student at the Royal College of Music, with a promising soprano voice; Ann Bolton, a secretary at the estate agency at which Sarah Spencer also worked; and Virginia Pitman, studying to be a cordon-bleu cook. They were an attractive quartet (although inclined to be 'a little on the plump side' on too much junk food, reflects Carolyn Pride) and there was no shortage of gentlemen callers, often Old Etonians and Guards officers, many with names that would later become familiar to readers of the world's tabloid press.

But Diana's innocence was unquestionable (as Charles would no doubt have been assured by the Palace vetters in the summer of 1980). Nevertheless, she was not exactly Goody Two-Shoes either.

She had plenty of admirers, but no lovers. She adored riding round London in her red Mini Metro after midnight mobbing up men friends, on one occasion covering James Gilbey's Alfa Romeo in eggs and flour (he had stood her up on a date). But according to Rory Scott, a frequent visitor to Coleherne Court when he was a handsome young lieutenant in the Royal Scots Greys, 'She was sexually attractive, tremendous fun, but absolutely off-limits, totally unobtainable....' Another boyfriend called her, 'Always a little bit ... ethereal really.'

Less ethereally, to pay for her keep, and to buy the petrol to run her little car, she was on the books of a couple of employment agencies (Solve Your Problems; Knightsbridge Nannies), and hired out as babysitter, cleaner, and maid-of-all-work at private dinner parties. She worked for £1 an hour as a menial at her sister Sarah's house in Chelsea; she was also a part-time minder tending well-to-do infants at the Young England kindergarten run by Victoria Wilson and Kay Seth-Smith in a church hall in London's Pimlico district.

A friend of the Prince who was at the New Grove barbecue that weekend, and who probably knew as much about what was going on at that time as anybody around, said with unusual candour, 'Charles was still a catch for any girl, but his was not a face that would come good with age. When he tried to look tender he merely looked agonized. I felt rather sorry for him. He had a string of conquests, but he did not win hearts. I remember thinking, He has all the makings of a curmudgeon. If he doesn't find a suitable wife soon – and, my God, what exacting standards had to be met – even the Prince of Wales may find he has a very serious problem on his hands.'

Even then, Diana had a deep and natural understanding of people. During their conversation on the haystack, she told the Prince that she had watched the funeral of Lord Mountbatten on television. She told him that her heart had bled for him when she watched him – looking so alone – following the coffin out of Westminster

Abbey. 'It was the most tragic thing I've ever seen,' she said. 'I thought: It's wrong, you are lonely, you should be with someone to look after you.'

The Mountbatten speech could not have been better chosen, of course, although it seems genuinely to have come from the heart. To those who knew the Prince well, and he was always predictable in his relationships with women, it came as no surprise when he asked Diana to drive back to London with him before lunch the following day; the only surprise was that she turned him down. 'It wouldn't be very polite to our hosts,' she told him sweetly.

'What did you make of Diana Spencer?' a friend asked him a few days later.

'She's got kid's knees,' he answered cheerfully.

The Prince, it was noticed around the Palace in the weeks that followed the New Grove barbecue, was in an upbeat mood – 'As if he had made up his mind,' thought Stephen Barry, whose intuition was never more busy than when the Prince was trying to keep things from him. But by this time, too, a kind of momentum had built up: Charles had taken her to a performance of Verdi's *Requiem* at the Royal Albert Hall, and he had invited her to join him aboard the royal yacht *Britannia* during Cowes Week. She accompanied him to Balmoral* for the Braemar Games, and a little fishing.

At this point, the press caught on to the relationship. Diana, perhaps aware that her sister Sarah had ruined her chances by saying too much, said almost nothing at all. But her smile was wonderful; her smile suggested that there was plenty more to come. Reporters besieged her apartment, followed her everywhere. When photographers turned up at the Young England kindergarten, she agreed to pose with several small children, on condition that she would then be left alone. Without make-up, her hair tumbling into loose waves, she posed in the bright sunlight for fifteen minutes

---

* Diana did not stay in the main house but with her sister Jane and her brother-in-law Robert Fellowes, a member of the Royal Household, in their grace-and-favour cottage on the estate.

with her small charges. She did not realize that the light was behind her, and her long legs were tantalizingly defined through the pretty pastel cotton skirt. It made picture editors very happy, and some photographers rather rich. The Prince, already rich, was not made happy. 'I knew your legs were good, but I didn't realize they were that spectacular,' he is said to have told her. 'But did you really have to show them to everybody?'

There is no question that at this stage Diana had acquired the backing of someone almost as influential as the Queen Mother herself – Camilla Parker Bowles. When friends enquired what Diana was like, Camilla, as always, would answer with a smile of deep satisfaction: 'Like a mouse.'

The re-emergence of Camilla in Charles's life had been growing apace since January. Andrew Parker Bowles, now a colonel, had been posted to Rhodesia as ADC to Lord Soames, who had been appointed governor of the former renegade colony with the brief of guiding it to independence. Camilla elected to stay in England with their children (Tom, five; Laura, eighteen months).

This arrangement in no time at all came to the notice of Charles. In the words of one of Camilla's girlfriends, 'Her availability was irresistible.' Abandoning her ambition for a career of wifely devotion, ignoring the advice of friends who said she was making a mistake, and perhaps aware that Andrew was being less than faithful to her in the Rhodesian heat, it was all on between them again. A male friend put it succinctly, 'Only Camilla Parker Bowles could find a way to reheat a soufflé.'

And so, when the Prince was invited to preside over the Independence Day celebrations in Rhodesia in April, Camilla decided that she would be in Salisbury to greet him. It was a situation that their friends watched with interest, and some amusement. (When Parker Bowles conscientiously decided to test-drive a tame buffalo named Ziggy which the Prince was to be invited to ride, the beast became unusually amorous, and gored his thigh.)

Lord and Lady Soames, however, viewed the approaching arrival of Camilla with something less than equanimity. Not only were they aware of the close relationship between Camilla and Charles, they were also conscious of an equally warm and close relationship that had sprung up between their own daughter, Charlotte (the recent ex-wife of banking heir Richard Hambro), and the wounded Parker Bowles.

The idea of entertaining these four people together at Government House was almost too appalling to contemplate, even by such experienced diplomats as Mary and Christopher Soames. Their relief was patent when Charlotte decided to return to England before Camilla and the Prince arrived.*

Meanwhile the boys from Fleet Street had the bit between their teeth. They had the phone number of the Coleherne Court flat and would start calling at six in the morning and still be calling at midnight, badgering whoever answered for details of the romance. The apartment was staked out twenty-four hours a day; Diana was hounded everywhere; there were switchback journeys across London, secret rendezvous, decoys, car switches and exits through kitchen windows, to try to shake off the pursuing pack. 'I love working with children, and I have learned to be very patient with them,' she said. 'I simply treat the press as though they were children.' Most of the time it was a game – 'a hoot' – but sometimes it was a game that went too far, and ended in tears. Diana's agony, said a friend, was the agony of a woman of shy and private feelings thrown into a situation of immense publicness. Her mother, Mrs Shand Kydd, wrote a letter of protest to *The Times*. The press apologized, but the game went on.

There was a small respite of a kind at Christmas, which Diana spent at Althorp with her father, and Raine. Her stepmother was still not liked by the family but she had earned their grudging

*In a remarkable display of sportsmanship, Colonel Parker Bowles invited former girlfriend Louise Grubb, a blonde Rhodesian-American photographer for Associated Press, to be his companion at the Government House dinner for the Prince. Contemplating this new *ménage à quatre*, Mary Soames said, 'And pray God may the claret be good.'

respect and their gratitude for the way in which she had cared for their father after he had suffered a massive cerebral haemorrhage in 1978. It was Raine who had learned about and tracked down a new German drug called Aslocillin, at that time unlicensed in Britain, which doctors said probably saved his life.

In January 1981 it was back to the old routine. Although Diana still addressed Charles as 'sir' – they had reached some degree of intimacy but still not enough it seems for Diana to be invited to call him Arthur – she knew that he was fond of her in his own way, and she, in her own way, was becoming rather more than a little fond of him. But she also knew and resented the fact that she was still obviously 'on approval'.

Could marriage really work? There were so many differences between them. His humour was Goonish; she had never heard of the Goons. She liked Pink Floyd, Blondie and Abba; he preferred a night at the opera. And his friends seemed so *old*. And why were so many of his close women friends married? She asked him that once, and he had simply shrugged: 'It's safer that way.' That answer should have alerted her, but it didn't. She was so naive.

She was a mouse.

Charles was skiing with friends in Klosters. He had his doubts too. He wasn't convinced she would say yes, or was ripe for the plucking if he really wanted her, as the Queen Mother continued to tell him in her own grandmotherly fashion. 'No matter how much he tried to be funny, a sense of foreboding kept breaking through,' one of his skiing companions would recall of his changing mood in Switzerland. 'He didn't know what to do ... but I think he knew he'd be missing a bet if he didn't ask her.'

And when he returned from Switzerland, he proposed, and she said, 'Yes, please.'

And although neither of them understood it then, his look of exhilaration was the exhilaration of confronting disaster.

Chapter Eleven

If Diana had no idea of what she was getting into – a complex royal web of deceit, infidelity and serial cuckoldry – the Prince was also travelling into areas of experience and challenge that he contemplated with immense wariness and worry.

Twice since their engagement had been announced at 11 a.m on 28 February 1981, according to one of his few lifelong friends, he had been on the brink of calling it off.

He had always been a man of muddled feelings, of course, but what had caused his gravest doubts was a question Diana had asked him shortly after the marriage was announced.

'Would you marry me if I were not a virgin?' she had said.

She was teasing him, he knew that, but he was surprised by the question and troubled by his answer: 'I don't know,' he had said.

It was the second time he had told her truthfully what he felt.

In love? asked an interviewer at the press call following the announcement of their engagement. 'Of course,' said she. 'Whatever "in love" means,' said he with that sudden withdrawal into puzzled aloofness which she was beginning to know so well. (Did she never ask him what he *meant* by that? a friend would later ask her. 'I just thought: least said, soonest mended,' she answered simply.)

It was at that moment, after his second truthful answer, that Charles Philip Arthur George Mountbatten-Windsor, Prince of Wales, heir to the British throne, knew that he had a problem.

And nobody would listen to him.

The night before the engagement was to be announced, Diana packed her bags and left Coleherne Court to take refuge in Clarence House, with the Queen Mother. 'I just want you to know,' her new Scotland Yard bodyguard, Chief Inspector Paul Officer, told her as she closed the door behind her for the last time, 'this is the last night of freedom in your life, so make the most of it.'

'Those words,' she would say, 'felt like a sword through my heart.'

Within twenty minutes of arriving at Clarence House she received an invitation to lunch from Camilla Parker Bowles. It was a friendly note, written several days before the engagement had been announced. Diana realized at once that Camilla must have already known exactly where she would be staying after the announcement was made, although it was something she herself had not been told until a few hours before Paul Officer came to collect her from Coleherne Court. It puzzled her at first, then it hurt. It was as if she herself had not been trusted with her own arrangements, although Charles must have known about them for days. But she said nothing. And again she said nothing when after she had moved into her own suite at Buckingham Palace she had lunch with Camilla. But she became puzzled by the older woman's line of questioning. She could not understand why Camilla was so insistent on finding out whether she planned to hunt when she moved to Highgrove. She wasn't. She told Camilla about the riding accident she had had as a child which had put her off riding for good. Later Diana would recall Camilla's 'look of satisfaction and relief'. For hunting (Diana would later learn) was the time when Charles and Camilla could meet without being furtive.

Diana was beginning to feel uneasy about Camilla. She was so ... *around*. On 30 March, Charles flew to New Zealand for a four-week tour which would end in Australia. Diana was left 'rattling around' the Palace with plenty of time to think. She was losing weight at an alarming rate. Stephen Barry fretted: 'She picked like a bird at chocolate, yoghurts and cereal … She was always running down to the kitchen to ask the chefs for an apple or any sweet leftovers.…'

'And then the tears started,' recalls Carolyn Pride, who had also been watching Diana grow thinner and thinner as the preparations for the wedding became more intense. 'This little thing got so thin. I was so worried about her. She wasn't happy and it was becoming a nightmare for her. She was dizzy with it, bombarded from all sides. It was a whirlwind and she was ashen, she was grey.'

Some people derive a sort of courage from despair, but Diana simply grew more nervous and more tense. Underweight and under stress, she was a time-bomb waiting to go off. And in July, less than a week before the wedding, something happened which caused her almost to call the whole thing off. On Friday the 24th, she had wandered into the Buckingham Palace office she shared with Michael Colbourne, who was in charge of the Prince's financial affairs and much beside. She noticed a small package addressed to Camilla – and it was clearly from Charles. Unable to stop herself, she opened it. Inside was a gold chain bracelet with a blue enamel disc bearing the initials G.F.

It has been reported that the initials were entwined and stood for Fred and Gladys, reputedly the pet names Charles and Camilla used for each other. But this is wrong. 'The Prince always called Camilla Girl Friday and that's what the initials stood for,' says Michael Colbourne, who has known the Prince since he was a chief petty officer on HMS *Norfolk*, the guided-missile destroyer which Charles joined in 1971 after leaving Dartmouth. 'There were certainly no tears … there was no confrontation in the office, as has been reported,' he insists.

But it was only the lull before the storm.

On the Monday of the week of the wedding, Diana was reaching the conclusion that the engagement had been a terrible mistake, and she wanted to call the whole thing off. Charles had left the

Palace, without his detective John McLean, to give Camilla her gift, now rewrapped. Diana was lunching in her rooms at Buckingham Palace with her sisters, Sarah and Jane, when she suddenly blurted out all her doubts, her fears that Charles did not love her – and her deep suspicions of Camilla Parker Bowles. But her sisters refused to take her seriously. 'Bad luck, Duch,' they made the now famous remark, using the nickname given her by stepfather Peter Shand Kydd, 'your face is on the tea towels so it's too late for you to chicken out now.'

Seldom was a marriage begun with such a shadow on it.

Chapter Twelve

The Queen Mother was an old pro. Monarchy was her business and her passion. All her life she had lived in palaces; she dined beneath gilded ceilings and slept in bedrooms with walls covered in silk damask; her popularity and her genius consisted of seeming to her subjects as ordinary as they. Gifted with self-control, perhaps by temperament, certainly by training, she would never shrink from the public eye; she was the best performer the royal family ever had. Behind her grandmotherly charm was as shrewd and calculating a mind as has ever ruled a kingdom. 'Her real cleverness is that she is never seen in what she does,' explains an admiring aide at Clarence House. But what she does is always for the good of the royal family. And it was to her an indisputable truth that weddings were good for the business of monarchy, for the House of Windsor PLC.

Although there is no question but that as a devoted, not to say a doting, grandmother, she longed to see her grandson married to a girl who would make him happy, she also knew that far more was at stake for the future of the monarchy than the mere happiness of those involved. She had single-handedly invented the royal wedding as the monarchical spectacular – the blockbuster that would always save the Palace. And once the royal-wedding juggernaut started to roll, she knew that nothing on this earth could stop it.

If there is a moment in the old age of a queen when she knows she can do no more to secure the future of her dynasty, for the

Queen Mother that moment came at eleven o'clock on the morning of 28 February 1981, when the Palace announced the engagement of Charles and Diana. Certainly she thought so. 'And now,' she told one of her oldest ladies-in-waiting, 'I can die happy.'

She and Bertie had been lucky. He had genuinely adored her. As he put it in a letter to their daughter Elizabeth in 1947, on the eve of her marriage to Prince Philip, 'Mummy is the most wonderful person in the world in my eyes.' And Mummy undoubtedly loved Bertie in return. Perhaps not with quite his adoration, but with the protective love the stronger member of a partnership can feel for the weaker. She had also loved him in his role as king, and understood as few others had understood the part their marriage played in strengthening the image of the modern monarchy. It was her own royal wedding in 1923 which helped to set the pattern for the future. Until then, marriages within the House of Windsor had been considered far too regal for the vulgar gaze and were celebrated privately at Windsor. But on her engagement to Bertie, she insisted on a full-scale wedding in Westminster Abbey. The last time royalty had married in the Abbey was when Richard II married Anne of Bohemia – and that was in 1382. But as usual Elizabeth got her way, and as usual Elizabeth was right. The marriage roused much loyal excitement and increased the popularity of the House of Windsor. None of this was lost on Elizabeth. Henceforth there could be no question of holding royal weddings anywhere but in great cathedral settings. And by 1947, when young Elizabeth married Philip Prince of Greece, the stately setting of the great medieval church seemed part of centuries-old royal tradition. Because of post-war austerity, the future Queen's wedding was, compared with later regal nuptials, somewhat drab; and the first royal matrimonial spectacular was not Her Majesty's but her sister Princess Margaret's in 1960.

It is still not realized quite how much this wedding of her younger daughter was the Queen Mother's personal creation, for without her connivance and support it could not have happened.

The Queen, much stuffier than her mother, and lacking her flair for royal publicity, believed that Margaret should marry someone 'suitable', if not an actual foreign prince, then at least an accredited grandee of pedigree and title, such as smug young Lord Blandford, who would one day be the Duke of Marlborough. Margaret, who was nothing if not headstrong, disagreed. She had already sacrificed her love for handsome and divorced Group Captain Peter Townsend, in theory to protect the moral image of the royal family (although more likely because the Queen Mother feared that to allow Margaret to marry Townsend and keep her royal status would open the door to the Windsors, and the granting of a royal title to the Duchess). Now in love with an even more 'unsuitable' character, a lively Old Etonian called Armstrong-Jones, she was emphatically not sacrificing herself again. The courtiers were aghast. The Queen had doubts. But the Queen Mother took a fancy to the young photographer and backed him to the hilt. But even she was surprised by the fervour and excitement created by her daughter's marriage.

This was the great performing monarchy at its zenith, and royalty had found an all-important role it had never had before on such a scale – as purveyors of irresistible romance for over 300 million television viewers. And it came at the perfect moment. The Swinging Sixties were about to begin, and the monarchy appeared to be in tune with them. After the wedding its popularity ratings rose significantly, and dropped only when the inertia of the Court began to reassert itself and the 1960s dwindled to a close. Charles's Investiture did something to revive the flagging popularity of his family, but the mid-1970s were soon recording another dip in the monarchy's fortunes when the occasion for another badly needed royal wedding arrived.

The Queen's daughter, Princess Anne, was in love with Captain Mark Phillips, the tight-lipped, straight-backed scion of a Wiltshire sausage-maker. Their marriage billed for the autumn of 1976 was a far greater challenge for the performing monarchy than Princess Margaret's. Here there was little romantic story-book appeal to excite the people. Anne was a royal anti-heroine, horsey, hoydenish and far too down-to-earth to make a fairytale Princess. And her bridegroom, a strong but very silent fellow member of her Olympic riding team, was privately referred to by Charles as 'Captain Fog'. Both seemed utterly resistant to romance.

But, after her success with Princess Margaret's wedding, the Queen Mother regarded Anne's as something of a challenge, and the elaborate machinery of a full-scale royal spectacular swung into action. This is one thing that courtiers are good at, and for once the Palace actually surpassed itself in sheer efficiency. Nothing was left to chance. On the eve of the wedding, Princess Anne, who had just returned from falling off her horse at the international horse trials at Kiev, found herself subjected to the *Vogue*-style beauty treatment normally reserved for the world's top fashion models. The Queen Mother arranged for her favourite photographer, Norman Parkinson, to take her pre-wedding photographs, and the old magician of the camera lens revealed a picturebook Anne no one imagined could exist.

With a worldwide audience of half a billion watching the event through satellite TV, the impact of Anne's wedding actually surpassed that of her Aunt Margaret's. It was, as *Time* magazine reported, 'the most public wedding that the world has ever watched'. And once again it did the trick. The popularity of the British royal family visibly increased. Its members had never been so talked about, had never been so famous. At a time when Britain's actual power was waning, its royal family basked in the attention – and possibly the envy – of the world.

And now it was clear that the world was waiting for the ultimate in royal weddings. Margaret and Anne had set the stage: it was up to Charles to fill it. Nobody knew this better than his grandmother – and the care and foresight she employed in guiding him towards his ideal bride were typical of how she always tried to mastermind relationships within the family. She understood the impact which this marriage would create, and its importance on the future of the monarchy itself. If it succeeded, as she intended that it should, the royal family could count upon a new and glorious season of popularity and goodwill. And after her death – she was in her eighties now – there would be her chosen candidate beside her favourite grandson to carry on her work, and see the crown of England as secure as ever in the next century. Much was at stake, not just for Charles, but for England and the monarchy, in the wedding which was fixed for 29 July 1981.

The wedding of Prince Charles to Lady Diana Spencer was the greatest ceremonial event ever mounted in the history of the British monarchy. Throughout the world, wherever there was a television set, someone was almost certainly watching the heir to the throne of England marrying his virgin bride. Since Westminster Abbey was not big enough to hold it, and presented problems for the television cameras, the service was held in the great baroque cathedral of St Paul's. If Princess Anne's wedding had been 'a Johann Strauss operetta', the wedding of her brother was full-scale royal grand opera. Even the audience possessed star quality: Nancy Reagan and the presidents of France and Germany rubbing shoulders with the kings of Sweden, Norway and the Netherlands, and Princess Grace of Monaco. There was a symphony orchestra; there was an aria sung by Dame Kiri Te Kanawa. The Prince was princely. His bride was everything a royal bride should be. This was a wedding of a splendour no other family on earth could equal. It was the supreme performance by the greatest performing monarchy in history. 'Here is the stuff of which fairy-tales are made,' intoned the Archbishop of Canterbury in his nuptial address. Here, indeed, was a story the whole world could warm to of a real-life Cinderella – a bride who had so recently been the unhappy child of a broken marriage, miraculously reborn as an instant princess.

But, more than that, this was the making of a global megastar, whose girlish looks and simple qualities would henceforth be enhanced with all the glamour and ineffable mystique of royalty.

Diana fever had started long before the wedding. Serious biographers had been at work weaving the story of her life from the gossamer of her existence. So far she had neither said nor done anything memorable in public, but already she was being hailed as the most famous woman in the world. Polls revealed that more women envied her – and more men fantasized about her – than any other female upon earth. Someone had called her the greatest silent star in history. In Italy the press was already speculating on her love life, and the sexual prowess she would use to keep the interest of that 'Principe Don Giovanni', her husband. In France they were writing of her skills at cooking and her taste in clothes. And in America she was being treated as a superstar. It is the way things work. In six short months she had effortlessly become an idol and an icon and a dream princess, not just for Britain, but for the whole world. And now that the combination of royalty and satellite television had let this most glamorous of genies out of the bottle of the British monarchy, time alone would tell what would happen to it.

Not that it seemed to matter to the eighty-one-year-old grandmother of the groom as that summer day in 1981 drew to its triumphant close. For now she could finally congratulate herself. In this regard, as in most others, the Queen Mother had been ahead of her time. Since that day in 1923 when she had married the shy young Duke of York in Westminster Abbey, she had also been at the centre of the total transformation of the British monarchy. She had witnessed its setbacks and created many of its triumphs. Now, like a famous actress turned director, she had brought the play to the conclusion she desired. Thanks to this wedding which she had had so large a part in making, the monarchy had never seemed stronger or more secure in the hearts and minds of the people, not just in Britain, but throughout the entire world. And she could feel happy for its future, because of this young couple on whom everything would finally depend. She knew them and she trusted them. One day Charles would make a splendid king, and this bride she had chosen for him would be a perfect mother for his children, and an admirable queen. And on and on it would go.

But it did not work out like that at all.

The time would come when that wise old lady would class Diana with that other great betrayer of the royal House of Windsor, Wallis Simpson – and then this day of days would become a nightmare in her mind, the marriage a disaster that would leave her numb 'by the very memory of what I have done'.

BOOK THREE

Chapter Thirteen

The wedding day was over. The chimes of Big Ben striking midnight were echoing across the park as the Queen Mother left the family behind her at the Palace, to be driven back to Clarence House in her claret and black liveried Daimler with the painted crown above the windscreen, the traffic lights fixed at green to allow her an unencumbered passage home. She had used the same official car for years, and it was rather like her – dignified and old and comfortable.

'I feel, Ruth dear,' she had told Lady Fermoy earlier that evening, as they watched the royal bride and groom, their grandchildren, depart in an open carriage for Waterloo Station, where a private train waited to take them to their three-day respite at Broadlands, 'we have much to celebrate and congratulate ourselves upon this day.'

At eighty-one – unlike the Queen, her daughter – the Queen Mother still relished life to the full, and saw no earthly reason to disguise the fact. She loved her drink and, since she enjoyed good food as much as ever, saw little point in dieting. If the press made gentle fun of her fondness for Gordon's gin and Dubonnet; what of it? It was part of her enduring popularity. She used to tell Elizabeth that the people expected royalty to look as if they were enjoying life. 'A smile costs nothing and can do so much,' she told her, and often quoted Queen Victoria's remark – 'Should not a queen be the happiest of mortals?' It still puzzled her, and saddened her a little too, that this was something her eldest daughter had always seemed to find so hard to understand.

As she descended from her car and entered Clarence House, which had been her home since Bertie died, she relished the luxury and comfort which had always meant so much to her. The house itself, an elegant white-stuccoed eighteenth-century mansion tucked away between St James's Palace and the Mall, was one of the most stylish and efficiently run private houses in London. She liked to think of it as a country house set in the very heart of the capital. Behind the high walls and closed-circuit security TV cameras, there was a summer house and a veranda leading out on to a perfect English lawn, on which her grandchildren had played croquet on summer evenings.

How much she had to be thankful for, how much there was to remember in her long life – and how much there was to protect. She had acquired beautiful paintings and fine furniture. She was rich in her own right. As well as Clarence House she had Royal Lodge in Windsor Great Park and her own apartment at Windsor Castle, and a castle she had bought in Scotland. It was called the Castle of Mey, and was an ideal spot to recharge one's batteries in the tranquillity of the long Scots summer evenings. She had one of the finest private chefs in London. She adored French food, and prided herself on serving the best food in any royal establishment (which, in truth, was not a difficult accomplishment).

Yes, all in all, her lifestyle was a good example of what the monarchy could offer those who served it well. These things were worth fighting for. But she also knew that one had to be realistic. Privileges like the royal yacht, the palaces, the private planes, the tax-free status of the Queen, could also make the royal family vulnerable, a target for republicans and the simply envious. She had lived long enough to see how very fragile royalty could be once it lost the love and interest of the people. She could still recall the shock she felt as a girl of seventeen on reading newspaper reports of the Russian revolution and the murder of Tsar Nicholas and his family in the cellar at Ekaterinburg. Since then she had seen the European monarchies topple one by one – the Kaiser, then the kings of Spain, Rumania, Yugoslavia, Greece, Italy, all of them falling like a pack of cards. And as for those who did survive in Scandinavia and the Low Countries – to her mind they were more like hereditary presidents than royalty. Didn't the King of Denmark ride a bicycle through the streets of Copenhagen? A king on a bicycle, indeed! She had never even learned to ride a bicycle, and on becoming queen had made a rule never to walk when she could go by royal limousine. No, the situation of the British monarchy was unique. And just as she had played so great a part in preserving its uniqueness, so she felt she had a right to warn them all against taking their way of life for granted. That was why this wedding had been so important to her. It was her masterstroke. Diana would bring new life and a young look back to the court. The camera loved her as it had once loved the Queen Mother herself (it had never loved Princess Anne, and would never love Princess Margaret ever again). The press warmed to Diana as they had never really warmed to the Queen. Through Princess Diana the royal family would be renewed, protected and loved for generations to come.

Diana was the key to everything.

Indeed, as the Queen Mother had said to Ruth Fermoy, she truly had much to celebrate and congratulate herself upon that day.

The first two nights of the honeymoon were spent at Broadlands, Earl Mountbatten's Hampshire estate, where the Queen and Prince Philip had begun their honeymoon thirty-four years before. And although Diana, the Princess of Wales, as she now was, expressed surprise, and perhaps some disappointment, when she learned that the groom had packed his favourite Hardy rods and boxes of flies in anticipation of some fishing in the Test, which flowed through Broadlands' 6,000 acres, she still believed that in the following weeks she would have the chance to begin to get to know her husband as a man, and not merely as a prince.

She knew that in the months she had known him, and been engaged to him, there had always been a barrier between them. He was defensive about emotions and his comment about love ('whatever "in love" means') on the day they got engaged was too objective for comfort. She couldn't get it out of her mind, although she attempted to rationalize it again and again. It had been his way of hiding his shyness, she told friends; she tried to laugh off his air of world-weariness as the last cynical refuge of a lifelong bachelor who had fallen in love.

But not many of her friends were convinced by her excuses, and some were afraid for her. 'Charles never *looked* remotely in love, he didn't even look comfortable,' said one of her platonic boyfriends from the Coleherne Court days. 'I mean, when a fellow can't project a convincing image at the announcement of his own engagement, what hope is there for the marriage?'

But Diana continued to find excuses for him. She knew that he had been raised to keep his distance and was wary not only of strangers but of the people around him too. 'A prince is condemned to a unique and lifelong loneliness,' her father had told her the day the engagement was announced. 'Don't expect too much in the way of friendship at first.'

She knew all about royalty. She knew it would take time to break down that inner wall of reserve that came straight from the Queen herself. She was conscious, too, of how little time she and Charles had spent together since their engagement had been announced in February. He had flown off almost immediately afterwards on a five-week tour of Australia and New Zealand, Venezuela and the United States. She still remembered the farewell at the airport when he had simply gripped her arm and pecked her on each cheek: a departure so aloof that it made her cry for a week. He had spoken to her a few times by phone, told her that he saw her face on newsstands and TV screens wherever he went – 'You are becoming quite famous,' he said – but the declarations of love she wanted to hear were lukewarm, or missing altogether, and her confidence dwindled with every passing week. (Allowing a blind woman at the Queen's garden party to feel her engagement ring a week before the wedding, Diana quipped, 'I'd better not lose this before Wednesday or they won't know who I am.')

It had been a bad time. Weakened by bulimia (the nervous disease, characterized by gorging and purging binges, which lay at the root of her rapid weight loss in the weeks before the marriage), tormented by self-doubt and increasingly suspicious of Charles's relationship with Camilla Parker Bowles, she had been prepared to walk away from 'Sir, his family, the Palace, the whole stupid bunch', she would later tell a girlfriend.

But those doubts, the bad times, were behind her now. She had even successfully excluded Camilla Parker Bowles and Kanga Tryon from the list of 120 select guests who attended the wedding breakfast at the Palace.* It was not an act of vindictiveness, but a simple statement of how she expected things to be from now on, she had told her husband (who seems to have yielded with a good grace, perhaps because he had never learned to plead). But in her heart Diana knew that it would never be as easy as that.

She was curious about sex, but it had never obsessed her; sex was okay, but it was not worth dying for. 'I knew I had to keep myself tidy for what lay ahead,' she had once said about her extended virginity, but, in truth, it had been no great strain on her. She had been merely fascinated by the number of affairs that Charles had had (although their brevity was beginning to strike her as ominous). But Camilla worried her. Camilla was far more important to Charles than the other lovers he had known. Theirs was more than the innocent friendship that he pretended to think it was. The lie was too big. 'When you saw them together, even if

---

* Lady Tryon, at whose Knightsbridge house Charles had frequently been discreetly entertained to tea, gave a luncheon party for sixty-five friends at San Lorenzo, the Knightsbridge restaurant which would later become a favourite of Diana's. 'I was not invited to the Palace and I know Mrs Parker Bowles wasn't either. She is also holding a party for friends. Obviously I cannot comment on why I wasn't invited [to the Palace lunch],' said Lady Tryon.

you didn't know the past, you could tell that there had been something between them, that something was still probably going on,' she would later say to a friend.

Charles would never be invulnerable to Camilla. Camilla would always be there: she had been an ungrudging adulteress before Charles wed and would always be game for a reprise of the act after he'd become a married man. Diana knew there was no question of that. But she had won the first round. She was confident. 'I had tremendous hope in my heart' is her favourite statement about that time. She utters it always with wry amusement.

The wedding night was spent in a smallish (five foot five inches by six feet) four-poster bed built for the Victorian Prime Minister, statesman and previous owner of Broadlands, Lord Palmerston (a.k.a. Lord Cupid, in recognition of his many mistresses). Diana was intrigued by an eighteenth-century print of a woman at her toilette with a suitor at her feet which hung above the fireplace in the bedroom. Her French still no better than when she was at the Institut Alpin Videmanette finishing school in Gstaad, she asked Charles to translate the French verse, '*Égard, tendresse, soins, tout s'épuisse en ce jour / Bientôt, l'Hymen languit et voit s'enfuir l'amour.*' He demurred. Is it rude? she asked. No, but it isn't very hopeful, he said. She persisted, and he translated: 'Consideration, tenderness, courtesy, all flow from this day. / But soon Hymen [the god of marriage] will languish and, behold, love will fly away.'

On 1 August, with Charles at the controls, the famous newly-weds flew in an Andover prop-plane of the Queen's Flight to join the royal yacht *Britannia* at Gibraltar, from where they would embark on a two-week cruise of the Mediterranean, the Greek islands and Egypt.

Early one morning, before the August sun got too high as they travelled along the North African coastline, the Prince's valet Stephen Barry saw the Princess standing alone at the stern of the *Britannia*, a sundress over her bikini, watching the broad white glistening track that followed in the wake of the royal yacht. The

Prince had sent Barry to tell his bride that he would like her to join him for breakfast in their suite on the Royal Deck. Barry delivered the message, but conscious of how very little time she had had to herself in the past weeks – what with the feverish preparation for the wedding, parties everywhere, supervising the decorations at Highgrove, commuting between the Palace and Gloucestershire in her little red Metro, wedding rehearsals at St. Paul's, endless Q & A sessions with the Palace prep team, and finally the wedding itself – he apologized for interrupting her solitude (taking the blame is the function of servants, a sardonic saying of Palace staff that he liked to repeat).

She told him, 'I was just catching my breath ... catching up with my feelings, that's all.'

'That was when I first cottoned on to what she was about ... Princess Diana was a *feeler* ... not a *thinker*,' Barry would say later. It was not meant to be a put-down. He had become genuinely fond of her, and, although he would always remain a loyal servant to the Prince, he was in agreement with many of the things his young wife said and did. 'She arrived at some sound conclusions and made some wise choices, but I don't think she ever worked things through intellectually. It was always something she *felt*. She had extraordinary instincts about things.'*

As she examined her feelings that August morning off the coast of Africa, Diana must have concluded that things had turned out rather better than she had thought possible only a few weeks earlier. She loved Charles. The wedding had been a triumph. The honeymoon was bliss. Her husband had even shown that he could be surprisingly romantic: on the eve of the wedding he had sent

* Diana was also given to premonitions. The day before her father collapsed in the courtyard of Althorp suffering from a massive cerebral haemorrhage she astonished a friend who had asked about his health: 'He is going to fall down. If he dies, he will die at once, otherwise he will survive.' Watching Prince Charles put his racehorse Allibar through its paces on the gallops early one morning at the Lambourn home of his trainer, Nick Gaselee, she turned to his detective and said that the horse was going to die. Seconds later the eleven-year-old collapsed and died of a coronary.

her a signet ring engraved with the Prince of Wales feathers and a tender note, 'I'm so proud of you and when you come up the aisle I'll be there at the altar for you tomorrow. Just look 'em in the eye and knock 'em dead.'

She treasured the note almost more than the ring.

The first week of the cruise was everything Diana had hoped for. They had privacy and time to themselves. Even her husband's eccentric honeymoon suggestion that they should read books by his mentor and friend, the South African philosopher and traveller Sir Laurens van der Post, and discuss them over dinner, simply made her laugh. Left discreetly alone, they took their meals *à deux*, usually in the small glassed-in sitting room, which led to a private veranda above. They even served themselves. One evening they watched *Chariots of Fire*, another evening the latest Bond movie, *For Your Eyes Only*. The sixth night they dined with Rear-Admiral Paul Greening and his officers in the main dining room, which doubles as a cinema. After dinner they watched video tapes of the wedding, flown in from the major television companies around the world.

It was the first time Diana saw just how truly stunning she had looked on her wedding day. She had been a bride of nonpareil luminance, wreathed in ivory tulle and trailing a twenty-five-foot silken train. The ship's officers applauded when she first came on to the screen. Then they watched in a kind of awed silence even more impressive than the wolf whistles and ribald comments with which the ratings greeted her appearance when the show was screened below decks. She was indeed the stuff of which fairy tales are made, but, more than that, she was a star of truly international magnitude. Her talent for reacting to a lens, for projecting herself as a purely aesthetic phenomenon, was unparalleled in royal memory.

'It's marvellous to see all the bits you missed,' murmured Charles as the video tapes continued to play back the wondrous scenes in London. But he seemed bemused by his bride's impact, slightly embarrassed by her beauty, as if he did not quite understand or condone her outright sensual allure. It quickly became known in

Palace circles as the Upstage Problem, or simply the Problem. 'Before Diana, Charles was popular,' one of their friends would sum it up later. 'After their marriage, he was second best. Everything Diana did, from buying a bag of sweets to having her hats retrimmed to show more of her face, became news. The Palace began to resent what they saw as her propensity for generating publicity for herself. But that was unfair. They were condemning the very star quality that had made her the number-one choice for the job.'

Stephen Barry was one of the first to recognize the Problem. The night the videos were screened aboard the *Britannia*, he felt a subdued vibration in the Prince that was impossible to describe but that conveyed a definite sense of concern. 'The Princess had everything going for her except the ability to not upstage the Prince,' Barry said.

After the wedding Diana knew exactly her strengths and what was expected of her by the people; if the Palace had other expectations, that was too bad. She had become a romantic legend. Asking her to fade into the background now was like asking the Mona Lisa not to smile.

Meanwhile, her own expectations and the early promise of the honeymoon were evaporating like the Mediterranean morning mists.

'A ship', Barry said, quoting Dr Johnson's definition one afternoon towards the end of the cruise when he thought he detected boredom in Diana, 'is a prison, with the chance of being drowned.'

She smiled sadly, recalled Barry, then answered enigmatically: 'But will we sink with anyone we know?'

The turnaround in her mood and in the fortunes of the marriage can be told in two short scenes aboard the *Britannia*.

One evening in their stateroom, while synchronizing appointments and commitments for the rest of 1981 in their respective diaries, two photographs of Camilla fell out of Charles's engagement book on to the floor. Diana demanded an explanation. Charles could offer none.

A few days later, entertaining the Egyptian President Anwar Sadat and his half-British wife Jihan in Port Said, Diana noticed that Charles was wearing a pair of gold cufflinks that she had not seen before: two Cs intertwined. Challenged, Charles resorted to royal insouciance, admitted the links were a present from Camilla, accused his wife of being naively jealous and refused to discuss the matter further.

It was the first indication that he had no inclination to budge from his bachelor lifestyle.

That night Diana made herself sick: the bulimia was back again.

Chapter Fourteen

And so Princess Diana returned from her honeymoon wiser, sadder and infinitely more mature. And maturity meant confronting reality. And the reality was that she had moved into a world of monarchical illusion, disinformation and manipulated fact, a world where candour is disapproved of and euphemism is *de rigueur*, where publicists and PR people are called assistant private secretaries, and anyone who fails to stick to the Windsor rules is simply excluded. 'You are either with them, or dead,' the Duchess of Windsor once said to actress Lilli Palmer. 'Look at the Duke, look at me.'

But Diana was determined not to become another Duchess of Windsor. She was too young to die. She understood the character and milieu of monarchy too well to buck the system so soon. And when she and Charles returned to Lossiemouth in Scotland to continue the honeymoon at Balmoral – 'dear Paradise', Queen Victoria had called it – she behaved publicly as if all was well and wonderful, even staging an impromptu walkabout among the thousands of people (and hundreds of press) who had turned out to welcome the happy couple home again. It was a convincing performance. 'She is so fresh, so blissful ...' feature writers gushed, and swooned. 'She is so natural, so happy ...'

'Docile Diana', as Prince Philip sometimes referred to her, had revealed unexpected single-mindedness in banning Camilla Parker Bowles and Kanga Tryon from the Palace wedding breakfast; she had shown even more courage in calling Charles over the cufflinks, and giving him so much flak over the pictures of Camilla he carried in his diary. And although he continued to display an air of equanimity – if he was conscious of guilt, according to the watchful Barry, there was no trace of it in his manner – he must have been taken aback by his young bride's willingness to stand up to him. Had he saddled the wrong horse, after all?

He welcomed the respite of Balmoral, a return to his home ground and to the bosom of his family. You always knew where you were with the Windsors – if it's Christmas it must be Sandringham, if it's Easter it must be Windsor. Now it was August and it was Balmoral. George V had rigidly maintained the schedule, and to the Duke of Windsor, when he was the Prince of Wales, the migration was 'as regular, as unchangeable, as permanent as the revolution of a planet in orbit'.

Diana quickly became aware of how important the highly ritualized existence of Balmoral was to Charles. In the morning, at 9.30 prompt, the men with their guns, and dressed in the grey–green tweed of the royal estate, would leave for the butts on the 'hill', as the family called Lochnagar, a rugged peak which had inspired Charles to write a boyhood fairy story for his younger brothers. There they would shoot the plump young *Lagopus scoticus*, or grouse, which would be flushed out of the heather and driven at speed over the butts by beaters. At noon the women would join the guns for a picnic lunch; afterwards the Queen would lead a group of riders across the endless trails and paths on the 50,000–acre estate, while Charles would fish for salmon in the Dee with his grandmother. In the early evening before changing for dinner, the party would meet in the drawing-room and talk about the day's sport, enjoy a pre-prandial drink, play cards. For dinner the men with Scottish connections would dress in kilts, jabot and jacket, while the others wore black tie. The meal would end with the Queen's pipers parading around the table playing traditional airs, after which the women retired to the drawing room, leaving the men to their port and cigars. When the men rejoined them, they would engage in party games, or sometimes Princess Margaret would entertain them with show songs from her 1940s and 1950s repertoire.

'*Bor-ring*,' Diana, whose own tastes in music ran more to the Beach Boys and Elton John, would later tell James Gilbey.

Diana missed her old friends from Coleherne Court. The amusement of watching her new in-laws at play quickly lost its charm; Princess Margaret's singing voice, like the bagpipes, was an acquired taste. Being neither a rider nor an angler, much of the time Diana was left to herself. Isolated by distance from her friends and family in London and by protocol from those around her (she now had to be addressed as 'Your Royal Highness' on first meeting, and 'Ma'am' after that – it appalled her, it made her laugh: 'I was twenty years old, for goodness sake!' she became increasingly pessimistic about the future.

But when you are young, she would later say, 'Optimism keeps breaking through,' and when she left Balmoral that autumn she carried inside herself a secret that she was convinced would change everything, and everything would be fine.

Chapter Fifteen

They had been married fourteen weeks and one day when Diana's pregnancy was announced by the Palace on 5 November 1981. To produce an heir in line to the throne was, of course, the reason why Charles had so reluctantly succumbed to wedlock in the first place, but a child so soon had not been any part of his plan. 'Had Her Royal Highness shown some slight consideration he could have forgiven her precocity,' said a member of his office, only half in jest. Official adjustments had to be made, including the postponement of a royal visit to New Zealand.

The Prince found private adjustments more difficult to contemplate. He had still not learned to adapt his bachelor way of life to the binary circuitry of marriage. He had always done whatever he wanted to do and was reluctant to forgo his old freedoms and princely liberties to live and work in partnership with his wife.

Perhaps had Diana's pregnancy been a little more comfortable and the morning sickness a little less enervating she could have tolerated his insouciance in the matter. But he seemed unable to comprehend how awful she felt, or provide the husbandly comfort and reassurances she desperately needed. The Windsor women, too, took babies in their stride; they saw little need to make a fuss of the new young mother-to-be in their midst. She felt neglected. But, worse than that, she was beginning to feel undefended and unloved, too.

For much of her pregnancy she stayed at Buckingham Palace while the carpenters and decorators put the finishing touches to their new London home – a house on the north terrace of Kensington Palace, next door to the apartment where Princess Margaret and Lord Snowdon had begun married life twenty-one years before, and now occupied by Prince and Princess Michael of Kent.

But, however much Diana tried to look to the future, the more she resented the way Charles clung to his past. Perhaps it was her gift of prophecy at work again, but she believed that her husband's history – and the people in it – menaced both of them.

She could not rid her mind of Camilla Parker Bowles. She could not understand what her husband continued to see in this persistent ghost from yesterday.

But there was a quality in the older woman that, had she been French, would have led to her becoming a Simone Signoret or Jeanne Moreau – women who love, each time, with total commitment, and to whom passion is a need. Diana was too young to understand the earthly wiles of such women, or to know the challenge of conjugal boredom in their smiles.

Diana was an English rose, the daughter of a great house, a young woman who had proudly 'kept herself tidy' for her husband on their wedding night. There was no way she could compete with the elemental appeal of Mrs Parker Bowles.

The lachrymose fits that burst on Diana at the most inconvenient times during the early months of her pregnancy, and through which a clear strain of frustration was threaded, eventually gave way to more disturbing symptoms.

On a visit to the family home at Althorp in January 1982 – to collect the wedding gifts, including a cheque towards the swimming pool which was being built at Highgrove, from the estate workers and tenant farmers and their families – a tiff with Charles escalated to a level of such vehemence that the Prince of Wales suite, which had been redecorated for their stay, was, in the words of her father, 'somewhat damaged'; a precious antique mirror had been shattered, an eighteenth-century chair leg broken, a window smashed.

'There was no air in here,' Diana explained the broken window when Stephen Barry, in the final weeks of his royal service after handing in his notice in October, went into the bedroom to pack. 'It was an accident,' she added, ingenuously.

Later, Lord Spencer showed the wrecked suite to Minnie Churchill, wife of Tory MP Winston Churchill who was showing a party of constituents around Althorp, and admitted ruefully that there had been 'an almighty row' between Diana and Charles.

Diana's tantrums were becoming alarming, according to a Buckingham Palace source. 'She had fits which would last just a few minutes, during which she would go crazy and become uncontrollable,' said John Bowes-Lyon, a great nephew of the Queen Mother. 'And then it was all over as quickly as it began.'

Almost anything was enough to set her off, and the staff had learned to tread warily around her. Even the wedding presents — more than 10,000 had poured in from all over the world, filling the private cinema at Buckingham Palace — it was realized were a potential source of rage. In the beginning, Diana and Charles made a point of visiting the Palace several times a week to inspect the loot. A retired rear-admiral, with a staff of six, had been appointed to catalogue and acknowledge every single gift — from the bonbon dish from Charles's former nanny, Miss Helen Lightbody, and the His and Her terrycloth robes from their youngest bridesmaid Clementine Hambro, to the Raoul Dufy painting from President Mitterrand of France, and the magnificent set of diamond and sapphire jewellery from the Crown Prince of Saudi Arabia.

One morning amid the mountain of gifts Diana discovered next to a pair of saddles from the King of Tonga a small oil painting of Vopnafjördhur in Iceland, where Charles had often gone salmon fishing in his bachelor days. 'It was a perfectly sweet painting,' recalls one of the cataloguers. 'But Diana got into a terrible snit about it, screaming at Charles. We had no idea what had started her off, but it was over quite soon, and she left as sweet as pie.'

The stunned cataloguers later realized that the painting was from Lord and Lady Tryon. And Lady Tryon was now high on Diana's private black list, although not as high as Mrs Parker Bowles.

'At first doctors thought her outbursts might have been epilepsy, but that was discounted because she didn't swallow her tongue, or have other epileptic symptoms,' said John Bowes-Lyon. 'Apparently what she suffers from can be hereditary, and there have been other instances in the Fermoy family, so the royal family have been told.'

But Palace talk of hereditary maladies and dark frenzies on the Fermoy side of the family were hastily swept aside at 9.03 p.m. on 21 June 1982, when Diana produced the son and future heir to the throne: Prince William. (Charles had wanted to call him Arthur, the name he himself liked to be called in moments of passion; Diana's choice of first name prevailed.)

But it was not a piece of British history, the birth of a future king, so much as a piece of legal marginalia, the divorce of two old friends, that would most touch the private lives of Charles and Diana that summer.

On 9 August, banker Rick Hambro and his wife Charlotte were divorced on the ground that they had lived apart for more than two years, and not because Charlotte's affair with Andrew Parker Bowles was still the talk of the town.

Now commanding officer of the Household Cavalry, Colonel Parker Bowles was based at Hyde Park Barracks, Knightsbridge. Camilla remained mostly at their home in Bolehyde, Wiltshire. The arrangement gave immense latitude to the Colonel, and friends became accustomed to inviting him and Charlotte to dinner parties as a couple – their consciences eased by the knowledge that Camilla was once again the moving spirit in the curiouser and curiouser life of the Prince of Wales.

At the start of the hunting season of '83, it was swiftly borne in on Diana that her earlier suspicions of Mrs Parker Bowles had not been idle. She became convinced that her husband's enthusiasm for the Beaufort was not unconnected with the fact that Mrs Parker Bowles was also a keen and regular rider of the Hunt.

It was a difficult and depressing time for Diana. There was talk in the royal circle that her depression was caused by a miscarriage she had suffered a few months earlier while staying at Balmoral. However, her sister, Lady Sarah, told friends, 'Whatever the problem was, there was no miscarriage, she was never pregnant.' But her distress at her husband's infidelity was soon overtaken by resentment and a sense of indignity at Charles's behaviour.

And so at Highgrove, towards the end of November, Diana decided that enough was enough. And when Charles returned late on a Friday evening looking desperately tired but happy after a hard day in the saddle, pursuing foxes, she announced quite firmly that she expected him to spend the following day at home with her and their baby William.

A philanderer, the Prince lacked the philanderer's charm, and appears to have made some monosyllabic response which Diana, perhaps hearing what she wanted to hear and still clinging to the hope that his cavalier attitude towards their marriage would change if only she could be strong enough, accepted as agreement to her Saturday plans.

But Diana was awakened early the following morning by the sound of a Range Rover being driven up to the front door. She went to the window and was dismayed to see Charles, dressed for hunting, climbing into the vehicle.

'When Diana saw Charles slinking off, after he had promised to spend the day with her and William, she went mad,' says London insurance magnate Ronnie Driver, who, with his wife Misty, had become close to the Prince. 'She started screaming ... accusing him of being selfish, a bastard, and a few four-letter words into the bargain.'

If it was a moment that lacked a certain princely dignity, it was filled with considerable human interest. Charles was cheating on his wife, a middle-class sin, and friends were amused and titillated, not shocked, by the goings on between him and Mrs Parker Bowles.

But if the sin was his, the crime of inviting attention to it was Diana's, and it was she who must be blamed for not observing the rules.

'Deliberately,' Driver said, describing with awe the look of shameless serenity on the face of the Prince, and the disquieting sound of the Princess of Wales calling him a selfish unfeeling bastard from their bedroom window, 'the Prince got into the Range Rover and drove away.'

But if Charles drove off that day as if nothing in particular was hanging in the balance, it was a scene that defined as nothing else the state and the direction of the Wales's married life: Diana standing at the window screaming and screaming at him ...

It was like saying goodbye into a dead telephone.

Chapter Sixteen

But however unstable and unsatisfactory things were between Charles and Diana, the instinct to breed was strong in both ancient families, and in September 1984 Prince Harry was born. 'He's a boy,' Charles announced in a call to the Queen at Balmoral from Diana's bedside in London, 'and he's got red hair.'

Now the Prince, and his mother, could relax: they had the heir and they had the spare. The Crown's next generation was secure.

But while the public was treated to carefully leaked stories about Charles the family man and devoted father, who even enjoyed changing Prince Harry's nappies (an unlikely chore for a man who had never had to remove the top off his own toothpaste, or put a fresh blade in his razor), the tensions in the royal marriage were beginning to claim victims as the people around them were forced to take sides, or were unable any longer to handle the atmosphere of suspicion and continual sniping between the Prince and Princess.

Michael Colbourne, who ran the Prince's private office, had resigned in July. 'I was the only person there who would call a spade a spade, and Diana saw me as an ally,' he would later say. 'I was told that the Prince was upset when I resigned, because he was losing a good friend and we had built up an awful lot together. Let's face it, a man in his position doesn't have too many friends.'

Shortly after the departure of Colbourne, Charles's private secretary Edward Adeane announced his resignation. There was a considerable amount of uneasiness about the whole business. 'Every time somebody leaves, the window opens a little wider,' complained Prince Philip, who valued discretion above all else, and understood how vulnerable royals were to unfavourable publicity.

The Palace put its own smooth spin on Adeane's exit, but there was no hiding the deep disenchantment, and often undisguised disapproval, being expressed among the top people around the royal couple.

The Queen watched the situation with dismay, although she continued to welcome Mrs Parker Bowles socially, and could barely bring herself to speak to the Princess of Wales at all. Her daughter-in-law, she felt, was behaving with extraordinary naivety. Princess Anne sided with Charles, and declared Diana *persona non grata*; saddling up a horse, she had galloped off minutes before her brother and Diana were expected for drinks at Gatcombe, and did not return until after they had left. Prince Philip appeared to be angry with everybody, and was, as usual, even at war with himself.

In the beginning, he tried to discuss the problem with his son. But he lacked the peacemaker's touch, and made so many bad-tempered calls that finally Charles refused to take them. It was a difficult time for the family. 'When the Prince of Wales walks into a room, Prince Philip walks out,' said the well-connected Ronnie Driver.

There was a certain sympathy for Philip, even from people who in the past had never found him a particularly sympathetic figure. 'What he could not admit to his son was his own sense of failure as a husband, and a father,' says a former Palace aide. 'Charles was the product of a home every bit as broken as his own and Diana's had been – only nobody could admit it. And now it was happening all over again, two more people's lives were being ruined, and a lot of other people were being hurt, all because the monarchy could not admit to human frailty.'

Philip, said the aide, knew that he was the one man who could have stopped his son making the same mistake as he had made forty years before – the older, experienced man marrying an inexperienced virgin for dynastic reasons, for reasons of state. In 1981, he had a marvellous opportunity to make his voice heard, to make amends; instead he told Charles to go ahead, he *urged* him to go ahead.

'Philip made the biggest mistake of his life when he told Charles that he must marry Diana, and that there was no alternative. There was a lot of steam building up for a wedding, of course. And Charles was running out of options. But, looking back, I think Philip let his loyalty to the Crown transcend his duties as a father,' says one of his most affectionate friends.

'Is the sex good?' he is said to have asked his wavering son shortly before the wedding day. 'I don't know yet,' Charles reputedly answered, embarrassed by his father's frankness. 'If the sex is good, you've got a chance,' the Duke replied, father to son, man to man.

Sex with Elizabeth had been wonderful. Sex with Elizabeth had been … a revelation.

'Prince Philip complained that he could not keep Princess Elizabeth [as she then was] out of his bed, that she was at him sexually all the time,' said the Duke of Leeds. 'It was not what he had bargained for at all.'

The Duke had heard the story from an English friend named Doris, who had been the last and youthful mistress of the Italian poet, soldier and patriot Gabriele D'Annunzio, and at whose Monte Carlo apartment Philip often stayed with his first cousin, the Marquess of Milford Haven. The frank and easy way Philip discussed his young bride with the Marquess, who had been his best man and was a fellow naval officer, shocked the loyal sensibilities of the young Duchess of Leeds, the daughter of Brigadier Desmond Young, the soldier–author of the 1950s bestseller *Desert Fox*, the story of German Field Marshal Erwin Rommel.

'We all thought that Philip was singularly unpleasant to discuss his wife in such an open manner … he was a disgusting man,' remembered the Duke of Leeds, recalling the stories of the immense bliss the young Elizabeth had discovered on her wedding night, and

'In love?' asked an interviewer at the press call following the announcement of their engagement. 'Of course,' said she. 'Whatever "in love" means,' said he with that sudden withdrawal into puzzled aloofness which she was beginning to know so well. [Anwar Hussein]

'I knew your legs were good, but I didn't realize they were that spectacular,' Charles is said to have told her. 'But did you really have to show them to everybody?' [Rex Features]

Here is the stuff of which fairy-tales are made,' intoned the Archbishop of Canterbury in his nuptial address. [Anwar Hussein]

Forty years before – the older, experienced man marrying an inexperienced virgin for dynastic reasons, for reasons of state. [Illustrated London News]

His grandmother wholly approved of Lady Diana, who was the paternal granddaughter of Countess Spencer, her Lady of the Bedchamber; and maternal granddaughter of Ruth, Lady Fermoy, one of her Women of the Bedchamber, and a dear friend for over sixty years. If she had not conspired to put Lady Diana into his bed, Charles knew that she had done nothing to discourage those who had. [Anwar Hussein]

Anne was a royal anti-heroine, horsy, hoydenish, and far too down-to-earth to make a fairytale Princess. And her husband, a strong but very silent fellow-member of her Olympic riding team, was privately referred to by Charles as 'Captain Fog'. [Anwar Hussein]

Lady Tryon: another of his trusted women friends, whom he had nicknamed 'Kanga'. An attractive Australian blonde whose accent became broader and conversation more amusing after a glass or two of Krug. Kanga had also been an early and uncompromising supporter of Diana.
[Tim Graham]

Camilla Parker Bowles was far more important to Charles than the other lovers he had known. Theirs was more than the innocent friendship that he pretended to think it was.
[Rex Features]

The Prince's valet Stephen Barry (centre), to whom he would sometimes unburden himself in private. [Anwar Hussein]

Charles on the whole remained faithful to Uncle Dickie's dictum that he chose his women from among the wealthy upper classes.

Davina Sheffield: she was not a titled lady, but she was the cousin of Lord McGowan, and that was close enough. [Tim Graham]

Lady Jane Wellesley: the romance lasted eighteen months before she announced, 'My future lies in another direction.' [Tim Graham]

Lady Sarah Spencer: the sister Diana wanted to be. [Anwar Hussein]

Princess Marie-Astrid of Luxembourg: 'The Royal Family do not go in for arranged marriages.' [Anwar Hussein]

Amanda Knatchbull: precisely the kind of woman (brunette, small bosomed, rather serious) who fascinated the Prince barely at all. [Tim Graham]

Susan George: a loving relationship. [Rex Features]

Sabrina Guinness: 'I love being with him, but please don't try to marry us off.' [Anwar Hussein]

Jane Ward, assistant manager at the Guards Polo Club: 'We are very fond of each other ... sometimes I think things could have been different had I never married.' [Anwar Hussein]

Anna Wallace: his last great love affair before Diana ... her fearless horsemanship had gained her the interesting nickname 'Whipper'. She was fun, intelligent, feisty, and even more beautiful than Davina Sheffield. [Tim Graham]

The ritual balcony appearances – from birthday parades to royal weddings. [Anwar Hussein]

To the Queen Mother it was an indisputable truth tha
weddings were good for the business of monarchy, fo
the House of Windsor PLC. [Anwar Hussein

If not exactly a part of them, Sarah Ferguson had been hanging out with royals all her life. Father Ronald – 'Dads' – had played polo with Prince Philip, managed Prince Charles's polo affairs, and as a former Life Guard major, he had once commanded the Sovereign's Escort. [Anwar Hussein]

Andrew went down on both knees and asked her to marry him. 'When you wake up in the morning,' she answered carefully, 'you can tell me it was all a big joke.' But the next morning he asked her again. She accepted. [Anwar Hussein]

Sarah and Andrew were married in Westminster Abbey in July, 1986. For her wedding gift – beside the dukedom bestowed on their wedding day – the Queen leased them Sunninghill Park in Berkshire; five acres of choice Crown Estate on which their sprawling ranch-style home would be built at a cost of £3.5 million [Anwar Hussein]

Fergie was funny, irreverent; even her grin was contagious. [Rex Features]

The two brothers and their families enjoying happy days. [Tim Graham]

Two of the last guests to leave 'Southyork' that night were two Texans. One was tall and deeply bronzed, the better to show off his perfect white teeth. At first sight, his balding companion was less striking, but he had a friendly charm which Fergie once said 'could disarm a charging bull at a hundred paces'. Both men were courteous and attentive. They were also the principal architects in the Duchess of York's impending fall from grace. One was Steve Wyatt, the other John Bryan. [Rex Features]

Diana's male friends were mostly charming young men who wrecked fast cars. Among the steadier sort was James Gilbey, who in the euphemistic tradition of his class was a motor trade executive, but who in real life sold used cars from a mews garage in Knightsbridge.
[Rex Features]

The newspapers on the morning after the announcement that the Yorks were separating were nothing when compared with what happened when the *Daily Mirror* published photographs of the Duchess of York and John Bryan on holiday near St Tropez. 'Holy shit!' Bryan said, when reporters showed him the first edition of the next morning's *Daily Mirror* at 11.15 Wednesday evening, August 19. The poolside pictures were splashed across the front page beneath the headline *The pictures they didn't want you to see: FERGIE'S STOLEN KISSES: Truth about Duchess and the Texan millionaire.* 'Oh, God!' he said when he turned to the centre-spread and saw the pictures of him kissing the Duchess's toes. This time the headlines proclaimed, *PHOTOS BRYAN COULDN'T STOP.* [Rex Features]

For the Queen – as she said in a memorable phrase at a dinner in the Guildhall in the City of London – 1992 had been her *annus horribilis*: the year of the 'Squidgy' tapes, in which the Princess of Wales engaged in some dirty talk with James Gilbey, described as a man-about-town; and Andrew Morton's best-selling book, *Diana, Her True Story*, detailing her depression, bulimia, suicide attempts (velvet ropes now kept gawkers off the Sandringham staircase down which she was said to have flung herself) and estrangement from her prince; Princess Ann had been divorced; it was also the year of the break-up of the marriage of the Duke and Duchess of York; and the publication of pictures of the Duchess frolicking topless in the South of France with her 'financial adviser', John Bryan of Houston, Texas; and it ended no better than it began, with the Queen herself agreeing to pay income tax. Then Windsor Castle went up in flames. [Rex Features]

The Queen suggested that Charles and Diana should take six months to cool off and reconsider, they should take an official trip together, she suggested the South Korean tour, to demonstrate their togetherness, that sort of thing; all they needed was time ... [Rex Features]

the keen interest in sex she had continued to demonstrate to her startled young husband.

Sex, especially royal sex, was a subject that was not discussed with the same frankness that it is today. And concerned that these were not the kind of stories that should be circulating in Monaco or anywhere else about the future Queen of England, the Duke of Leeds reported Philip's caddish behaviour to his brother-in-law Oliver Lyttelton (later Viscount Chandos), a leading Tory member of Parliament, with a strong recommendation that a gag order should be put on Philip forthwith. Whether any government action was taken has never been revealed, but shortly after this incident the young Prince became altogether more discreet about matters so close to home.

'The thing about the Duke of Edinburgh is that he is such a strange mixture of things. He can be shockingly blunt but it isn't the bluntness of a bully or a braggart, it's the plain speaking of an honest man,' says a former member of Philip's private office at Buckingham Palace. Nobody understood better than the Duke did the fix Charles was in; nobody was more aware of the pressures that had made Charles the man he was. But whenever he tried to speak to Charles about the Parker Bowles situation, or the best way to handle Diana, or any of the other things that were going so wrong in his life, Charles simply shied away.

'A lot of grief could have been avoided if Charles had had the courage to pick up the phone and talk to his father about his problems,' said the former Palace man. 'After all, Prince Philip had been there himself... Sometimes he must have felt he was watching a cruel repetition of his own past.'

As a small boy, Philip watched the break-up of his own unhappy parents' marriage and the memory of it still troubled him. But perhaps the most significant and revealing fact about the Duke is that he had spent almost all his formative years in the role of poor relation. Only the most fortuitous train of events had brought him to the esteemed but often irritating position of husband to the

Queen of England. It was true that he shared with his wife a common great-great grandmother, Queen Victoria,* but the other connections in his ancestry were less impressive, its history more checkered.

His mother was Alice of Battenberg, Lord Mountbatten's sister; his father Prince Andrew of Greece. They married in 1903. Andrew was the seventh son of a Danish prince who, when the royal house of Greece was being set up after the Greeks had won their freedom from the Turks in the 1860s, was imported to wear the crown, apparently for no other reason than that he had a kingly bearing not readily available in Greece at the time. Shortly after his coronation – he was crowned George I, King of the Hellenes – he married the Russian Tsar Nicholas's daughter, Olga. Their third son was Prince Andrew, Philip's father. In 1913 George became an unfortunate statistic on the growing list of assassinated European royalty when one of his less than loyal subjects shot him dead in Salonika. He was succeeded by his son (Prince Philip's uncle) Constantine I. On the outbreak of the First World War, Constantine was suspected by the Allies of being in league with the Kaiser, with whom he had family links, and was swiftly deposed. Prince Andrew and Princess Alice, who by now had four daughters, spent the remainder of the war in exile in Switzerland. In 1920, Andrew's brother briefly regained the throne and the family returned to Greece.

One year later on the island of Corfu, Alice had a son. The child was christened Philip in accordance with the rites of the Greek Orthodox Church, and assumed the title Royal Prince of Greece. Prince Andrew was away when his son was born, for he was a professional soldier in the Greek army fighting the Turks. Philip was still only a few months old when his father was arrested and charged with treason. Princess Alice pleaded for his life in Athens

* His connection with Queen Victoria came from his great-grandmother, the Queen's third child, Princess Alice.

−154−

to no avail. She turned to her English relatives for help. King George v, shocked by the murder by the Bolsheviks of his cousins in the Russian royal family five years earlier, brought pressure to bear. A Royal Navy gunboat was despatched to Corfu to fetch the family to England – and a life of stateless exile. For having delivered his kinsman from the firing squad, King George felt he had done enough; there was no financial help and no encouragement for them to stay in England. They finally travelled to Paris, where they borrowed a house in St Cloud. There was very little money; wealthy relatives paid the children's school fees, and saw that they were fed and clothed, but nothing fancy.

But, if Philip felt himself the victim of a grave injustice, his reaction was not resentment but a determination to learn from his parents' mistakes, which seemed to promise an endless education. In the early 1930s, after all his sisters had married into the German aristocracy, his father decamped to Monte Carlo, the gambling tables and a wealthy mistress. His mother – Alice, Princess of Greece, as she continued to sign herself – assailed by deafness, a traumatic menopause and blighted hopes, turned increasingly to God. Religious mania followed, and eventually she suffered a complete mental breakdown from which she would never completely recover.

With neither parent in a position to care for him, Philip see-sawed between the two sides of his divided family; at first the English side prevailed and his mother's eldest brother, George, Marquess of Milford Haven, sent him to his own English preparatory school, Cheam. But in 1933 it was agreed that he should complete his education at the progressive Schloss Salem founded on the family estate by his sister Theodora's father-in-law and Germany's last imperial chancellor Prince Max of Baden. Philip stayed a year at Salem; had he continued longer he might well have had to fight for Germany five years later. But when the school's Jewish headmaster Kurt Hahn fled to Britain and set up an offshoot of Salem at Gordonstoun in Scotland, Philip followed, with Uncle

George's backing, so becoming one of Gordonstoun's first and most famous pupils.

It had been an extraordinary and a lonely life, the problem of personal identity – of belonging – was seldom far from his mind. He had a Danish name, which he never used, and rarely visited Denmark. According to his passport he was royal – Philip Prince of Greece – but judged by royal standards he remained an outsider. He spoke German better than he spoke English, used English more often than he used German, spoke Greek barely at all, and Danish never. And when he went to Monte Carlo in 1945 to wind up his dead father's affairs, he found that after funeral expenses had been paid and debts settled, the estate had completely disappeared. His inheritance, according to one friend, amounted to just a few family mementoes, a Savile Row suit which he had altered to fit him, and an ivory-handled shaving brush.

But virtually parentless most of his life, and often friendless, he had long before come to terms with his life. He was just seventeen when he realized that he had a very strong idea of what he wanted, and even more important, how to get it. And his mentor and role model was to be his mother's brother – Lord Louis Mountbatten (as he then was).

'Uncle Dickie' had it all. He was smart and shrewd and he was a winner. He had used his charm, matinée-idol looks, royal connections and amazing stamina to create a life of stunning glamour, achievement and enormous fun. His best friend was his cousin, the Prince of Wales, and the friendship connected him to the highest levels of London society. He was at the very centre of the action. He knew who counted and who did not. He dined with Douglas Fairbanks, Noël Coward and Charlie Chaplin; danced with Bebe Daniels, Gloria Swanson, Dolores Del Rio. His high profile and ready access to the Palace even impressed the Admiralty; by 1934 he had become the youngest destroyer commander with the Mediterranean fleet. Uncle Dickie seemed to have such control of his life. Everybody had expected him to marry a major royal. But he was smarter than that – he married the richest non-royal heiress in the land: Edwina Ashley. Simply the most sought-after girl in London, Edwina was the grandchild of Edward VII's favourite Jewish banker, and one of the richest and most powerful men in Europe, Sir Ernest Cassel. She had much to recommend her, but the bottom line was that she would inherit a yearly income of £50,000 after tax the day she married. In the 1920s that was serious money.

For Lord Louis it was love at first sight, and when he looked again there was a luxury yacht, a supercharged Hispano-Suiza, a string of polo ponies, a thirty-room penthouse in Park Lane and a splendid villa on a hill in Malta.

And the really nice thing was, Edwina was a dish to look at.

Yes, Philip, sixteen years old, had finally discovered exactly what he wanted out of life.

And when he thought about it, Uncle Dickie agreed that he was the man to help him get it.

Now, thanks to the shrewd and adventurous Uncle Dickie, Philip was married to the richest and most famous monarch in the world. He had achieved almost everything his sixteen-year-old heart had ever wanted. Marriage had given him a country, palatial homes, a magnificent yacht, a passport, a new religion, private planes and, most of all, a sense of belonging.

Only one thing still eluded him.

And that was a truly happy family.

Unable to reach his son, unable even to begin to understand his troubled daughter-in-law, excluded from his wife's affairs of state, he felt marginalized and, like his own father before him, became obsessed with a mordant sense of personal failure. His consciousness of being simply the Queen's husband became more compelling as he grew older; the reluctance of the Queen to make him her official consort – the title Queen Victoria had given to her beloved Albert – continued to rankle, and he now accepted that whatever success he had achieved, and he had achieved some, would never be properly recognized.

'The Palace was not a happy ship,' admits an aide. 'But at least unhappy ships can be tenacious of life. The problem was, the Palace was also becoming a rudderless ship – and that can be fatal.'

Adding to Diana's other problems was a bad case of postnatal depression that would not go away. Her sex life with Charles was now nonexistent, she told friends with a mixture of amused self-deprecation and aching susceptibility. 'He's seldom here to notice me,' she told one friend plaintively.

'Part of Diana's depression was caused by her realization that there was nothing she could do to change Charles,' says Michael Colbourne, whose understanding and calming presence she missed terribly. During the summer Charles was playing more polo than ever, up to sixty matches between May and August, and, when the hunting season began on 1 November, riding to hounds at least six times a month. Yet it was not simply her husband's expensive self-indulgences that Diana could not accept, 'but the sense of duty that he had been born with', says Colbourne.

'When she married, she could not imagine that he would not change, and she was naturally disappointed,' he continued with the born courtier's lack of bias, and deftly keeping a safe distance from the subject of the Prince's undutiful and increasingly incautious pursuit of Mrs Parker Bowles.

But not all of the Prince's friends were willing to show such diplomatic even-handedness and tolerance as Michael Colbourne. Many were quietly appalled by the humiliations Charles was continuing to inflict on his wife. Even when they agreed that Diana was undoubtedly a handful – and nobody could deny her tantrums, which had been witnessed by too many to be something Charles had dreamed up in his own defence – the Prince's by now quite blatant affair with Mrs Parker Bowles was too much to expect any wife to bear.

'He has a lot to answer for,' said Lord Beaverbrook, grandson of the Canadian newspaper tycoon, a former lord-in-waiting to the

Queen, and a first cousin of Andrew Parker Bowles. 'It was Charles who ran to Camilla when things began to go wrong with Diana. And, once Camilla was ensconced, she started throwing her weight around. When she saw the romance was a runner, she simply took a proactive role. Of course, Diana was upset. She had every right to be.'

Before the birth of Prince Harry, Charles's affair with Mrs Parker Bowles had been a secret known to only a few. Indeed, in the beginning, according to Beaverbrook, even Andrew Parker Bowles was not aware of what was going on. 'The first I knew was when Charlie Shelburne was getting married for the second time and his fiancée had to move out for the night from Bowood and went next door to Camilla's. Andrew wasn't there – but Prince Charles was. And, after dinner, Camilla made it pretty clear that the fiancée had to go up to bed pretty quickly, straight away.' Now it was a scandal being discussed as openly in London as the state of the Princess of Wales's obvious unhappiness. For the first time, too, the Parker Bowles marriage was attracting attention, as their *laissez-faire* arrangement began clearly to threaten the marriage of the Prince and Princess of Wales.

Even people of the utmost discretion were beginning to speak out. One evening at White's, the most urbane and decorous of St James's clubs, Charlotte Hambro's father, Lord Soames, accused Andrew Parker Bowles of turning his daughter into 'a common mistress'. There are few more calumnious accusations a clubman can make of a fellow member, and it must have hurt Lord Soames to make it, but Parker Bowles left the premises at once.

But on another night in another club, the altogether more raffish Turf Club in Carlton House Terrace, where his incorrigible lifestyle was generally counted to his credit, Parker Bowles allowed that he saw no reason why his present marital arrangement should not go on forever. 'Mark my words, it will end in tears,' said the Duke of Marlborough's younger brother, Lord Charles Spencer-Churchill, presciently. 'When you play around with the monarchy, you play with fire.'

Meanwhile, as things continued to go badly in this world, Charles was reputedly trying to find answers by contacting the next. According to his staff, he tried several times to reach his great-uncle Dickie Mountbatten through the medium of a ouija board.

But, this time, it seems that even Uncle Dickie did not have the answers.

Chapter Seventeen

The Princess of Wales began 1985 determined to overcome two problems: she had to defeat the bulimia that she knew had become a serious risk to her health; and, now that she had dutifully delivered 'the heir and the spare', she had to overcome the royal family's attitude that she was simply an ornamental but redundant bimbo in their midst. Princess Anne's observation that Diana's dresser Evelyn Dagley had eight O-level certificates of education whereas her mistress had but two – implying that the Princess of Wales wasn't even smart enough to dress her dresser – hurt Diana a lot.

At Sandringham that New Year, while her in-laws and the rest of the house party amused themselves riding and shooting, pursuits she abhorred – she could not understand how Charles could say, as he did, that he killed out of reverence for the thing he killed – she thought very hard about her future.

She had lost her way since the early days of her fame. She had let herself slip out of the popular limelight that she had naturally commanded at the beginning of their marriage. What she had to prove to the family, to her husband, and especially to the Queen, was that she still had a role to play in the royal show. That was what her father had told her a few months earlier when he warned her of the increasing part that Mrs Parker Bowles was playing in her husband's life.

The choice was simple: either the Windsors must embrace her –

or ignore her at their peril! What she must not become, her father had told her sternly, was another beautiful, vacuous, spirit-broken Queen Alexandra to Charles's Edward vii, the royal rake and lover of countless married women. She certainly must not give Mrs Parker Bowles a free run to reprise the role of her great-grandmother Alice Keppel as Charles's mistress.

But how did anyone even begin to challenge the Windsor family apparatus?

Lord Spencer, who in many ways was the embodiment of the aristocrat of the past and a keen student of old-fashioned backstairs politics, had been impressed by the way in which his mother-in-law Dame Barbara Cartland had used the modern media, and especially television, to boost her popularity and to sell her books. 'If the public likes you, it gives you tremendous power over your publishers,' Dame Barbara had remarked to him once. And if television worked for Dame Barbara why shouldn't it work for Diana, who was young, modern, telegenic? If she was going to stand up to her husband and the Windsor mafia she would first have to win the hearts of the people, Johnnie Spencer told his daughter. And to reach the people she had to take route 1 – and that was television.

The opportunity to launch the new, confident Diana came in April when after a long break from international duties – she had been devoting herself to motherhood, was the official line; in reality she had been sidelined by the Palace because of her unreliable relationship with Charles – she was invited to accompany the Prince on a state visit to Italy. The Italian Job, Diana called it, and she was determined that it would also be a hatchet job on Mrs Parker Bowles's continual portrayal of her as 'a mouse'.

During the visit they were to stay at La Pietra, the magnificent Florence home of the author and artful old aesthete Sir Harold Acton. British royalty has always had a strong emotional connection with Florence, and L'Ombrellino on fashionable Bellosguardo had for many years been the home in retirement of Mrs Keppel. The villa passed on to Mrs Keppel's daughter, Violet Trefusis (the lesbian lover of Vita Sackville-West, for whom Virginia Woolf wept copious tears of jealousy), who was not averse to being addressed as 'Highness', being convinced that she was the old King's daughter.

Violet's great enemy for years in the Florence expatriate pecking order was the Waleses' host, Sir Harold. He was a splendid raconteur and settler of old scores, and Diana took great delight in egging him on to tell them scandalous and unflattering stories about Mrs Keppel's daughter, whom he clearly disliked as much as Diana disliked her niece Mrs Parker Bowles. 'What a dreadful family they seem to have been,' Diana said with mock-solemn glee at the end of a particularly scurrilous story about Violet's 'ungentlemanly behaviour' in Florence. 'I must say that Mrs Keppel's daughter was a subject that Charles appeared most anxious to change,' said a guest at that private dinner at La Pietra.

Her spirits revived by the Italian sun and the warmth of her reception, Diana began to glow again. She even started being funny again. When Charles told her to mind her head as she ducked beneath an arch in Sir Harold's magnificent garden, she said, 'Why? There's nothing in it.' That should have warned him that things were changing. The Italians loved her. Never had the great divide between Diana, superstar, and Charles, supporting player, been exposed so deeply. She had a knack for picking up the gestures that define a personality. Her own mannerisms – the half-swivel on the back of her heel, the raised hand touching the tip of her nose to cover an untimely giggle, the up-and-under smile, like Bogart's lisp or Monroe's walk – were enough to supply that extra quality of recognition which a star must have. And even though her wardrobe still left much to be desired (it was criticized for being 'dowdy and frumpy', and at La Scala in Milan to see Puccini's opera *Turandot*, she wore the same Victor Edelstein pink chiffon gown with shoestring shoulder straps she had worn two years before in Australia and Canada), the Italians could not get enough of her. Graffiti proclaiming *Di ti amo* became so prolific on the ancient walls of Florence that the local anti-British neo-fascist party claimed that the British Council was paying young unemployed Italians to paint the slogans in the dead of night. Everyone called her Lady Di – a name she professes to dislike – but which possesses magical overtones in Italy, which has several hundred princesses but no ladies.

Charles could never handle Diana's public persona. He had never really recovered from their first public tour together in Wales, after their honeymoon – the crowds chanting her name, wanting to touch her, as if she were a pop goddess, or a movie megastar. Which in a sense she was. But it was her reaction, the extraordinary way she handled the adulation that impressed him and somehow troubled him, too. 'My dad says give us a kiss,' called out a small boy. 'Well, then, you had better have one,' she said, and kissed him. She actually kissed him. Charles had never heard a crowd cheer so much. It had always been obvious who the people had come to see. In every walkabout, they would work opposite sides of a street. But they always wanted Diana. 'Over here, Diana, over here,' they would call over his shoulder. He smoothed away his embarrassment with remarks like, 'I haven't got enough wives. I've only got one, and she's busy over there.' He tried self-deprecating humour – 'I'm sorry, you must make do with me' – but it never worked for him, it never humanized him, it never sounded right.

Diana could reach the people in a way the Queen never could, no other royal ever would. She would walk in the rain to greet the people who had waited for hours to catch a glimpse of her. 'Darling, don't walk about in the rain, you will get so wet,' he would say as he tried to rescue her. But the people loved her, they wouldn't let her go. Despite the cold she would not wear gloves because she knew the women wanted to see her rings. The Queen *always* wore gloves, never reached out; the Queen was never touched the way the Princess of Wales was touched. 'Have you been waiting long? Have you travelled far?' Her Majesty might enquire in her regal voice, always standing ten feet away. 'That morning sickness is awful, isn't it?' Diana would say to a pregnant woman as she walked *among* the crowds, just as she would walk through the kitchen at any hour, whenever she was hungry, and help herself from the saucepans, chatting to the cooks and the serving people, who were the ones she seemed to like best and could relax with most. Charles had tried to be like her. But the task was beyond him. And in Italy nothing had changed.

A former private secretary on the British Embassy staff in Rome at the time recalls how dichotomized the official Foreign Office observers were about the Italian visit. 'It was a huge success – but not necessarily for Charles,' he recalls. 'He wore the horns. He was as Florentines so delicately put it, *il vecchio cornuto* – the old cuckold. He was seriously boring. It corresponded exactly to the age-old Italian fantasy – old, rich, impotent husband ... cool exterior, furnace-hot interior, beautiful young wife ... Knowing winks from the worldliest old eyes in the world. They loved the way she would slip her shoes off beneath a restaurant table ... They pitied the way he had to roll up his spaghetti with the help of spoon ... '

Charles knew, and Diana knew that he knew, that he had been completely upstaged again. It was like old times: she was the star. 'He, poor duck,' said the former Embassy staffer, 'having been brought up on this public appearance thing, knew better than anyone the nuances and warmth, or lack of it, of a public reception. There was no kidding him over exactly what was happening.'

In London, as reports and television coverage of the royal visit came back, the Palace knew that the Upstage Problem had returned. 'But this time', said one of Diana's former boyfriends, 'Diana knew *exactly* what she doing. She may not have had as many O-levels as her dresser, but she was a fast and thorough learner.' After Italy, each week she seemed to grow more confident – as Charles, some thought, grew uneasier.

The distance that had come between the Prince and Princess of Wales since their marriage was nowhere better reflected than in their choice of friends. Diana's attempts to introduce a younger, jollier crowd into their company was never on the cards. Always a man for the status quo, at the top of Charles's A list – 'the wrinklies', in Dianaspeak – were his venerable unpaid advisers Sir Laurens van der Post, Dr Armand Hammer, who also gave generously to the Prince's causes, and British Airways chairman Lord King. These were the men he invited to dinner when he wanted the conversation to be profound. But these were not the evenings Diana's people fought to get invited to. 'Charles likes to think of himself as a serious thinker,' says one who was not an admirer, as Diana's friends seldom were. 'He takes his thinking seriously, but this is not the same thing as being a serious thinker.' Others on Charles's A list were the Palmer Tomkinsons, the Tryons, the Parker Bowleses, and Camilla's sister Annabel and her husband Simon Elliott. The landed aristocracy was always within the sound of a hunting horn: the Earls of Shelburne and Halifax; the Duke of Westminster, the Marquess of Douro, whose wife Antonia was the great-grand-daughter of the German Kaiser Wilhelm, who had started the First World War. 'The grub is not always the best at Charles's table,' an occasional guest once remarked. 'But the company is usually very rich, very exclusive, and the history's always first class.'

The women Diana counted on were Catherine Soames, a member of the Jardine Matheson trading family who ran Hong Kong, and whose husband Nicholas, a Tory member of Parliament and grandson of Sir Winston Churchill, was a former aide to Charles; Kate and Sarah Menzies, whose father John Menzies owned a national chain of high-street newsagents; Carolyn Bartholomew, her old Coleherne Court flatmate; and Julie Samuel, younger sister of Sabrina Guinness, and whose husband Michael was the younger son of Viscount Bearsted. Her male friends were mostly charming young men who wrecked fast cars. Among the steadier sort were Captain David Waterhouse, a Household Cavalry officer and nephew of the Duke of Marlborough, and James Gilbey, who in the euphemistic tradition of his class was a motor-trade executive, but who in real life sold used cars from a mews garage in Knightsbridge.

And in June 1985 Sarah Ferguson entered her life.

Diana called her a breath of fresh air. She was divine. She was hysterically funny. She was outrageous. Everybody admired how close to the edge she would go. Risk was her quick fix, her adrenalin rush.

'Everybody adores her,' said Diana, whose fourth cousin by marriage she was.

But Sarah Ferguson was more than a breath of fresh air.

She was the wind of change.

Chapter Eighteen

If not exactly a part of them, Sarah Ferguson had been hanging out with royals all her life. Father Ronald – 'Dads' – had played polo with Prince Philip, managed Prince Charles's polo affairs and, as a former Life Guards major, had once commanded the Sovereign's Escort. An Old Etonian, and a scion of a family which could trace its ancestry back to the squirearchy of Ireland, he was it would seem a man to be trusted.

After so narrowly failing in 1954 to win the hand of Diana's mother – the beautiful younger daughter of the fourth Baron Fermoy, remember – he promptly fell in love with Susan Wright, a niece of the ninth Viscount Powerscourt. They married shortly before her nineteenth birthday. Sarah was born on 15 October, 1959, two years after her sister Jane. Almost as soon as they could walk, the two girls were put on ponies, making a modest name for themselves in gymkhanas and agricultural fetes around the Berkshire countryside.

Ronald Ferguson, whose army rank, and affinity with fillies, both equine and human, had earned him the title Galloping Major, resigned his Guards commission after failing the Staff College exams which would have taken him to senior echelon. And like many Guardees who had cultivated contacts and polished social skills while serving the Queen, he went to work for a Mayfair public-relations firm, which numbered Aristotle Onassis among its clients.

On the death of Ronald's father, the Fergusons moved from their suburban Edwardian residence near Sunningdale to Dummer Down House, an 876–acre farm in Hampshire. The change of scenery and distinct improvement in their circumstances could not save the marriage, however. And Ronald's dalliance with a twenty-two-year-old woman who had been his wife's bridesmaid sixteen years before was an affair too far for Susie Ferguson, who anyway had become attracted to an Argentine polo pro named Hector Barrantes, who played for the Stowell Park team of meat baron Lord Vestey. The attraction deepened at a polo tournament on the Côte d'Azur in the summer of 1973. Although London insurance magnate Ronnie Driver, patron of the San Flamingo team, felt that 'Ferguson was virtually throwing his wife at Barrantes,' Ronald expressed shock and hurt when Susie told him that she had fallen in love with the widowed Argentine – a man of no noticeable substance whose life revolved around the international polo circuit – and wanted to marry him.

Sarah was fifteen when her parents divorced in 1974. Old enough to understand the reasons why marriages like her parents' so often end in the way they do, young enough to be hurt all the same. But soon Ronald was in love again – her name was Susan Deptford, the twenty-eight-year-old daughter of a wealthy Norfolk farmer – and in 1976 Sarah had a new mother.

That year she didn't go back to Hurst Lodge, her weekly boarding school in Sunningdale. Her school days were over. She liked and trusted her stepmother Sue and, free of the worry she had felt over Dads, she flew off to join her mother and stepfather in Argentina, where the Barrantes had built a small ranch in Trenque Lauquen on land owned by the family of Hector's late wife, who had been killed in a car accident, when eight months pregnant.

In Buenos Aires she fell in love for the first time in her life with the spontaneity and unexpectedness that was to become a troublesome pattern. His name was Kim Smith-Bingham and, although he was working as a lowly ranch-hand, he was an adventurous Old Etonian. When he returned to England, Sarah followed. When he took off for the Swiss ski resort of Verbier, Sarah was not far behind. It was in Verbier that she met Paddy McNally.

McNally was rich, a widower with two teenage sons, and twenty-two years older than Sarah. A former journalist with a special interest in motor sport, he had joined the Marlboro sponsorship team handling the Grand Prix. Sarah's love for him was instant, passionate, inexplicable and totally one-sided. 'She loved not only Paddy but his sons, and they in turn regarded her as their stepmother,' recalls art dealer Nigel Pollitzer. McNally's first wife, textile heiress Ann Downing, had died of cancer, and he was in no hurry to marry again. 'Fergie couldn't understand that,' says Pollitzer. 'She wanted to marry, have children of her own. She couldn't understand why Paddy didn't feel the same. It made her quite desperate.'

Distressed by McNally's lukewarmness towards the idea of marriage, or any sort of commitment, Sarah returned to London, and sublimated herself in work. But she still could not get McNally out of her mind. Employed to run the Mayfair office of Geneva-based Richard Burton, a former racing driver who now published fine art books, her first commission was a book on the Impressionists, which sold an impressive 155,000 copies and grossed $5 million. But things looked even brighter when 'her new best friend in all the world' the Princess of Wales recommended her to the Queen as a suitable guest of good breeding to be invited to the traditional Royal Ascot week party at Windsor Castle.

When Prince Andrew saw her – the explosion of Irish red hair, the fall-out of freckles, the figure that an Edwardian showgirl would have killed for – it was love at first sight. At least on his part it was. With Diana's connivance, Andrew and Sarah were seated next to each other at lunch in the State Dining-Room. By the time the dessert came around Andrew felt he knew her well enough to hand-feed her profiteroles. And she believed that she understood him well enough to eat them all up. 'They were two young people who would never ask how much elastic there was in the rubber band,' said a courtier who had watched their audacious antics at the table that day with distaste, and some alarm.

During the afternoon at the races Sarah and Andrew were never apart. Their liveliness and obvious sense of enjoyment in each other's company was the talk of Ascot. 'Within days he said he was going to marry me,' Sarah would later reveal. But with unfinished business in Verbier still on her mind she laughed it off as she might a schoolboy joke.

The story of Andrew and Fergie was never a secret. The press were on to it at once. When a handsome Prince hand-feeds a glorious redhead profiteroles bathed in hot chocolate sauce in the State Dining-Room of Windsor Castle in the presence of two dozen guests and the Queen herself it does not go unnoticed.

Sarah was thrilled. The publicity could not have been more timely. She waited for McNally to call, to react, to beg her to marry him after all. But to McNally the whole thing was simply a vicarious pleasure, a wonderful joke.

'I'm pleased for you,' he told her.

'I don't want you to be *pleased* for me – I want you to *marry* me,' she stormed.

Towards the end of the summer, Sarah made her last play. She joined McNally at the Villa d'Este, an exquisite hotel on the shores of Lake Como. He was involved with the Italian Grand Prix at Monza. The Marlboro–McLaren team and its top driver Alain Prost had already won four races and there was celebration in the air.

So it was that in the most romantic of settings Sarah's ill-starred romance reached its final crisis as Prost roared home to his fifth win of the season and an unassailable lead in the driver's championship. As the champagne flowed she confronted McNally for the last time. 'Marry me – or else,' she said. McNally, happy with his life, his sons, his wonderful career, did not even bother to reply.

Sarah returned to England, determined – in her own favourite clarion call – to 'go for it'.

Chapter Nineteen

Prince Andrew Albert Christian Edward Windsor was born at Buckingham Palace on 19 February 1960. Born a whole decade after the Queen's last child, Princess Anne, the devotion of his mother during his early years was such that the royal circle privately referred to him as 'the love child'.

Unquestionably, his arrival healed a long dry period in his parents' marriage that began, according to Mountbatten, with the removal of his name from the family title in 1952 when, under pressure from the Churchill government, the Queen proclaimed that it was her Will and Pleasure that She and Her Children should be styled and known not as Mountbatten-Windsor but simply as the House of Windsor. 'Philip retaliated,' Mountbatten liked to tell friends with sly amusement and evident satisfaction, 'by moving out of her bed.'

What happened in 1959 to return him to Her Majesty's bedchamber is not known. But when he returned from a six-week world tour in the spring of 1959, the Queen was at London Airport to greet him, and for the month of May she barely left his side in a display of togetherness that left royal watchers breathless and amused. Together they attended a soccer cup final, watched a cricket match, toured the Chelsea Flower Show, welcomed the King of Norway, attended a dinner at the Guildhall, and hosted a state visit by the Shah of Iran. Apart from a brief respite in Northern Ireland, Philip was never alone.

'Andrew,' according to the Queen's photographer cousin, the Earl of Lichfield, 'was the favourite in his mother's eyes. He could do no wrong.' And when four years later Edward was born, he was perceived at Court to be 'a companion for Andrew'.

But in no time at all it was 1977 and Andrew was a student at Lakefield College in Ontario and his companions were pretty girls with pretty Canadian names like Cally, Kirstie, Sandi and Jenni. Canada, however, was simply a brief interlude – to broaden his mind, said the Palace – between leaving Gordonstoun and beginning a twelve-year engagement with the Royal Navy. At twenty-one, he qualified as a helicopter pilot and joined 829 Naval Air Squadron, flying Sea Kings from the carrier HMS *Invincible*.

He had worked hard and done well, and now it was time to collect the princely rewards. He was different from Charles, who would be king. Without his elder brother's sense of destiny, he had an altogether lighter touch. He was dedicated to his navy career; he did not fret, as Charles sometimes fretted, about the career he might be missing elsewhere. Charles always wanted to do too much. Andrew did not have that problem. He always did just enough – to pass his exams, keep his father off his back, make his mother happy – to get by. It was the secret of happiness, he liked to tell his friends.

Like his brother before him, he entertained a number of beautiful women to candlelit suppers in his second floor Buckingham Palace apartment. But in 1982 he fell truly, madly, deeply in love. The girl of his dreams – as she was no doubt the girl of thousands of young men's dreams – was American actress Koo Stark. They met at a dinner party in a Chelsea restaurant. There were many attractive women in the group – including Jocelyn Gray and Lady Camilla Dempster, daughter of the eleventh Duke of Leeds – but it was Koo who caught his imagination. She was the date of publisher John Ricketson-Hatt, but when the party moved on to the nightclub Tramp, it was Andrew who monopolized her.

Why Koo? he had asked, just like everybody else. It was the

name her young brother had given her because he could not say Kathleen Dee-Anne. She had done other movies, but *Emily* was the one people remembered. Directed by Henry Herbert, who was also the Earl of Pembroke and Montgomery, it was a soft-porn movie so soft it was practically chaste, she told him.

She was beautiful, with long dark hair. She was funny about herself; she had an openness that Andrew liked. Four years older than the Prince, she was a romantic young woman whose liaisons had been unsuitable rather than scandalous.

A few days after Koo met the Prince, she left her lover, Turkish born textile entrepreneur Touker Suleyman.

Their affair flowered unsuspected through the spring and summer of 1982. It was interrupted only by the Falklands War, in which Andrew flew dangerous missions decoying Argentine Exocet missiles away from the British task force warships; and by a somewhat smaller incident in Chester Square when police, summoned by neighbours anxious after hearing a woman screaming, ordered an upset Mr Suleyman to leave Miss Stark's apartment.

By 18 June, the war in the Falklands was over. Andrew and Koo picked up their affair with the urgency of lovers who never expected to see each other again. In September, he took her to Balmoral to meet the Queen. According to Andrew, his mother knew about Koo's interesting career and considered her to be a very nice young woman. But now their secret was out and the press took a dimmer view of Koo than Her Majesty seems to have taken of her favourite son's loved one. Nude scenes from *Emily* were soon being used to illustrate stories about Koo's past amours. By year's end the affair was over.

'I was desperately fond of Koo,' Andrew would later tell a friend. 'But marriage would have been an awful mistake. I was terribly spoony in those days. I needed to do some more larking about before I settled down.'

For a man in search of some larking about, he certainly got lucky in Barbados. When the *Invincible* paid a courtesy visit on the West

Indian island, he was invited to stay at the palatial plantation house of Mrs Janet Kidd, daughter of the late press baron Beaverbrook. Living in a cottage on the estate was former top English model, Vicki Hodge, thirty-five-year-old sister-in-law of Janet's son, Johnny Kidd. Setting eyes on the young Prince sitting beside the pool, Miss Hodge was immediately smitten. Within hours, she had seduced him and assiduously spent the next two days educating Andrew in the ways of love. Later photographs were taken of Vicki's twenty-one-year old girlfriend Tracie Lamb necking with the obviously delighted royal. But, soon after the Prince had sailed away, the story and pictures of the encounter were being hawked around Fleet Street, eventually selling for £25,000.

Andrew lived the scandal down, by royally ignoring it. But it had upset his mother dreadfully, and his father flew into a rage Andrew never wanted to live through again. 'I became a lot more cautious after that Barbados business,' he later admitted ruefully. 'I was a bloody fool. I would still give my left one for it not to have happened.' And so his liaisons after the Hodge episode were squeaky clean, a little boring. There was a flurry of excitement when he showed a brief interest in Lord Porchester's attractive daughter, Carolyn Herbert. 'Porchie' was the Queen's racing manager, and it was generally agreed in Court circles that, other than Prince Philip, he was the only man she would have wanted to marry. 'Porchie was awfully keen for Carolyn to marry Andrew,' said a fellow trainer, as shrewd a judge of the human condition as he was of horse flesh, 'but they had known each other far too long – the chemistry simply wasn't there.'

And so Andrew was not only available but positively aching for something good to happen in his life when he found himself sitting beside Sarah Ferguson that day at Windsor.

It took almost no time at all to forget Paddy McNally when Sarah put her mind to it, and by Christmas 1985 he was such a distant memory that she was sure that there had never been anyone else in her life but Andrew. She accepted an invitation from the Queen to join the royal family for the New Year at Sandringham; she was thrilled when Charles and Diana asked her to join them skiing in Klosters in January. It seemed not to matter that she smoked like a chimney (Princess Margaret was the only other royal tobacco addict) and enjoyed her wine (Charles and Diana, and even Andrew, were virtual teetotallers, sipping an occasional celebratory drink). The family seemed to love her. 'Also the press, always anxious for new heroines, of course, had taken a tremendous shine to her,' said a Palace aide, perhaps explaining the Queen's unexpected enthusiasm for the most unroyal guest to shake up the exquisite calm of Sandringham in years.

But she had to wait until February – 23 February, when they were staying with the Duke and Duchess of Roxburghe at their wonderfully romantic Floors Castle in Scotland – before Andrew went down on both knees and asked her to marry him. 'When you wake up in the morning,' she answered carefully, 'you can tell me it was all a big joke.' But the next morning he asked her again. She accepted.

It seemed somehow exactly right that they should appear on television to talk about their engagement, to talk about their love, to talk about each other, and the wonderful future they planned to share together. It was not so much an interview as an arm-punching celebration of happiness, affection and sheer exuberance. From that moment on the British people were as much in love with Fergie as was the Prince himself. They loved the way she looked, and her eye-rolling talent for silly faces. She was funny, irreverent; even her grin was contagious. And they loved the way she dressed. The sartorial code of good British families has always been that the best-dressed people are the people you notice least. Fergie disagreed. She heliotroped her way through the social scene in frills and flounces – 'adding bells and whistles for good measure should the mood so take her', said a friend admiringly. And when she persuaded Diana to gatecrash Andrew's stag party with her, both dressed as policewomen, nobody was surprised. They failed to break through the heavy security at Aubrey House where the party was being held, and repaired to Annabel's nightclub in Berkley Square for a glass of Buck's Fizz, still in uniform.

It is remarkable that it was a Frenchman, seeing the Princess of Wales and the future Duchess of York at Annabel's that night, who expressed the doubt that nobody in the royal family appears to have felt. 'C'est magnifique, mais ce n'est pas la royauté,' he said parodying a military forebear who had witnessed another great British error of judgement more than a century before, the Charge of the Light Brigade.

Sue Ferguson was turning out the pockets of one of her husband's jackets before sending it to be cleaned. A book of matches fell out with the cover turned back; on it had been written the room number of a hotel opposite the Victoria and Albert Museum with a time and a date which, Sue noticed, was that very day one hour hence. She got into her car, drove to London, went straight up to the hotel room and knocked at the door. It was answered by her husband wearing a towel. Inside was a woman Sue knew. The Galloping Major suggested they should discuss the matter later. Later he admitted everything, told Sue she had every right to ask for a divorce, but then proposed a strange accommodation. Divorce proceedings would jeopardize Fergie's romance with the Prince, he said. 'If they don't marry,' he negotiated, 'you can have a divorce. If they do, I promise never to be unfaithful again.' There was a certain charming ruthlessness to him, she thought, still wondering why she had agreed to such a deal.

Sarah and Andrew were married in Westminster Abbey in July 1986. For her wedding gift – beside the dukedom bestowed on their wedding day – the Queen leased them Sunninghill Park in Berkshire, five acres of choice Crown Estate on which their sprawling ranch-style home would be built at a cost of £3.5 million. While the house was being completed, King Hussein of Jordan offered them the rent-free use of Castlewood, a twelve-bedroomed house he owned in Surrey. The couple moved into their sprawling new home – dubbed Southyork by the press – during the winter of 1987 and settled down to married life.

But 'settled down' is a comparative term. Andrew's naval duties meant he was infrequently at home and, though staff tried to fine-tune their engagement books, there were often clashes which conspired to keep them apart. 'She was absolutely madly in love with Andrew and when he was at sea she wrote him letters every day, but in effect she was abandoned because of his job,' a later lover would say, when others were blaming her for the break-up of the marriage. 'She was deeply in love. She really wanted the fairy tale.'

Shortly before the wedding, Fergie summoned clairvoyant Maureen Conway to Andrew's apartment at the Palace for a reading. It was the beginning of a professional relationship and a friendship that would last as long as her marriage. On that first visit to the Palace, sitting in Andrew's study surrounded by his teddy bears and scatter-cushions embroidered with slogans like 'It's tough being a Prince', Conway sensed that, behind Fergie's bubbly public persona, something was troubling her.

'But she was one hundred per cent convinced that nothing could go wrong with the marriage,' says Conway now. 'I have never met anyone so certain of anything. But I warned her that there were problems ahead. She said, "What kind of problems – anything to do with Koo Stark?" She knew I had read for Koo, and I realized that was why she had sent for me, to pump me about her. Koo still worried her. I said that Koo would never be a problem to her.

'Sarah said, "Then I have no problems. All my problems are over!" I still didn't think so. I told her that the problems I saw would be of her own making. The problem would come from her, from her relationships. She said, "You mean if I had an affair with someone? That kind of problem? You don't think I'm stupid? Do you think I'd jeopardize *all this*?"'

Shortly afterwards, Prince Andrew joined them and gave Conway the wedding ring to hold. 'What do you get from that?' he asked. She gave them a reading that was genuinely hopeful; she did not mention her doubts about Sarah. 'I truly did feel good about them together. But I knew that everything depended on Sarah.'

The following morning, Sarah called. 'Thank you,' she said.

'Be careful,' Conway said again.

'Yes, I know,' Sarah told her.

Friends noticed quite early in the marriage that, though Andrew did his best to continue to appear as fun-loving as his still exhaustlessly bubbly wife, he ducked eating out in her favourite restaurants whenever he could, he took more and more rainchecks on parties. 'He seemed to prefer to sit watching golf videos, his supper on his lap,' said a friend, puzzled by the change in him. Golf had become Andrew's passion, and much of his time ashore was spent playing at Swinley Forest, the exclusive Berkshire club owned by the Earl of Derby.

But, if Fergie was disappointed to discover that her husband's style had become so out of keeping with her own, she appears to have sensed no immediate threat. 'Oh, Andy's suffering from a little mettle fatigue, nothing serious,' she told old friends who wondered why he had twice failed to accompany his wife to a dinner party at their home.

But it was not as simple or as funny as that. 'He exuded not just tiredness but ... regret,' said one of Fergie's very closest friends. 'The change in him since the days he was chasing her all over Windsor was just amazing. He had been so dazzled by her then, and now all the dazzle had gone. He just didn't seem to be the same man. And the odd thing was, Sarah accepted it.'

There were also stories of Andrew's frugality, which bordered on meanness, as he went around Sunninghill switching off lights and turning down radiators. Unlike Charles, who had a vast personal fortune from the Duchy of Cornwall estates, Andrew was not an immensely wealthy man, although he was far from poor. He received £250,000 a year from the Civil List, and he had his Royal Navy salary of £34,000 a year; there was also an allowance, unspecified, from his mother. But he had no capital and no other assets other than a life insurance policy worth around £600,000. 'Money was definitely on his mind. When he talked about his expenses he was beginning to whine,' said one of the Yorks' friends on the Duchess's side. 'It was difficult to sympathize.'

But despite the distance that was clearly growing between Andrew and Sarah, and the increasing awkwardness and uncertainty they showed whenever they were together, in a period of just seventeen months Sarah gave birth to Princess Beatrice and Princess Eugenie. Andrew was present at the birth of his second daughter, delivered by Caesarian section at a private London clinic. 'The baby is lovely, very well, and the mother is fine,' he told waiting newsmen. 'I've promised to come back tomorrow.'

But his voice showed no delight, and almost no interest. It rose barely a half-tone above the flat, unfeeling voice he used when he read out official statements, or talked to the ground victims of the Lockerbie airline disaster in Scotland. Nevertheless, royal watchers, aware for some time that all was not well between the Yorks, hopefully interpreted his words as meaning there would be a change of direction in the marriage, and that the new baby would bring a fresh stability to the relationship, encouraging Andrew to spend more time at home.

Nobody knew it then, but it was already far too late for that.

By now Prince Andrew knew that his wife had made the biggest mistake – committed the greatest indiscretion – in the whole of her amorous, wayward, headstrong young life.

In October 1990, the Yorks gave a party for 200 friends to celebrate the official opening of Sunninghill. Guests filed through the thirty-five-feet-high white-painted entrance hall with its glass-domed ceiling and rustic-beamed minstrels' gallery, without which no ranch was complete. On the second floor of the two-storey building were the twelve main bedrooms. The main suite was thirty-five feet long, with two master bathrooms and separate dressing rooms, with bow windows overlooking the garden. They each had their own office suite. A cinema, pool room and swimming pool completed the entertainment section.

The guests were impressed, and those who were not were polite. On an earlier visit after studying the edifice for several minutes in silence, Prince Charles told his brother, 'Well, there's no place like home – at least, not like yours, Andrew.' Among the guests that night – 'I kept thinking of it as an opening night, it was so showbizzy,' said one of the guests – were Michael Caine and his wife, Shakira; David Frost and his wife, Lady Carina; Scottish comedian Billy Connolly and his Australian-born actress wife, Pamela Stephenson (a close Fergie friend); the Pakistan cricket captain Imran Khan; and Princess Margaret's son, Viscount Linley.

Two of the last guests to leave Southyork that night were two Texans. One was tall and deeply bronzed, the better to show off his perfect white teeth. At first sight, his balding companion was less striking, but he had a friendly charm which Fergie once said 'could disarm a charging bull at a hundred paces'. Both men were courteous and attentive. They were also the principal architects in the Duchess of York's impending fall from grace. One was Steve Wyatt, the other John Bryan.

> Last week, lawyers acting for the Duchess
> of York initiated discussions about a
> formal separation for the Duke and Duchess.
> These discussions are not yet complete and
> nothing will be said until they are.
> The Queen hopes that the media will spare
> the Duke and Duchess of York and their
> children any intrusion.

The news came as no surprise to the six accredited Court correspondents who had been summoned by the Queen's press secretary

Charles Anson to hear the statement. Indeed, the *Daily Mail* had been sitting on the story for almost a week, its editor Sir David English demanding 'twenty-four-carat proof' before he published. But what the correspondents could not help remarking was the date the announcement was made: Thursday, 19 March 1992. It was six years to the day that Andrew and Sarah became engaged.

While final details were being worked out by the lawyers – 'In the end even a royal divorce comes down to who gets the fish knives and who keeps the old Elton John records,' said a courtier – it was agreed the couple would remain under the same roof at Sunninghill. Sarah would be relieved of all further royal engagements. But Charles Anson, a former diplomat who had arrived at the Palace via merchant bankers Kleinwort Benson in July 1990, did not seem inclined to let the matter stand as a simple press release. Speaking with the apparent authority of the Queen in an informal chat with BBC Court correspondent Paul Reynolds, he declared that Sarah 'was unsuitable for royal and public life' and had 'behaved foolishly'. He did not spell out the precise nature of her foolishness, but he blamed her for leaking details of the private lunch she had had with the Queen to discuss her problems.

Later that day, Reynolds began his story on the BBC: 'I can only say that the knives are out for Fergie at the Palace. I have never known such anger here at what has been going on.'

The 'knives are out' story went around the world. But exactly what had been going on? What on earth had gone so wrong with a marriage that had started out so full of hope and filled with so much happiness?

BOOK FOUR

Chapter Twenty

Though the separation of the Duke and Duchess of York was not officially announced until March 1992, the dragon's teeth which spawned the drama had been sown two and a half years before in the Lone Star State of Texas.

Some four and a half months pregnant with her second child, Her Royal Highness, the Duchess of York, flew to the States early in November 1989 on a semi-official five-day visit to Houston, accompanied by her lady-in-waiting, an equerry and the Queen's press secretary, who had been seconded to the Yorks. It was exactly the kind of royal trip Sarah liked best. It was not simply the attention that she had grown to love, but the social kowtowing was also good for her ego, although she had not yet lost her sense of humour and it could still occasionally make her laugh, too.

Among her none-too-demanding official duties was a visit to the first night of the Houston Grand Opera's British season, which she attended wearing an off-the-shoulder yellow dress, cunningly cut to disguise her condition, and patterned with roses, in tribute to her host state. Her hostess was Lynn Wyatt – 'the vibrant Lynn Wyatt', she was usually referred to in the Houston press – who later entertained the royal party at her mansion home, Allington, next to the exclusive River Oaks Country Club.

Lynn had been born Lynn Sakowitz, and her family had set up a chain of stores to rival Neiman Marcus. In the 1950s, she had married real-estate heir Robert Lipman, a six foot seven inch giant of a man who had given her two children – Steven and Douglas. In the 1960s, Lipman left her and the children and moved to London, where he entered the swinging scene with the zeal of a religious convert. 'He was completely out of his head on LSD most of the time, and had enough money to keep half of London in drugs,' recalls property developer Frank Duggan, who with his wife, actress Viviane Ventura, knew him well and whose Chester Street home became a popular Sunday rendezvous for Lipman and celebrities like Roman Polanski and Sharon Tate.

While on an 'acid trip to hell' with his eighteen-year-old French girlfriend, Claudie Delbarre, who had gone to London to learn English and teach tired businessmen French, Lipman bludgeoned her to death and fled back to America. Extradited to England, he was charged with murder. After a brief but sensational trial in October 1968, the Old Bailey jury acquitted him of murder, but found him guilty of manslaughter. He was sentenced to six years' imprisonment. Meanwhile, Lynn had divorced Lipman and married the wealthy Oscar Wyatt. Wyatt adopted the two Lipman boys, giving them his name, in 1963.

Fergie and the Palace knew nothing of this lurid tale. Indeed, the Duchess was so taken by Steve Wyatt it is questionable whether it would have mattered anyway. Wyatt was a handsome man of thirty-five with a mock sort of movie-cowboy humility and a way of walking that betrayed that he was not unconscious of how much he was observed. 'There was an instant attraction, and the moment they set eyes on each other the Duchess was smitten,' says a Texan who was present at that first meeting.

During her entire Texas stay Sarah was rarely apart from Wyatt. There was almost something mesmeric in Wyatt's hold on her, one of the Texans observed; and she, by some strange alchemy of snobbery and sex that transcended even her interesting condition, beguiled him.

'They were definitely an odd couple,' says one of Wyatt's business associates who had watched the romance develop in Houston. 'She enjoyed her wine, Steve never touched a drop. He kept away from drugs. I guess it's not hard to understand why. At that time he was into a sort of New Age philosophy – his talk was full of words like "karma" and "aura" – and he had a crystal which was supposed to alert him to people's psyches. But I think the Duchess took that stuff with a pinch of salt, his talk about astral bodies ... It was his body she was interested in. He kept himself in terrific shape.'

At the weekend, when they visited his family's 20,000-acre ranch near Corpus Christi, she impressed Wyatt by taking the controls of one of the helicopters owned by his stepfather's Coastal Corporation. 'Did your husband teach you to fly?' he asked her, impressed. 'He is too busy these days to teach me anything,' she said. She added that in the previous year, Andrew had managed to spend only forty-two nights at home. Wyatt, who recognized an opening when he saw one, said he thought that was an awful waste.

By this time, the Duchess must have known what she was doing, and where it was taking her.

A few months earlier the clairvoyant Maureen Conway had moved to Texas, and she now had an apartment in Dallas. The two women had become friends since that first meeting amid Prince Andrew's teddy bears at the Palace before the wedding. The Duchess now dialled her number. 'Do you remember what you told me back in 1986 – nothing could go wrong unless I let it?' she said, coming straight to the point when Conway answered the phone. 'You told me that only I could spoil things ... if I ever let myself get involved?'

'Yes,' said Conway, already knowing, fearing what was coming next.

'I'm getting involved,' Sarah laughed nervously.

'Well, stop it,' Conway told her, speaking not as a clairvoyant but as a friend. She understood both the confidence and the trust Sarah had in her, and she knew that the Duchess was not looking for prophecies this time. 'Sarah already knew better than anyone what was going to happen,' she would say later. 'She knew herself very well. She knew the course she was on. She must have already accepted the consequences.'

And Conway felt sad for her. 'I think that was the moment I first understood how little control she has over her impulses, her blind instincts ... whatever it is that makes her behave the way she behaves. She holds nothing back. There is such a passion in her ... she has almost no consideration for herself at all when a thing like that happens to her. I remember I told her again that it was not too late. She could still back out, I said.'

'I can't,' Sarah said, miserable and defiant at the same time.

'Why can't you?' Conway asked.

'It's my nature,' Sarah said, apparently recognizing that there was now a pattern to her behaviour from which she could not escape and had no resources to resist.

'Then I told her that she must accept the consequences,' Conway would later recall the poignant conversation in Texas, it was the last time the two friends, the Duchess and the clairvoyant, talked. 'I'm sure there must have been times when she would have liked a respite from her own demons,' Maureen Conway said.

Sarah returned to London via New York, using one of the Wyatts' private jet planes; in the Big Apple she stayed at the Plaza Athenee Hotel, paid for by the Wyatts. Apart from their mutual affection, the Duchess was the social catch of the season, and Steve Wyatt was understandably thrilled. They dined at Mortimer's in a group which included John Bowes Lyon, the Queen Mother's great-nephew who lived in New York at the home of designer Halston. They went to dinner with Norman Mailer, whose books Sarah confessed she had never read. 'Which one should I begin with?' she asked the famous author. He suggested *Tough Guys Don't Dance*. She asked what it was about. 'Pussy,' said Mailer.

She left New York, on 9 November, carrying some fifty parcels and packages in addition to her suitcases. Asked what the packages contained, she answered, 'Christmas presents.' The trip had been a great success. Sarah had given Wyatt her private number before she left New York and told him to call her as soon as he got to London.

Wyatt called at the end of November, hoping that it was not one of the forty-two nights that her husband might answer the phone. His luck was in. He told her that he had been invited by London advertising supremo Frank Lowe to join him pheasant shooting in Yorkshire on 7 and 8 December. Remarkably, she told him, she would be in Yorkshire on 8 December; as Patron of Opera North she had agreed to attend a gala charity performance of *Show Boat* at the Grand Theatre, Leeds.

Each December Frank Lowe took over Constable Burton, a 3,500-acre sporting estate north of York, owned by Charles and Maggie Wyvill, and invited a group of friends to join him for a couple of days of sport. Among his guests that year were the Earl of Lichfield, banker Nicky Villiers, actor Nigel Havers, Charles Allsopp, who was the head of the auction house Christie's, Wayne Eagling, principal dancer with the Royal Ballet, and Princess Anne's former beau and manager of Mustique, Brian Alexander.

Lowe, who had known Wyatt for some years and had shot with him in Mexico, says he was not pleased when the Texan asked if the Duchess of York might join them at dinner. 'It was the first I knew that the Duchess was a friend of his,' he said. 'I agreed reluctantly because that sort of presence can spoil a jolly party. But there wasn't much I could do without being rude.'

A clearly pregnant Fergie duly arrived for dinner, and returned to London early the following morning for a private lunch date. That afternoon she flew back to Yorkshire in an aircraft of the Queen's Flight, accompanied by her equally pregnant lady-in-waiting, Carolyn Cotterell. Following the gala première in Leeds, they drove the thirty miles to Constable Burton, arriving shortly towards the end of dinner. She had telephoned Maggie Wyvill earlier to say that a technical hitch with the aircraft had delayed her return to London, and could she come over?

Lord Lichfield was one of the first to go to bed. 'As far as I knew Sarah and Carolyn were returning to Sandringham that night, but next morning when I was alone having an early breakfast, there she was, still wearing the long black evening dress she had worn the night before. She said the plane had not been able to fly, so she had had to stay the night.'

As the guns prepared to go out that morning, Lichfield suggested a group picture on the steps of the fine eighteenth-century mansion. 'I thought it would look great. Sarah looked very dramatic in her black gown and cape,' he said. He posed the other house guests around her, with Wyatt at her feet. Unfortunately, these interesting pictures were lost to posterity when Lichfield dropped his camera and ruined the film. A set of pictures taken by Maggie Wyvill at the same time became the subject of intense newspaper bidding when the extent of Sarah's involvement with Wyatt became known two years later. Wyvill refused the offers, and even removed a framed enlargement of one shot which had hung unnoticed for two years in the main hall of Constable Burton.

Wyatt had now moved to London permanently to work out of the Pall Mall offices of Delaney Petroleum, associated with his stepfather's empire. Soon Sarah became confident enough to introduce her Texan admirer to her royal husband. The two disparate men, probably with only one thing in common in all the world, met at Castlewood, the house in Surrey that had been lent to the Yorks by King Hussein while their own house was being built. Andrew was impressed by the tall American, and particularly interested in his stories about the wheeling and dealing in the international oil game, and his talk about the cutting edge, corporate takeovers, acquisitions and the power wielded by men whose names were unfamiliar to him. Particularly sensitive about his own financial situation at that time – money, or the lack of it, had become a frequent topic of conversation with the Prince – he was incredulous to learn that Wyatt's stepfather had a fortune variously estimated at between five and eight billion dollars.

In royal reckoning, a man whose stepfather is that rich is a man you can respect. Certainly Andrew at this point had no problem trusting Wyatt with his wife, although that was soon to change when stories of Sarah's familiar behaviour with Wyatt in America began to filter back to him from New York. 'It is naive in the extreme to imagine that you can go out to dinner with your boyfriend in New York in the same company as the Queen Mother's great-nephew and not expect tongues to wag in London,' said a Clarence House aide.

The romance was becoming well known by people in the know; you could hear the stories for the price of a meal with the right people in London, Houston or New York. But still it did not get into the papers.

And still Andrew did not act to stop the burgeoning relationship. Perhaps he simply could not believe what he was hearing. Perhaps Sarah had convinced him that the rumours simply were not true. 'It is a mystery to me how Andrew put up with Wyatt for so long. He seemed to have no particular feeling for him, either for or against. Apparently he could not see what was happening under his nose. The only one who could have stopped that dalliance was Andrew, and he did nothing. But he could be very ingenuous where Fergie was concerned,' says a friend of the Duchess who would later recall a night at Harry's Bar in London when the marriage was beginning to wobble. 'Andrew isn't a drinker, and he disapproves of people who do. Nobody was permitted to smoke, because he doesn't smoke. Fergie was drinking vodka and tonic, and pretending it was mineral water, and making silly comments like, "This is delicious water ... what is it, French? Italian?" We all knew that it was Russian vodka, except Andrew. It was very awkward. You felt you had to laugh at her joke, but you didn't want to embarrass him.'

Shortly after the birth of Princess Eugenie, by which time even Andrew had his suspicions about Wyatt, the Texan arranged a five-day break for Sarah at the Gazelle d'Or, a chic French hotel just outside the walled city of Taroudant, in Morocco. Wisely, perhaps in a bid to allay Andrew's fears, Wyatt did not accompany her to Morocco. Instead he suggested that their mutual friend Pricilla Phillips should go along to keep Sarah company. Pricilla, a tall American actress, was one of the many beautiful women who had been involved with Wyatt. The Duchess enjoyed grilling her about Wyatt, and especially enjoyed hearing stories about his other girlfriends.

In July, Lynn Wyatt invited Sarah and her children to Cap Ferrat in the South of France, where she had rented Somerset Maugham's old villa, La Mauresque, before moving on to the equally magnificent Les Rochers Fleuries, on the Chemin de Roy. And it was at Les Rochers Fleuries, which Lynn was renting for $75,000 a month, where the photographs were taken (possibly by Pricilla Phillips) that would finally sink the marriage of the Duke and Duchess of York. They showed Steve Wyatt with two-year-old Princess Beatrice naked on his lap. Other pictures showed him with his arms around Sarah on a swing-seat, and horse-riding knee to knee.

But just how close Wyatt and Sarah had become, and just how prepared he was to involve her in his business affairs, was revealed later that summer when the Duchess was invited to dinner at Le Gavroche by construction heir Lord McAlpine and his wife Romilly. The Duchess pleaded a previous engagement, but asked whether she might come on later. In fact, she had been asked by Wyatt to give dinner in her second floor Buckingham Palace apartment to Dr Ramzi Salman, Iraq's oil-marketing chief, with whom Oscar Wyatt was closely involved. Iraq had invaded Kuwait on 2 August and the Saddam Hussein regime was vastly unpopular throughout the world.

Nevertheless, out of ignorance or sheer bravado, or perhaps she was a little intoxicated, Sarah suggested that all three go on to Le Gavroche. Their arrival at the smart restaurant caused understandable consternation. For not only was McAlpine the Treasurer of the Tory Party but among his guests were Lord Palumbo, a godfather to Princess Beatrice, and his Lebanese-born wife Hayat, who refused even to be introduced to Dr. Salman – 'I do not see you,' she told him with the kind of glacial disapproval you could skate on.

The comedy of manners continued with Lady McAlpine desperately trying to seat her unexpected and quite unwelcome guests. The noble Lord McAlpine discreetly made room next to him for Sarah, while Wyatt was motioned to another table. But Wyatt was having none of it. Grabbing the Duchess's hand he sat down and pulled her on to his lap. 'Mah woman and I sit together,' he said with Texan pride and a sense of possession that alarmed the English diners.

For the rest of the evening the McAlpines and their guests, wearing that glazed and inscrutable look only the English can assume when deeply embarrassed, were treated in the words of one guest to 'a display of mutual fondling I have never seen before in a three-star restaurant'.

Late in the spring of 1993, after he had become Sarah's lover and financial adviser, John Bryan said of that extraordinary incident, 'Wyatt was using Sarah. It was his idea to bring the Iraqi oil minister to the Palace. But remember, Sarah would not have done it unless it had been cleared by the Palace. Sarah was naive but she has a generous spirit. Wyatt had been nice to her and she wanted to help him.'

Although Steve Wyatt might have believed it impossible to top his social triumph at Le Gavroche, he knew he had truly hit the jackpot when he was invited to Buckingham Palace for a Christmas ball to celebrate the birthdays of the Queen Mother (ninety), Princess Margaret (sixty), Princess Anne (forty), and Prince Andrew (thirty).

'Hi, I'm Steve Wyatt. Friend of Sarah,' he was heard introducing himself to guests in the Palace ballroom. Later he told friends that he had been seated next to the Queen at supper. 'He was on a real high for days afterwards,' said an American colleague who had heard Wyatt's Palace stories several times and was beginning to worry about his unhealthy illusions of grandeur. 'I got the impression that if he had had a mobile telephone with him at the Palace he would have called Oscar and Lynn to tell them about it there and then. He thought he had really made it in London.'

Unfortunately, the reverse was true. Wyatt had not made it in London. Not the London that was so important to him anyway. The Queen was considerably less impressed by her Texan supper guest than he was by her. And although she was curiously fond of Sarah, and generally amused by her exuberance, the Queen was now slowly becoming impatient with her too, and there were signs that she was beginning to withhold the total support she had once given. In a rare move of direct intervention, she called her daughter-in-law and asked whether she thought that Mr. Wyatt was 'quite the sort of person you should be encouraging, dear'.

Sarah's mother, Susan Barrantes, was more direct: '*Chill him,*' she said.

And even the Duchess got the message.

Chapter Twenty-one

It was a devastating time for Steve Wyatt, whose fame in café-society London rested squarely on his royal connections. Disconnected from Sarah – literally, she would not accept his calls, and eventually changed her private number – he sought solace in the way he knew best: in the company of beautiful women.

But society London is a small and surprising place and the beautiful woman he met at a dinner party in the spring of 1991 put him on an entirely new collision course with the Ferguson family. Her name was Lesley Player – an apt name as it turned out.

Lesley Player was petite, attractive, middle-class, and had the kind of history of which mini-dramas are made.

Ten years earlier she had married Jim Player, a record producer who also owned an employment agency specializing in chauffeurs. The demand for chauffeurs in booming London was substantial and very soon Lesley was riding around in her own chauffeured Bentley (later there was a Rolls Royce Silver Spur) and living in a million-pound mock-Tudor home on the River Thames, in the royal borough of Kingston.

But when the economy crashed so did the chauffeur market. In 1989, the business and the marriage went into liquidation, and the dream house was put up for sale. Personally owing £42,000, but still hanging on to her Rolls (she believed in keeping up appearances), Lesley Player cast around for a new way to make her fortune.

She found it by accident one evening when, channel hopping on her television set, she saw a programme about the sport which was to change her life – polo. Totally taken by the excitement and glamour of the game, especially its aura of money and sophistication, she signed on at the local Epsom Polo Club for lessons. A fast learner, within a few months she was playing in friendly mixed matches. On a trip to America, she got the idea of using a women's polo tournament to raise money for charity. On her return to England, she set about trying to interest polo clubs and sponsors in her idea. She had little success, but one name kept recurring: Major Ronald Ferguson.

Ferguson, she decided, was the key to everything. He was not only the Prince of Wales's personal polo manager (no salary but plenty of prestige), he was also the £32,000–a-year director of sponsorship – controlling some £750,000 worth of billings a season – at the Royal County of Berkshire Polo Club, an exclusive outfit co-owned by Bryan Morrisson, who had made a personal fortune by publishing the music of rock groups like Pink Floyd, Wham! and the Bee Gees.

Calling cold, Player was surprised to get an appointment the following week. Ferguson listened to her ideas and liked what he heard – and saw. A tournament to be held at the Berkshire was set for August 1991.

'Many people say I'm not the most intelligent of men, and perhaps that's true. But I'm loyal and trusting and I have been hurt so many times, because I am naive in many ways,' Major Ferguson said, cantering slowly up to the first fence over tea at Claridge's a few weeks later. 'I want you to know I care about you, and I only wish things could be different. If only I were twenty years younger and circumstances were different, then perhaps I could have what I wanted.'

Two days later, Player says that Ferguson did get what he wanted when they made love at her Kingston home. Afterwards they talked. He told her about his life, his problems; he talked about his daughter the Duchess of York (whom he called G.B.: for Ginger Bush), and her problems, especially about the unwise affair she had been having with a rich Texan named Steve Wyatt.

And now sitting right next to Lesley Player at a dinner party in Chelsea was Steve Wyatt. Whaddya know! She was charmed by his crystal which was alert to people's psyches; she was fascinated by his theories about karma and the New Age philosophy. She also noticed, just as the Duchess of York had noticed in Houston before her, that he had a very nice body.

The next day Wyatt called her and invited her to dinner at his apartment in Cadogan Square. She arrived at seven for pheasant casserole and four hours later, by way of a *digestif*, they were making love.

That summer, shortly after Steve Wyatt found out about Player's ongoing affair with Ferguson – and, as if to square this remarkable triangle, Player had confessed to Ferguson what she was doing with Wyatt – the Texan moved to Washington ('Mr Misdeeds goes to Washington,' said one of Sarah's most faithful friends), leaving a time-bomb of 120 photographs taken at Cap Ferrat carelessly ticking on top of a wardrobe at his £500–a-week apartment.

Chapter Twenty-two

B ut it was the season of rich Texans. And as Steve Wyatt exited
stage left, his old schoolfriend John Bryan decided it was time
to emerge from the opposite wing.

A tall, lean, prematurely bald man, Bryan was an above average
golfer and squash player, a fine skier; he was also a highly energized
businessman of considerable imagination. In 1987, with a bachelor
of arts degree in economics from the University of Texas, and a
masters in business administration from the University of Pittsburg
Graduate School, he went to London to take up an appointment
with York Trust Group, an investment banking firm.

He acquired a company called Oceanics in late 1987 and was
quickly recognized as a player to watch. Perhaps because his father
had been born in England (educated at Ampleforth, the country's
leading Roman Catholic public school: alma mater of Andrew
Parker Bowles), Bryan was fascinated by the London social scene −
in which he very soon became a minor but busy participant. He
dated, among others, Geraldine Harmsworth, the beautiful estranged
wife of Lord Ogilvy and daughter of media magnate Viscount
Rothermere and his late wife, the society hostess known as 'Bubbles'.

It was a world in which John Bryan felt good. A world of old
titles, older money and beautiful young women, it was filled
with opportunities for a young man with a masters in business
administration. And when he met the Duchess of York, through his
good friend Steve Wyatt, he knew at once that with his charm and

credentials he would be the perfect candidate should she ever need a financial adviser.

And the way things were developing, it looked as if she soon might.

Over Christmas and the final days of 1991 at Sandringham, Sarah and Andrew discussed their future and agreed that they had come to the end of what had been a short and bumpy road. The Prince had somehow persuaded himself that the rumours about Wyatt had been only rumours, and the American played no part in their discussions. They were, the Yorks now recognized with sadness, simply 'incompatible souls'.

But it was generally agreed among those closest to the Duchess that most of the sadness was on Andrew's side. 'Fergie had a lot of regrets about a lot of things, but freeing herself of Andrew – I don't think that was one of them,' says a woman who has been one of Sarah's friends since her days in publishing, and who blames the Prince's 'serious attitude problem' for the difficulties in the marriage.

'He always wanted to be the centre of attention,' says another friend, whose husband was telling an anecdote one evening at Harry's Bar when Andrew started tapping his knife on his glass and shouting, 'I want to tell a story, I want to tell a story.' Her husband abandoned his anecdote. 'Andrew then told a joke that was utterly unfunny, very long and extremely filthy,' recalls the interrupted anecdotist's wife. 'He might be a prince, but he is an extremely boorish man. One's heart went out to Sarah when she had to sit there and watch him behaving like that.'

If Andrew was a nightmare to have to live with, he was no better to have to work alongside. When volunteers were invited to join his helicopter service team aboard HMS *Hermes*, not one sailor came forward. He was, says a former navy colleague, the master of the wrong foot. 'You can call me H,' he is reputed to have told a venerable rear-admiral. 'And you can call me sir,' was the withering reply.

'The biggest single factor in the break-up of the Yorks' marriage was Andrew's plain awfulness,' says this same woman.

And so that Christmas Sarah and Andrew told the Queen of their decision to separate. This was the moment that Sarah had dreaded most. Andrew was so in awe of his mother that he would often stammer to a halt in mid-sentence if he thought she had lost interest in what he was saying. 'He is still like a little boy in front of the Queen,' Sarah had told friends. 'She's always a monarch first in his eyes.' Nevertheless, the meeting with the Queen went well. Sarah explained the situation; Andrew said very little. The Queen did not try to dissuade them. She simply expressed her 'disappointment' and asked them to wait six months before making any announcement, or taking any irrevocable decision.

They agreed.

On 2 January 1992, Sarah took her daughters to Klosters to ski for the first time. Her marriage problems had been frankly discussed and admitted to the Queen. Steve Wyatt was out of her life. It had been a tricky couple of years but now she was truly happy at last.

Then a window-cleaner and odd-job man named Maurice Marple ruined everything. Hired to clean up Wyatt's rented apartment in Cadogan Square long after his departure to Washington, DC, Marple found on top of a dusty wardrobe the photographs that had been taken in the South of France two years before.

Recognizing the long red hair and laughing face of the Duchess of York — a friend supplied the added information that the hunk with his arm around her was Steve Wyatt; she had recognized his face from a gossip column picture — Marple promptly took the pictures to the *Daily Mail*. The *Mail* advised him to take the pictures to Scotland Yard. Very shortly the story of the pictures discovered on top of Wyatt's dusty wardrobe in Belgravia was in the papers; some of the pictures would soon mysteriously turn up in *Paris Match*.

Prince Andrew was now furious.

By this time Sarah had gone to Florida to receive a cheque on behalf of a charity for motor neurone disease. She was accompanied by her father, and Lesley Player, acting as her lady-in-waiting (a role she occasionally affected in order to be close to the galloping Major). Player had flown to Palm Beach straight from a skiing holiday in Aspen, and had no idea of the crisis that had arisen in London over the photographs. When she asked Ferguson what was going on – she had never seen Sarah in such a foul temper; she was screaming at her father for the least thing – Ferguson told her the story.

'Andrew's hit the roof,' he said. 'He *thinks* they're having an affair!'

The six month period of reflection suggested by the Queen was not yet halfway over. 'I don't need any more time to think, Mother,' Andrew now told the Queen, with an obduracy and anger he rarely displayed in her presence. 'My mind is made up.'

On Sunday, 15 March, Sir Matthew Farrer, the Queen's solicitor, and Charles Doughty, a distinguished lawyer retained by the Duchess to represent her interests, gathered at Sunninghill. It was the first meeting with the Duke and Duchess of York to discuss the ramifications of their separation and to establish an agenda for a financial settlement prior to divorce.

One other man present that day was John Bryan.

Sarah introduced him as 'my financial adviser'.

'Everything looked better after that meeting,' she would say later. 'John was a wonderful tower of strength.'

Everybody loved everybody. Bryan had nothing but praise for the Prince. 'Andrew wanted what was best for Sarah,' he later recalled of that first summit meeting at Sunninghill. 'He was in a sense on her side against the Palace lawyers. Right from the beginning Sarah never made any demands. She said, "I'll leave it up to you. You tell me how much I should have for the future of me and my children."'

But it was not as easy as that.

Prince Andrew's money worries, it seems, were not as unfounded as his friends thought. 'Unlike Charles, who has a vast fortune, we discovered that Andrew really did have nothing but his Royal Navy salary. No other income, no capital, no assets, nothing', said Bryan, overlooking the £250,000 from the Civil List. We were told that all he had was a life insurance policy worth around £600,000.'

More distressing to Sarah was the realization that even Sunninghill did not belong to them but was still owned by her canny mother-in-law. 'The Queen paid to have it built, she used her own architects, she made all the fundamental decisions. It was not a gift to Andrew and Sarah ... they were just allowed to live there,' said Bryan, the awe of one financial pro for another still in his voice a year later.

Sarah needed kindness at that moment and John Bryan was kind. 'I was sure he would take care of me,' she said. 'He had a brilliant mind and a kind heart. People like John are rare in the world.'

Even today Bryan is chary of putting a precise date to when he added lover to his duties as financial adviser and honest broker to the Duchess. But it clearly suits his book to place it well after the official announcement of the Yorks' separation on 19 March 1992. But there was at least one significant sighting earlier that month when they were seen lunching together at L'Incontro, an expensive Italian restaurant in Belgravia. 'They were playing footsie-footsie under the table, rubbing their legs up against each other and looked very intimate,' recalls Andrew Langton, a leading London property dealer who was at a nearby table. 'If I had not known who they were, I'd have sworn they were having an affair.'

Still John Bryan's identity and his important role in the Duchess's life remained unknown to the press. Yet the previous December they had been seen dancing together at Annabel's when Taki Theodoracopulos, the millionaire who writes a society column for the *New York Observer* and the *Spectator* magazine in London, bumped into them. 'I knew Bryan from New York,' recalls Theodoracopulos.

'I originally met him in Xenon with Fred Hughes, who was Andy Warhol's best friend and executor, and Bryan got me to invest $50,000 in a business deal, something to do with satellites. I never saw a cent again.'

Nevertheless, Bryan was sufficiently unabashed about the satellite deal to greet the Greek millionaire when they met at Annabel's. 'He punched my arm and said, "Hey, Taki! Come and say hello to the Duchess." I believe he was her man from around that time – three, four months before the official separation,' said Taki, whose instinct in these matters is very fine indeed.

A few weeks after the Sunninghill summit Sarah, her children, a nanny, two Scotland Yard bodyguards, and John Bryan flew to the island of Phuket in Thailand for a holiday. Nevertheless, Bryan continued to insist that he was 'an honest broker' within the divided House of York, and sought only to bring the unhappy couple together again. Andrew believed him, appeared even to trust him, and the two men spent a Sunday together at Sunninghill trying to work things out when Bryan hurried back from Thailand after pictures of him carrying Princess Eugenie on his shoulders had appeared in the London papers.

As if having the sins of the father visited upon her were not enough, the Duchess of York was now being blamed for the problems of the sister-in-law. Princess Anne, who had been waiting for some time for her own divorce from Captain Mark Phillips, sent Sarah a stinging letter claiming that the Yorks' announcement – and Sarah's unseemly behaviour – had set back her own proceedings by several months.

'Her tone', said a person close to the Duchess, and who had read the letter, 'was that of a peevish airline pilot who is stacked up over a busy airport and has been told that somebody else has moved ahead of him in the queue.'

'It was a horrible letter,' says Bryan, astonished by the vehemence of its unsisterly and unroyal tone, which added new pain to the anger Sarah felt about the Queen's claim on Sunninghill, the wedding gift and family home Sarah was now being asked to surrender.

Anne's fears, however, turned out to be greatly exaggerated. One month after writing the letter she was granted an uncontested 'quickie' divorce on the ground that she and Captain Phillips had been legally separated for more than two years. The decree, which took less than four minutes to hear, was made absolute in six weeks. Neither party was in court. Shortly before Christmas that year, Anne married Commander Tim Laurence in a low-key family ceremony at the remote Crathie Parish Church, near Balmoral.*

In May the Duchess of York moved out of Sunninghill, taking the little princesses and their nanny to live in Rowenda Lodge, a six-bedroomed mock-Tudor house (with pool, sauna, tennis courts and a staff annex) on the Wentworth golf club estate. She had clearly lost the first face-off with the family. Nevertheless, she continued to call Andrew her 'best friend', and appeared to be keeping her options open. She was photographed in her new home before a desk filled with framed pictures of Andrew and the children. It was hard not to notice the legend embroidered on the cushion beside her: 'Anyone can be a mother, it takes someone special to be a mummy'.

The signs of Sarah's fall from grace, small at first, quickly gathered pace. When she returned from a visit to her mother in Argentina in June (Bryan went along too) she learned that since she was no longer considered 'royal' she had lost her PPOs.† Nevertheless, the Texan minder continued to believe in her as she had been and refused to recognize what she had become. And what she had become in the eyes of the royal family was a non-person. On the opening day of Royal Ascot – exactly seven years after that fateful first lunch with Andrew at Windsor – she returned with Beatrice and Eugenie to picnic on the grass, then stand in the crowd to

*The Church of England, of which her mother is titular head, had held that she could not remarry in an Anglican church during the lifetime of her ex-husband.
† Scotland Yard Personal Protection Officers.

wave to the Queen as she passed in her coach on the royal procession to the racecourse. It was a cruel and poignant moment as the small girls rushed forward to wave to their grandmother. One can only imagine how hurt and excluded they must have felt. 'Can we come too?' Beatrice cried out.

The Queen waved. She waved to everybody.

In the following months, Sarah and her business adviser showed up in various places around the world: nightclubbing in Paris (where they were reported smooching on the dance floor to the old Chris de Burgh number 'Lady in Red', which had been her favourite song when Andrew was wooing her); VIPing it at EuroDisney ('Another freebie, Fergie?' taunted British tourists as, surrounded by a small army of Disney bodyguards and public relations people, she went to the front of the long lines for the main attractions). 'Freebie Fergie' quickly became a familiar cry in the British press. Riled and protective, Bryan says, 'Everything she does is paid for out of her own pocket. She even paid for half the decoration at Sunninghill, and that cost a packet. Unlike Andrew, she has no Civil List support. The only real income she has is from her books,* and from television. She does have a small stipend from the Queen, but that's entirely at the Queen's discretion.'

Meanwhile, encouraged by Andrew's apparent uninterest in their increasingly *outré* relationship, Bryan started to get careless. He organized a holiday in the South of France for what now appeared to be his adopted family. He rented Le Mas de Pignerol (House of the Little Pine), a secluded five-bedroomed villa with pool, situated in the middle of a forest just outside St Tropez. It cost £4,000 a week, but that's the price you must pay for privacy these days, he told Sarah.

Only it wasn't enough.

* A series of children's books featuring Budgie the Helicopter.

Not when you are going into the lion's den.

For this was the summer territory of Europe's most experienced, and probably most feared, paparazzo, Daniel Angeli.

On Sunday, 9 August, Fergie, her two daughters, their nanny, John Bryan and a bodyguard assigned to the two princesses put down in a chartered Kingair turbo-jet (£8,000 return) at the tiny airstrip of La Mole, a twenty-five minute drive west from St Tropez. They were met by two hired Mercedes and a second Scotland Yard man, who had travelled ahead. Warned that two paparazzi were waiting in a black truck, Fergie, wearing a blue jacket and floral shorts, slipped on a pair of dark glasses and tied a large floral scarf over her head. The photographers put on a show of taking their pictures as the party disembarked, but when the black truck made no attempt to follow them, Bryan and Fergie relaxed. Nobody noticed the motorbike which appeared some way behind them. When the Mercedes turned off the main road five miles later, the motorcyclist turned back and told Angeli the good news: there were only three villas off that track, and all of them were sitting ducks.

The following morning, 500 yards from the villa, in the trees, Daniel Angeli and his assistant were focusing their 1,200mm lenses on their quarry. The villa was set in the middle of a natural amphitheatre, screened on all sides by woods. 'The sun was on their faces. No way could they see me. It was like sitting in a stadium, the best seats, the best view,' Angeli would say later. For three days, starting at 10 a.m., they shot roll after roll of film, breaking for lunch only when Sarah and Bryan went inside for lunch, resuming again at 3.30 p.m., and continuing until dark.

At this stage, the paparazzi did not know the identity of the tall bald figure in the frame with the Duchess. But, whoever he was, Angeli knew that he was soon going to become very famous indeed.

A week later, the Duchess was back again at Balmoral and contemplating the thought that the invitation to the Queen's favourite summer retreat might be a step towards her own rehabilitation with the royal family. It was like old times: Charles and Diana were there with William and Harry; she and Andrew were together again, with their daughters.

'Holy shit!' Bryan said, when reporters showed him the first edition of the next morning's *Daily Mirror* at 11.15 on Wednesday evening, 19 August. The poolside pictures were splashed across the front page beneath the headline 'The pictures they didn't want you to see: FERGIE'S STOLEN KISSES: Truth about duchess and the Texan millionaire'. 'Oh God!' he said when he turned to the centre-spread and saw the pictures of him kissing the Duchess's toes. This time the headlines proclaimed, 'PHOTOS BRYAN COULDN'T STOP'.

The pictures could not have been more embarrassing, nor more incriminating. 'Poolside embrace: Arms entwined, Fergie and Bryan kiss and cuddle on a sun lounger at their holiday retreat', read the captions. 'Topless in Tropez: Fergie peels off for a session by the pool with her Texan pal', 'Loving Touch: Little Eugenie looks on as Bryan gives Fergie a kiss.' And, 'Tender touch: Bryan kisses Fergie as she dresses daughter Eugenie after a session in the pool. Princess Beatrice looks on'.

The most amazing royal pictures ever taken, the paper called them. And if they weren't that – since Fergie was no longer royal – they proved beyond all doubt that the Duchess of York and her financial adviser were much, much more than the just good friends that Bryan had always insisted they were.

Tipped off about the pictures, which had been sold to the *Mirror* for £60,000 twenty-four hours earlier, Bryan had tried to get a High Court injunction to prevent their publication (although he still did not know what the pictures actually showed). What they showed was far worse than anything he had imagined. He was absolutely appalled. Despite the lateness of the hour, unhappily, reluctantly, nervously he called Sarah at Balmoral.

'The pictures are appalling ... far worse than I thought possible,' he remembers blurting out. 'They show *everything*.'

'Oh shit,' Sarah said bleakly, as she felt herself slipping deeper and deeper into a nightmare world.

Later Bryan recalled, 'Actually, there were no recriminations at Balmoral at all. In fact, you could hear a sigh of relief from the others, the feeling of there but for the grace of God ... And Andrew was remarkable, he really showed his colours. He was just as supportive as could be. You must remember that what happened was between a woman who had separated from her husband and intended to divorce him. It was a totally different situation to those tapes between the Prince of Wales and Camilla Parker Bowles, and the Diana and James Gilbey tapes. Sarah was separated from her husband, she was already out of the royal family.... It was a whole different ballgame. Sarah and I were ... I don't want to use the words lovers, or falling in love, or any of that kind of stuff because it sounds so indiscreet and inappropriate. But we had become close, definitely by July. The photos are self-evident, but that still doesn't imply love.... We were just having a good time, just lying around....'

But that August the scandal and Sarah's ordeal looked as if it would run and run.

Then she had an amazing stroke of good luck.

On Monday, 24 August, just four days after the Fergie pictures broke in the *Mirror*, the story of the taped conversation between Diana and James Gilbey – 'Squidgygate' – broke in the *Sun*.

MY LIFE IS TORTURE: Dianagate tape of love call reveals marriage misery.

Chapter Twenty-three

James Gilbey said, 'And so darling, what other lows today?'
And The Princess of Wales said, 'I was very bad at lunch. And
I nearly started blubbing. I just felt really sad and empty, and
I thought: Bloody hell, after all I've done for this fucking
family.'

'Squidgygate was a catharsis, really,' Diana would tell a friend
after the tape of the twenty-three minute conversation,
recorded on New Year's Eve 1989, finally found its way into print
in August 1992. But it was a catharsis Charles did not welcome. He
was horrified that his wife's mildly dirty and rather banal phone
conversations with her old chum Gilbey should be splashed across
newspapers, making her look like an idiot and he, Charles, like a
total cuckold. 'His behaviour was a man in a state of shock,' said a
Palace aide, who had known the Prince for fifteen years and
understood his moods, and had never seen him so shaken by
anything. 'The Palace was in total disarray, of course. They realized
now that they had no control of events at all. Nobody seemed to
be in control. Charles was stunned. The idea that his wife might
have been doing with Gilbey what he had been doing with Mrs
Parker Bowles seemed to deeply offend him.'

Nevertheless, he seemed detached from the panic at the Palace.
A lot of time was spent in quiet visiting with old friends, not only
Mrs Parker Bowles, but men like Conservative MP Nicholas

Soames, his former equerry and childhood friend – people he could talk to and trust.

'In the past he would often arrange meetings at a moment's notice. He would never question whether the summons was inconvenient or stop to consider whether his friends had to break other engagements to see him. But now he would simply *show up*. Once he arrived on the doorstep in the middle of a dinner party,' a friend said, recalling his dazed behaviour in the weeks after the Squidgy tape was published. 'He was completely lost ... sort of bereft.'

But, if Charles showed clear signs of deep depression, Diana behaved as if the tape had broken a spell. All that year the rumours had been growing, the stories getting closer to the truth. Every day another bit of the jigsaw, another piece of the puzzle that was their marriage got printed in the papers. Sometimes Charles and Diana even leaked the stories themselves. They both knew it, they both used their friends to inform the press about those things which made them look good, or would put the other in a bad light. It was the game they played.

It was to her credit that she did not permit herself the gaucherie of denial, but how far had she permitted herself to go with Gilbey? He was a man she trusted utterly. He was, after all, the man she had used to spill so much of the riveting detail about her private life to author Andrew Morton. He clearly knew her well, but did he know her intimately? ('He may know her intimately, but he does not know her well,' sniped one of Charles's friends, when he heard that Gilbey had been a major source of so many of the frankly prejudiced stories in Morton's book.)

Even their closest friends wrangled interminably about whether Diana and Gilbey had been intimate and, if they had, had they gone all the way? 'I don't want to get pregnant,' she tells him on the tape. 'Darling, it's not going to happen. Don't look at it like that. It's not going to happen. You won't get pregnant,' he assures her.

It is a puzzling conversation if they are not lovers, or contemplating becoming so.

An old woman friend of Gilbey's, convinced that they were lovers, claims that they often met at High House, a hundred-year-old redbrick Norfolk farmhouse in a small village called Bradenham, halfway between Sandringham and the Lotus car HQ at Ketteringham where Gilbey now worked. Some insisted that the couple made love only in Diana's 500 Mercedes SL – and that it never progressed beyond heavy petting. (A part of the tape suppressed when it was first published contains this revealing exchange: 'It's just like sort of – ' Gilbey says. 'Playing with yourself?' Diana suggests. 'What?' says Gilbey. 'I said it's just like – ' Diana says. 'Playing with yourself,' Gilbey finishes the sentence. 'Yes,' she says. 'Not quite as nice. Not quite as nice,' he says. 'I haven't played with myself actually, not for forty-eight hours. Not for a full forty-eight hours.') Another rendezvous was thought to be an apartment owned by Mara Berni, whose San Lorenzo around the corner in Beauchamp Place, Knightsbridge is one of Diana's favourite restaurants in London, and where it was reported she had arranged to receive private mail.

'My daughter Diana has only ever slept with one man, and that is her husband,' her father had once confidently told an old friend one evening when the two men were discussing the morals of the young, before the Squidgy tape became an issue. 'In any case,' the old Earl added sadly, 'the trouble with her is she tells me she doesn't like sex.' Spencer men, it must be said, have either an unusually intimate knowledge of Spencer women, or a poignant trust in their absolute fidelity. For shortly after the scandal of the Squidgy tape divided their friends – did they or didn't they? – Charles Spencer stoutly defended his sister's honour: 'Hand on heart,' he said, 'I can tell you that Diana has only slept with one man in twelve years, has only slept, in fact, with one man in her life. She's not interested in that at all. I know that Prince Charles is the only man she has ever slept with. James Gilbey would have loved to have slept with her, but I can assure you he has not.'

In June the publication of the Andrew Morton book had elicited sympathy throughout the land for Diana, but she knew that even that was not the whole truth, although it was largely her truth, and a fairly good shot across the bows of Charles and the monarchy itself.

'I wish they would write one big story that said it all,' she had told a friend a year before, when almost every day a new story would appear in the press reflecting the state of her marriage. If Squidgygate did not say it all, it said enough for the world to realize that the end of the marriage was now a matter of time. And after the Morton book the Palace was readier for the final split than it had been one year earlier when it was still insisting that there was nothing wrong with the marriage at all.

Diana was on a skiing holiday in Lech, Austria, when she heard of her father's death at the end of March. It was one of the rare moments when her intuition let her down. Although he had been unwell, she left England convinced that he was in no immediate danger. She had wanted to fly back to England alone, leaving Charles to stay with the children. Aware of how bad this would make him look in the press, he insisted on accompanying her. She reacted as often only the grieving can react, with extreme anger. It was, she screamed, too late in the day for him to start behaving like a loving husband. The stand-off lasted several hours before his private secretary called the Queen at Windsor, explained the situation, and requested her to intercede. Only then did Diana agree to travel home with her husband. Met by the gathered media at London Airport, Charles's close attention to his grieving wife was duly reported. Shortly after the couple arrived at Kensington Palace, Charles left for Highgrove, leaving Diana to mourn alone.

Earl Spencer's funeral took place on 1 April at the thirteenth-century church of St Mary the Virgin at Great Brington, where the vaults held nineteen generations of Spencers. Diana arrived alone;

Charles flew in a few minutes before the service began in a red Wessex helicopter of the Queen's Flight. It was a bleak melancholy day, but it was a Spencer tradition to entertain the mourners to a champagne buffet at Althorp after the burial. Although Charles was clearly anxious to get back to London, he agreed to return to the house to drink the final toast to the departed Earl. But at the house his mood seemed to change again. He said he wanted to talk privately to his brother-in-law, the new Earl Spencer.

Charles Spencer, aware of the crisis in his sister's marriage and suspecting that the Prince wanted to discuss some delicate family business, invited him into the library where half a century before the fastidious seventh Earl had ripped a cigar out of the mouth of Winston Churchill. But the Prince did not want to talk about Diana, or their deeply troubled marriage, but about himself. It was a poignant conversation, and one that clearly revealed the disturbed state of the Prince of Wales's mind.

'He did not seem to appreciate how I felt at my loss,' the new young Earl would later tell his family. 'We had just buried my father and he kept telling me *how lucky I was to have inherited so young!*'

'I wish I had inherited when I was young,' Prince Charles told him, exposing the grievances and emotional conflicts in him that made his life so difficult and almost unbearably painful at times. 'My parents don't trust me with anything.'

The Queen's extraordinary tolerance of Charles's private life, and her continued determination to gloss over his blatant affair with Mrs Parker Bowles, continued to astonish many courtiers, who saw this as being at the very heart of all their problems. 'It was more than idle tolerance,' said one aide, who had watched the affair growing more dangerous every year. 'The Queen actually seemed to go out of her way to show her approval of the whole Parker Bowles set-up.'

And it was not only the Queen, but the influential Queen Mother herself who 'let it be known' that the Parker Bowleses had her full approval. Every autumn the couple continued to be invited to Scotland to spend a weekend as her personal guests. 'What do they *talk about?*' asked one Palace aide, at a loss to explain the fascination the Queen Mother had for the adulterous pair, who more and more were threatening the stability of her beloved grandson's marriage. 'It isn't surprising that Diana is so bloody paranoid about the Queen Mother on that tape.'

On the tape Diana tells James Gilbey:

'His grandmother is always looking at me with a strange look in her eyes. It's not hatred. It's sort of interest and pity mixed in one. I am not quite sure. I don't understand it. Every time I look up, she's looking at me, and then looks away, and smiles. I don't know what's going on.'

And so nobody was surprised when Andrew Parker Bowles was chosen personally by the Queen to escort Princess Anne to Royal Ascot that June. Some people at the Palace, still struggling to keep the lid on the scandal of the Prince and Mrs Parker Bowles, nonetheless found irony in the explanation that Andrew Parker Bowles would be a more discreet escort for the newly divorced Princess Royal than her real lover, Commander Tim Laurence.

But at Ascot the Palace would pay a small but embarrassing price for the arrogance of its thinking.

Accompanying Princess Anne from the Royal Enclosure to the Paddock to inspect the horses, Brigadier Parker Bowles (now in charge of the army's Veterinary and Remount Services) encountered Lord Charles Spencer-Churchill, younger brother of the Duke of Marlborough, who was partaking of a glass of champagne or two with a group of friends. Living up to his reputation as a ready wit, but rather more to his nickname 'Nutty', Churchill called out to his friend, 'Ernest Simpson. Ernest Simpson. Why don't you join us over here, Ernest?' A reference to the hapless husband of Wallis

Simpson, before she became the Duchess of Windsor, it was a cruel, unfunny but rather too accurate jibe which Parker Bowles sensibly refused to hear.

But when, on his return from the Paddock, Parker Bowles was subjected to a similar harangue from an even more exuberant Nutty, he excused himself from the Princess Royal and had a conversation with Spencer-Churchill, the severity of which varies in the telling.

But, according to Spencer-Churchill himself, Parker Bowles 'was very angry indeed. He pummelled my right arm and my shoulder *extremely* hard. The next day I was black and blue with bruises. I thought it was a good tease, but obviously Andrew was not very amused.'

But after the Morton book – even after the Squidgy tape, which embarrassed her deeply, and might have done her great harm, but merely enhanced her reputation as a megastar – Diana was on top again. 'Nobody realized just how tough she was, or what a highly defined sense of survival she had,' admitted one of Charles's very closest people, with grudging respect. And if, as many of their friends now think, it was Mrs Parker Bowles who first started Diana on the way to being her own woman, Charles could only blame his mistress for the fact that Diana was now clearly running her own show.

And all the Palace could do now was to wait for Diana's next move.

Because she was on top did not mean that she intended to relax. As she became stronger and more secure, she also became tougher and more sure of what she wanted. The publication of the Squidgy tape had changed her image in a subtle way. She knew that men reacted to her in a different fashion. It had not changed the way she felt about sex. Sex was still something she could take or leave. But she enjoyed the new interest men showed in her as a woman. 'I suppose most men dream of bonking a princess,' she told a girlfriend after Squidgygate.

But she was still convinced that the royal family was determined to destroy her. 'Who released that tape?' she would ask friends over and over again. 'Ask yourself: who stood to gain most from doing that?'

'The last period they were together, leading up to the trip to South Korea the Queen so ill-advisedly sent them on in November, was the worst time of all. Diana proved that she was still a Spencer. She could still be utterly hysterical when thwarted,' admits one of the few admirers she had kept at the Palace. ('Courtiers are just like anyone else,' admitted one aide ruefully. 'When the chips are down, you go with the money.')

But Charles sometimes saw the funny side of the extreme touchiness that had come between them, and would later embroider an incident into an anecdote for an old friend. 'Diana asked him – or rather ordered him – to pour her a cup of tea,' says Diana's step-grandmother, an old friend of the Prince, Dame Barbara Cartland, remembers one of his self-deprecating stories. 'Charles replied something about – "We have someone to do that for you, if you care to ring" – at which, my dear, she simply *hurled* the teapot straight at him. Imagine that!'

Diana was in Paris, and Charles was all alone at Highgrove when Mrs Parker Bowles telephoned him on 15 November 1992 – his forty-fourth birthday – to wish him many happy returns. Twenty-four days later, on 9 December, the Palace issued a short statement:

It is announced from Buckingham Palace that, with regret, The Prince and Princess of Wales have decided to separate. Their Royal Highnesses have no plans to divorce and their constitutional positions are unaffected. This decision has been reached amicably, and they will both continue to participate fully in the upbringing of their children.

Their Royal Highnesses will continue to carry out full and separate programmes of public engagements and will, from time to time, attend family occasions and national events together.

The Queen and the Duke of Edinburgh, though saddened, understand and sympathize with the difficulties that have led to this decision. Her Majesty and His Royal Highness particularly hope that the intrusions into the privacy of The Prince and Princess may now cease. They believe that a degree of privacy and understanding is essential if Their Royal Highnesses are to provide a happy and secure upbringing for their children, while continuing to give a wholehearted commitment to their public duties.

Thirty-six days later Camillagate broke.

Chapter Twenty-four

The publication of Charles's private conversation with Camilla, the anguished meeting at Sandringham and the onslaught from the press, the people – the whole world – had almost become a familiar ache. Then at the beginning of April 1993, Prince Charles faced a new, painful encounter. Two days earlier the IRA had placed bombs in litter-bins in a crowded shopping mall in a small town called Warrington, killing two small boys and wounding dozens of shoppers. It had been another bleak reminder of the misery caused by the same senseless terrorism which had robbed him of his beloved Uncle Dickie a dozen years before.

'Christ, will this bloody war never end?' he had asked a friend the night before he went to Warrington.

'But what war?' his friend would ask later. 'The war that killed his uncle? The war with his father? The war within himself? The never-ending war with Diana? It was all very well for his mother to describe the previous year as her *annus horribilis*. For Charles it was a time of total nightmare.'

Charles's marital skirmishes with Diana in the 1980s had become in the 1990s nothing less than a battle for the hearts and minds of the British people. And so far his estranged wife had won every round. Her timing, her visibility and sense of energy, her instinct for a headline, were infallible. When Charles was skiing in Switzerland, Diana was talking to lepers in Nepal. 'Where is everyone?' he asked, surprised to be greeted by only two photographers when he strolled out on to the slopes. 'With your wife in Nepal,' he was told. Diana could reach the hearts of the people as Charles never could and, despite all the Palace machine's attempts to repackage him, probably never would.

Studying the tapes of his Warrington visit with his public relations people a few days later he was all too well aware of how inadequate and strangely awkward his own words of sympathy had sounded. 'Your courage has made my day,' he said to a young mother who had lost a leg in the explosion. There was gloom in the Palace screening room when the tapes from the BBC, ITN and CNN came to an end. With his winter-holiday tan (February, polo in Mexico; March, skiing at Klosters), and smiling throughout the visit 'as if he were opening the Chelsea Flower Show', his attempt in that bereaved northern town to come across as a concerned, reassuring presence totally misfired.

'He was bitterly disappointed by his performance,' admitted one of his own Palace aides after the screening. 'He accepts that he doesn't have Diana's sure touch in those situations. He just about got by in Bosnia [where he visited British troops engaged in the United Nations operation]. But his touch in Warrington was totally wrong. Although the similarity in ages of the two murdered boys to his own sons upset him deeply, he just could not express his feelings. He is embarrassed and tongue-tied in the face of people's suffering. Diana will spontaneously comfort a dying old woman, she can instinctively hug a young man with AIDS. Charles can't do that. He is not a tactile person. He can never show his true feelings in public.'

But he has changed, and is changing, according to a woman who has known him since his days at Cambridge, and was his lover one summer in the 1970s. 'Whether he can admit it even to himself, Diana has had an enormous influence on the way he now thinks and feels about things,' she says. 'The Palace is doing the repackaging job it has to do if he is to be king, but he is making changes in his life, too. He has ended his association with the embarrassing Ronald

Ferguson. He has finally given up high goal polo. He is subtly, quite slowly, changing his own image as a man.'

Once he rarely discussed his problems with even his closest friends. 'But since Diana left him – and Diana left him, make no mistake about that – he has talked about himself with halting but extraordinary frankness to three people I know. The point he has made to each of them ... *he never intended any of it to happen.*'

Right up until the final communiqué from the Palace announcing the separation he had hoped that cooler heads would prevail. 'Having suffered in his own childhood, the last thing he wanted was to inflict unhappiness upon his own children,' his former love said.

Years before, Aunt Margaret had told him not to read the newspapers when he knew they were attacking him or being nasty, but during those last months he had found it impossible not to. They had been hard to take. He tried to take his mind off his worries with a series of private dinner parties with some of his favourite people. 'They were mostly the people Diana could not get along with, and who his father dismissed as eggheads,' says a friend. 'They discussed the problems of the world, as they always did, but Charles's heart wasn't in it any more.'

Royalty can live with all the scandal in the world, said one of the younger Palace aides, but the mockery that followed the publication of the Camillagate tape was insufferable. Prince *Tampacchino* they now called him in Italy – Little Prince Tampax – and in America girls were reported to be asking for 'Charlies' when buying tampons. 'He has, I promise you, heard all the stories. What is harder to take is people's pity,' the aide said. 'He has had truly thousands of letters of sympathy. But the thought of all those loyal, kind people he feels he has let down is far worse for him than the humiliation of it.'

A sense of shame tormented him for months. He seemed staggered, complained that he slept little and was obviously using every ounce of his will-power to carry on. In the office, his aides complained that they had an increasingly difficult time getting him to make decisions. He had always called his friends at odd hours, but the late-night calls became more common, and some worried about his state of mind. At a dinner party in London in April, four months after the Camillagate tape was first published, he unnerved friends by talking about Mayerling. Mayerling was the shooting lodge in the woods outside Vienna where Crown Prince Rudolf, heir to the throne of Austria, shot himself and his mistress, at the end of an unhappy love affair, a hundred years ago. 'Wouldn't the media have a field day if I took the same way out?'

'I don't think he was serious. But who could tell?' said one of the guests that evening. 'He laughed and said that he was no Rudolf – and, of course, one could not get much further from Rudolf's neurotic mistress than down-to-earth Camilla. Fortunately, he still has Camilla. And Camilla is one of life's survivors. If she has anything to do with it, and nobody imagines that she is going to go away, Charles will rise like a phoenix from the ashes.... Anyway, that's the theory!'

Diana had moved all her personal possessions from Highgrove to Kensington Palace. And, although Charles knew that he could never completely expunge the memory of her from his life, he set about removing all traces of her from their Gloucestershire home. Her first-floor study, known as the Princess's sitting room, was totally gutted. At the suggestion of Mrs Parker Bowles, he hired a decorator to give the entire house a 'more masculine' atmosphere.

But there were also times in the difficult months after the Camillagate tapes were published when he had seriously contemplated leaving England. 'He was emotionally exhausted. He did feel he had been treated dreadfully unjustly by the press. There was a moment when he seriously wanted out,' says one of his friends.

Tuscany beckoned. He talked wistfully about buying a house in the beautiful countryside where he had gone to paint with his portly equerry, Nicholas Soames puffing up the hills beside him, far from Diana and Camilla and the press and all the worries of the world.

'A very strong rumour went round the Palace in the spring that he was about to buy a house near Florence,' says an aide. 'It made people very nervous. What do they call Florence – the paradise of *exiles?*'

The Queen Mother became upset and anxious when she heard the story. The idea of the Prince of Wales seeking refuge far from Britain came too close for comfort to memories of Great-Uncle David and the Abdication.

According to a reliable Clarence House source, she invited Charles to lunch. During the lunch at the beginning of April, she did not mention Tuscany or Florence at all. She never let on that she had heard the rumours about his desire to buy a house abroad. She never pressed him on his intentions. Instead, she asked him to tell her about the occasion he visited the ex-King in his mansion off the Bois de Boulogne. It was a strange request. She had never visited the famous Paris home; she could barely bring herself to speak the Windsors' name. But she spent almost the whole lunch quizzing Charles about his meeting with the Duke, completely ignoring his obvious discomfort with the conversation and her line of questioning. He left the lunch, according to a footman, 'looking far less happy than when he arrived'.

'She is such a wily old bird. She knew that his meeting with the Duke had depressed Charles enormously. She wanted to remind him of the sense of waste and desolation in that empty life – a life utterly tormented by regret,' says one of the Queen Mother's friends, to whom she had cheerfully confessed her ploy.

It was a remarkable meeting, and in a way rather sad. 'At ninety-two, it was a touching expression of her love and concern for Charles, but she must have also recognized that it was possibly the last time that she would play a role in the affairs of the Crown,' said a friend.

There has been no more talk of Tuscany.

Great-Uncle David and the Abdication had always been held up to Charles as the dread example of how easily the monarchy could be damaged by one individual's selfishness and irresponsibility. He, personally, had done his best to avoid his great-uncle's failings. Yet he is privately convinced that future historians will almost certainly pick on him, rather than the Duke of Windsor, as the real disaster that befell the monarchy in the twentieth century. How had it happened? 'One only did what everybody wanted by marrying Diana,' he has said to friends, not with any sense of self-pity, but with genuine puzzlement and concern.

Chapter Twenty-five

August at Balmoral had always been a special time for the Queen. However scattered and fallen out the family may have been for the rest of the year, August at Balmoral was the time they came together: Margaret returned from Turkey and Corfu, Princess Anne arrived with her family from Gatcombe Park; although they had been separated, in 1992 Andrew brought Sarah to be with their daughters there; and Charles and Diana put on a show of togetherness for the Queen. Even Philip knew that it was a family date he dare not miss. From the Queen Mother to the youngest Windsor infant, August at Balmoral had always been something special.

But in 1993, for the first time in all her forty years on the throne, the Queen did not look forward to that summer gathering of the House of Windsor. It would, she knew, be a sad affair, reminding her how many of her children's homes were broken, how many faces were missing. Balmoral would depress her, she knew that; no Princess of Wales, no Duchess of York, not even Princess Anne's friendly old Fog. The Queen was not a sentimental woman, far from it, but how could she not be reminded at Balmoral that August how empty their ranks had grown and how loosened the ties that bound them were?

Balmoral had always been the time to gossip about their private lives, to become nostalgic, recalling incidents from the Windsors' more happy days, and to discuss and plan the year to come: from family weddings and births, to royal tours and state occasions. 'That is going to be hard for all of them this year,' admits an aide. 'Nobody will want to dwell on the events of the past year, none of them will want to be reminded of the fact that both Charles and Andrew are heading like their sister before them to certain divorce. Balmoral this year will be a sad and bleak place.'

But there was at least one small ironic glimmer of relief for the Queen in the affairs of Edward. The Prince, who had once found it necessary publicly to protest that he was not gay, was finally, at the age of twenty-nine, taking a noticeable interest in beautiful women. And when his mother read the Sunday tabloid memoirs of a young model named Romy Adlington, who claimed that she had lost her virginity to Edward at Buckingham Palace, while the Queen slept next door, it is easy to imagine that a feeling of relief transcended Her Majesty's displeasure at yet another royal scandal.

In April, Andrew finalized his settlement with Sarah. She would collect a lump sum of £600,000, half of which would be in trust and be handed back in the event of her remarriage. A further £1.4 million would be put in trust for Beatrice and Eugenie, with £650,000 of this sum allowed towards the purchase of a house, which would be in the children's names. The balance of the trust would be invested but, at best, could be expected to yield no more than £25,000 a year. Given the original numbers bandied about in the media at the time of the separation – ranging from £4 million to £10 million – the settlement could not be construed as generous. But, as John Bryan had warned Sarah, Andrew had little money of his own, and at all times she was in the hands of the Queen – whose own income was about to be taxed for the first time.

Signing the agreement was effectively the end of the marriage, although Sarah would not be free to petition for a divorce until January 1994.

'For the fairy tale to end this way is very sad,' says John Bryan. 'But now they are no longer living together their bond seems almost stronger. They behave impeccably towards each other, and there are no recriminations. It could have been a great love story, but the royal family just got in the way.'

Sarah's relationship with Bryan remains one of the great enigmas of the whole story. Sarah tells friends that she is not in love with him, and that the friendship is fading. But, shortly after the settlement with Andrew was announced, one of her oldest friends, Lulu Blacker, had tea with her at Romenda Lodge. Did she see Bryan very often these days? Lulu asked. Hardly at all, said Sarah. Driving back to London, Lulu's small daughter, Iona, discovered that she had left her teddy bear behind and began to cry. Lulu returned to the house and slipped into the drawing room to retrieve it without bothering Sarah – only to find the two lovers locked in a friendly embrace, just like old times.

Just like old times, too, Prince Andrew was back on the town with a beautiful blonde beside him: Caroline Neville, known to her friends as Cazzy, the twenty-nine-year-old daughter of Lord Braybrooke. 'It's not a hot and heavy romance,' Cazzy told friends cautiously at the end of April, as the Prince returned to sea to take up his first command on the minesweeper HMS *Cottesmore*.

And the Princess of Wales?

In the most explicit statement she has made about her future to date she says, 'I will continue to do my public duties, and when two years are up, I will simply stop and get a divorce. As for a financial settlement … I am not a greedy person.'

Earl Spencer, speaking on his sister's behalf, explained the present situation and the Princess's future intentions in the clearest detail since the announcement of the separation in December 1992: 'As for the royal family, it's all over as far as Diana is concerned. Completely. There is no vengeance, remarkably, possibly because our own parents went through a particularly unpleasant divorce and subsequent unhappy life. Charles has been amazed at the lack of vengeance.

'Diana is reorganizing her life, but at the moment she is not a hundred per cent there. As I see it, and I'm a big fan of hers, she's not half as manipulative as she is painted. If Ken Wharfe, her detective, tells her the photographers want a particular angle, she does it. She is perfectly straightforward.

'As for the marriage, she feels she did her best.'

One of her very closest friends says, 'She's got it all worked out. She'll lead a classic Sloaney [Sloane Ranger] life. She's looking for someone to love her, she wants to have more children. A title or someone famous is not necessary.

'Right now, she feels uncertain about the future of the monarchy. She wants William to be king, but Charles is not certain that he wants to be king. Diana offered to step down when they separated, but the Queen was desperate for her to stay. She's determined not to let people down. The Queen and Prince Philip have been very supportive.'

Despite such contentions, there are those who feel Charles indeed sees himself as a strong and determined future monarch. 'She must know I have no intention of ever, ever giving up my role as heir to the throne,' he recently told a friend, when he seemed stronger and less daunted by past humiliations. 'He said that he had learned much about Diana that he never knew before – and the more he learned, the stronger was his resolution.'

But if he has learned new things about Diana, he has also discovered much about himself and the institution of which he is a part. According to those who know him well, he is determined not to let those lessons go to waste. 'He has finally faced up to the degree to which his own conduct and behaviour destroyed not only his marriage but undermined the monarchy itself,' insists a friend, who helped him through the traumatic months after Camillagate.

'Charles now admits that Diana was justified in objecting to Mrs Parker Bowles, and claims that he had always respected the way she protected her position. What he still cannot forgive is the way she sought revenge on him at the cost of the monarchy,' says a friend.

But his melancholy side and his mood swings continue to confuse those close to him. 'His optimism in the morning can turn to deep gloom by the evening,' says one friend after spending a weekend with him at Highgrove. 'On Sunday about twenty people came to lunch. Mostly his hunting friends, and a couple of polo people were there. But no Camilla. He was relaxed, and extremely funny about Diana's possible settlement demands. 'Will she want Sandringham, do you think?' he said. Somebody suggested she could ask for Buckingham Palace. He said, 'Oh, she's welcome to that.' He was in wonderful spirits. But after everybody had gone, he was in another mood entirely. Of course, he is aware that this will be no ordinary divorce. Whatever happens it will not mark the end of Diana's influence upon the monarchy, or on his family. He knows that.'

'Since the split in December,' says one of his most trusted friends, 'it has been one long post-mortem. He accepts that Diana will marry again. That doesn't bother him. As for Mrs Parker Bowles, the fact that they are still so close after so much scandal and so many humiliating blows, it's obviously a relationship of extra-ordinary depth.'

Camilla's sister, Annabel Elliot, says it more clearly: 'Charles cannot live without her.'

Privately, it is understood by their friends that Camilla and Andrew will eventually separate. 'Camilla has money of her own, but Charles will want to help her buy a house not too far from Highgrove,' says one of their closest friends. 'They will never marry, of course ... but they will never be apart.'

APPENDIX

The 'Camillagate' Tape

The following is a transcript of a telephone conversation between the Prince of Wales and Camilla Parker Bowles, recorded during the night of 17 December, 1989.

Charles: ... he thought he might have gone a bit far.

Camilla: Ah well.

Charles: Anyway you know, that's the sort of thing one has to beware of. And sort of feel one's way along with, if you know what I mean.

Camilla: Mmm. You're awfully good at feeling your way along.

Charles: Oh stop! I want to feel my way along you, all over you and up and down you and in and out.

Camilla: Oh.

Charles: ... particularly in and out.

Camilla: Oh, that's just what I need at the moment.

[Man who recorded conversation speaks over couple to record date].

Camilla: I know it would revive me. I can't bear a Sunday night without you.

Charles: Oh God.

Camilla: It's like that programme, *Start the Week*. I can't start the week without you.

Charles: I fill up your tank!

Camilla: Yes you do!

Charles: Then you can cope.

Camilla: Then I'm all right.

Charles: What about me? The trouble is, I need you several times a week.

Camilla: Mmm. So do I. I need you all the week. All the time.

Charles: Oh, God. I'll just live inside your trousers or something. It would be much easier!

Camilla: What are you going to turn into, a pair of knickers? [both laugh] Oh, you're going to come back as a pair of knickers.

Charles: Or, God forbid, a Tampax. Just my luck! [laughs]

Camilla: You are a complete idiot! [laughs] Oh, what a wonderful idea.

Charles: My luck to be chucked down a lavatory and go on forever swirling around the top, never going down!

Camilla: [laughing] Oh, darling!

Charles: Until the next one comes through.

Camilla: Oh, perhaps you could just come back as a box.

Charles: What sort of box?

Camilla: A box of Tampax so you could just keep going.

Charles: That's true.

Camilla: Repeating yourself. [laughing] Oh, darling, Oh I just want you now.

Charles: Do you?

Camilla: Mmm.

Charles: So do I.

Camilla: Desperately, desperately, desperately. Oh, I thought of you so much at Garrowby.

Charles: Did you?

Camilla: Simply mean we couldn't be there together.

Charles: Desperate. If you could be here – I long to ask Nancy sometimes.

Camilla: Why don't you?

Charles: I daren't.

Camilla: Because I think she's in love with you.

−232−

Charles: Mmm.

Camilla: She'd do anything you asked.

Charles: She'd tell all sorts of people.

Camilla: No she wouldn't because she'd be much too frightened of what you might say to her. I think you've got ... I'm afraid it's a terrible thing to say, but I think, you know, those sort of people feel very strongly about you. You've got such a great hold over her.

Charles: Really?

Camilla: And you're ... I think as usual, you're underestimating yourself.

Charles: But she might be terribly jealous or something.

Camilla: Oh! [laughs] Now that is a point! I wonder, she might be, I suppose.

Charles: You never know, do you.

Camilla: No. The little green-eyed monster might be lurking inside her. No, but I mean, the thing is you're so good when people are so flattered to be taken into your confidence, but I don't know why they'd betray you. You know, real friends.

Charles: Really?

Camilla: I don't. [pause] Gone to sleep?

Charles: No, I'm here.

Camilla: Darling, listen, I talked to David tonight again. It might not be any good.

Charles: Oh no!

Camilla: I'll tell you why. He's got three children of one of those Crawley girls and their nanny staying. He's going, I'm going to ring him again tomorrow. He's going to try and put them off till Friday. But I thought as an alternative, perhaps I might ring up Charlie.

Charles: Yes.

Camilla: And see if we could do it there. I know he's back on Thursday.

Charles: It's quite a lot further away.

Camilla: Oh is it?

Charles: Well, I'm just trying to think. I'm coming from New-market.

Camilla: Coming from Newmarket to me at that time of night, you could probably do it in two and three quarters. It takes me three.

Charles: What to go to um, Bowood?

Camilla: Northmore.

Charles: To go to Bowood?

Camilla: To go to Bowood would be the same as me really.

Charles: I mean to say, you would suggest going to Bowood, uh?

Camilla: No, not at all.

Charles: Which Charlie then?

Camilla: What Charlie do you think I was talking about?

Charles: I didn't know, because I thought you meant ...

Camilla: I've got lost ...

Charles: Somebody else.

Camilla: I've got lots of friends called Charlie.

Charles: The other one. Patti's.

Camilla: Oh! Oh, there. Oh that is further away. They're not ...

Charles: They've gone ...

Camilla: I don't know, it's just, you know, just a thought I had, if it fell through, the other place.

Charles: Oh right. What do you do, go on the M25 then down the M4 is it?

Camilla: Yes, you go, um, and sort of Royston, or M11, at that time of night.

Charles: Yes. Well, that'll be just after it will be after shooting anyway.

Camilla: So it would be, um, you'd miss the worst of the traffic. Because I'll, we, you see the problem is I've got to be in London tomorrow night.

Charles: Yes.

Camilla: And Tuesday night A's coming home.

Charles: No ...

Camilla: Would you believe? Because, I don't know what he is doing, he's shooting down here or something. But darling, you wouldn't be able to ring me anyway, would you?

Charles: I might just. I mean, tomorrow night I could have done.

Camilla: Oh darling, I can't bear it. How could you have done tomorrow night?

Charles: Because I'll be [yawns] working on the next speech.

Camilla: Oh no, what's the next one?

Charles: A Business in the Community one, rebuilding communities.

Camilla: Oh no, when's that for?

Charles: A rather important one for Wednesday.

Camilla: Well at least I'll be behind you.

Charles: I know.

Camilla: Can I have a copy of the one you've just done?

Charles: Yes.

Camilla: Can I? Um, I would like it?

Charles: O.K., I'll try and organize it ...

Camilla: Darling ...

Charles: But, I, oh God, when am I going to speak to you?

Camilla: I can't bear it. Um ...

Charles: Wednesday night?

Camilla: Oh, certainly. Wednesday night I'll be alone, um, Wednesday, you know, the evening. Or Tuesday. While you're rushing around doing things, I'll be, you know, alone until it reappears. And early Wednesday morning. I'm mean, he'll be leaving at half past eight, quarter past eight. He won't be here Thursday, pray God. Um, that ambulance strike, it's a terrible thing to say this. I suppose it won't have come to an end by Thursday.

Charles: It will have done?

Camilla: Well, I mean, I hope for everybody's sake, it will have done, but I hope for our sakes it's still going on.

Charles: Why?

Camilla: Well, because if it stops he'll come down here on Thursday night.

Charles: Oh no.

Camilla: Yes, but I don't think it will stop, do you?

Charles: No, neither do I. Just our luck.

Camilla: It just would be our luck. I know.

Charles: Then it's bound to.

Camilla: No it won't. You mustn't think like that. You must think positive.

Charles: I'm not very good at that.

Camilla: Well, I am going to. Because if I don't, I'd despair. [pause] Hm – gone to sleep?

Charles: No, how maddening.

Camilla: I know. Anyway, I mean, he's doing his best to change it, David, but I just though, you know, I might ask Charlie.

Charles: Did he say anything?

Camilla: No, I haven't talked to him.

Charles: You haven't?

Camilla: Well, I talked to him briefly, but you know, I just thought – I just don't know whether he's got any children at home, that's the worry.

Charles: Right.

Camilla: Oh … darling, I think I'll …

Charles: Pray, just pray.

Camilla: It would be so wonderful to have just one night to set us on our way, wouldn't it?

Charles: Wouldn't it? To wish you a happy Christmas.

Camilla: [Indistinct] happy. Oh, don't let's think about Christmas. I can't bear it. [pause] Going to go to sleep? I think you'd better don't you? Darling?

Charles:	[sleepy] Yes, darling?
Camilla:	I think you've exhausted yourself by all that hard work. You must go to sleep now. Darling?
Charles:	[sleepy] Yes, darling?
Camilla:	Will you ring me when you wake up?
Charles:	Yes I will.
Camilla:	Before I have these rampaging children around. It's Tom's birthday tomorow [pause]. You all right?
Charles:	Mm, I'm all right.
Camilla:	Can I talk to you, I hope, before all those rampaging children ...
Charles:	What time do they come in?
Camilla:	Well usually Tom never wakes up at all, but as it's his birthday tomorrow he might just stagger out of bed. It won't be before half past eight. [pause] Night, night, my darling.
Charles:	... Darling ...
Camilla:	I do love you.
Charles:	[sleepily] Before ...
Camilla:	Before half past eight.
Charles:	Try and ring?
Camilla:	Yeah, if you can. Love you darling.
Charles:	Night darling.
Camilla:	I love you.
Charles:	Love you too. I don't want to say goodbye.
Camilla:	Well done for doing that. You're a clever old thing. An awfully good brain lurking there, isn't there? Oh darling. I think you ought to give the brain a rest now. Nightnight.
Charles:	Night darling, God bless.
Camilla:	I do love you and I'm so proud of you.
Charles:	Oh, I'm so proud of you.
Camilla:	Don't be so silly, I've never achieved anything.
Charles:	Yes you have.
Camilla:	No I haven't.

Charles: Your great achievement is to love me.

Camilla: Oh darling, easier than falling off a chair.

Charles: You suffer all these indignities and tortures and calumnies.

Camilla: Oh darling, don't be so silly. I'd suffer anything for you. That's love. It's the strength of love. Night night.

Charles: Night darling. Sounds as though you're dragging an enormous piece of string behind you with hundreds of tin pots and cans attached to it. I think it must be your telephone. Night night, before the battery goes. [blows kiss] Night.

Camilla: Love you.

Charles: Don't want to say goodbye.

Camilla: Neither do I, but you must get some sleep. Bye.

Charles: Bye, darling.

Camilla: Love you.

Charles: Bye.

Camilla: Hopefully talk to you in the morning.

Charles: Please.

Camilla: Bye, I do love you.

Charles: Night

Camilla: Night. Love you forever.

Charles: Night.

Camilla: G'bye. Bye my darling.

Charles: Night.

Camilla: Night night.

Charles: Night.

Camilla: Bye bye.

Charles: Going.

Camilla: Bye.

Charles: Going.

Camilla: Gone.

Charles: Night.

Camilla: Bye. Press the button.

Charles: Going to press the tit.

Camilla: All right darling, I wish you were pressing mine.

Charles: God, I wish I was. Harder and harder.

Camilla: Oh darling.

Charles: Night.

Camilla: Night.

Charles: Love you.

Camilla: [yawning] Love you. Press the tit.

Charles: Adore you. Night.

Camilla: Night.

Charles: Night.

Camilla: [blows a kiss]

Charles: Night.

Camilla: G'night my darling. Love you ...

Charles hangs up.

The 'Squidgy' Tape

The following is a transcript of a telephone conversation between the Princess of Wales and James Gilbey, recorded 31 December 1989.

James: And so darling, what other lows today?

Diana: So that was it ... I was very bad at lunch. And I nearly started blubbing. I just felt really sad and empty, and I thought, 'Bloody hell, after all I've done for this fucking family.'

James: You don't need to. Cause there are people out there – and I've said this before – who will replace the emptiness. With all sorts of things.

Diana: I needn't ask horoscopes, but it is just so desperate. Always being innuendo, the fact that I'm going to do something dramatic because I can't stand the confines of this marriage.

James: I know.

Diana: But I know much more than they because ...

James: Well, interestingly enough, that thing in *The People* didn't imply either one of you.

Diana: No.

James: So I wouldn't worry about that. I think it's common knowledge, darling, and amongst most people, that you obviously don't have ...

Diana: A rapport?

James: Yeah, I think that comes through loud and clear. Darling, just forgetting that for moment, how is Mara?

Diana: She's all right. No. She's fine. She can't wait to get back.

James: Can't she? When's she coming back?

Diana: Saturday.

James: Is she?

Diana: Mmmmm.

James: I thought it was next Saturday.

Diana: No, Saturday.

James: Not quite as soon as you thought it was.

Diana: No.

James: Is she having a nice time?

Diana: Very nice.

James: Is she?

Diana: I think so. She's out of London. It gives her a bit of a rest.

James: Yeah. Can't imagine what she does the whole time.

Diana: No.

James: The restaurant. If you have a restaurant, it's so much a part of your life, isn't it?

Diana: I know, people around you all the time.

James: That's right. The constant bossing and constant ordering and constant sort of fussing. And she hasn't got that. She's probably been twiddling her fingers wondering what to do.

Diana: Hmmmmm.

James: Going to church every day.

Diana: I know.

James: Did you go to church today?

Diana: Yes, I did.

James: Did you, Squidge?

Diana: Yes.

James: Did you say lots of prayers?

Diana: Of course.

James: Did you? Kiss me, darling. [Sound of kisses being blown]

Diana: [laughing, returns kiss]

James: I can't tell what a smile that has put on my face. I can't tell you. I was like a sort of caged rat and Tony said: 'You are in a terrible hurry to go.' And I said, 'Well I've got things to do when I get there.' Oh God, [sighs] I am not going to leave the phone in the car any more, darling.

Diana: No, please don't.

James: No, I won't. And if it rings and someone says, 'What on earth is your telephone ringing for?' I will say, 'Oh, someone's got a wrong number or something.'

Diana: No, say one of your relations is not very well and your mother is just ringing in to give you progress.

James: All right, so I will keep it near me, quite near to me tomorrow, because her father hates phones out shooting.

Diana: Oh, you are shooting tomorrow, are you?

James: Yeah. And darling, I will be back in London tomorrow night.

Diana: Good.

James: All right?

Diana: Yes.

James: Back on home territory, so no more awful breaks.

Diana: No.

James: I don't know what I'd do. Do you know, darling, I couldn't sort of face the thought of not speaking to you every moment. If fills me with real horror, you know.

Diana: It's purely mutual.

James: Is it? I really hate the idea of it, you know. It makes me really sort of scared.

Diana: There was something really strange. I was leaning over the fence yesterday, looking into Park House and I thought, 'Oh, what shall I do?' And I thought, 'Well, my friend would say go in and do it,' I thought, 'No, cause I am a bit shy' and there were hundreds of people in there. So I thought 'Bugger that.' So I went round to the front door and walked straight in.

James: Did you?

Diana: It was just so exciting.

James: How long were you there for?

Diana: An hour and a half.

James: Were you?

Diana: Mmmmm. And they were so sweet. They wanted their photographs taken with me and they kept hugging me. They were very ill, some of them. Some no legs and all sorts of things.

James: Amazing, Leonard Cheshire.

Diana: Isn't he.

James: Yeah, amazing – quite extraordinary. He devoted himself to setting up those homes. To achieve everything, I think it's amazing. Sort of devotion to a cause.

Diana: I know.

James: Darling, no sort of awful feelings of guilt, or …

Diana: None at all.

James: Remorse?

Diana: None. None at all.

James: Good.

Diana: No, none at all. All's well.

James: O.K. then, Squidgy. I am sorry you have had low times … try darling, when you get these urges – you just try to replace them with anger, like you did on Friday night, you know.

Diana: I know. But do you know what's really quite, um … whatever the word is? His grandmother is always looking at me with a strange look in her eyes. It's not hatred, it's sort of interest and pity mixed into one. I am not quite sure. I don't understand it. Every time I look up, she's looking at me and then looks away and smiles.

James: Does she?

Diana: Yes. I don't know what's going on.

James: I should say to her one day, 'I can't help but ask you. You are always looking at me. What is it? What are you thinking?' You must, darling. And interestingly enough, one of the things said to me today is that you are going to start standing up for yourself.

Diana: Yes.

James: Mmm. We all know that you are very capable of that, old Bossy Boots.

Diana: I know, yes.

James: What have you had on today? What have you been wearing?

Diana: A pair of black jodhpur things on at the moment and a pink polo neck.

James: Really. Looking good?

Diana: Yes.

James: Are you?

Diana: Yes.

James: Dead good?

Diana: I think it's good.

James: You do?

Diana: Yes.

James: And what on your feet?

Diana: A pair of flat black pumps.

James: Very chic.

Diana: Yes [pause in tape]. The redhead is being actually quite supportive.

James: Is she?

Diana: Yes, she has. I don't know why.

James: Don't let the [garbled] down.

Diana: No, I won't. I just talk to her about that side of things.

James: You do? That's all I worry about. I just worry that you know she's sort of ... she's desperately trying to get back in.

Diana: She keeps telling me.

James: She's trying to tag on to your [garbled]. She knows that your PR is so good, she's trying to tag onto that.

Diana: Jimmy Savile rang me up yesterday and he said: 'I'm just ringing up, my girl, to tell you that His Nibs has asked me to come and help out the redhead, and I'm just letting you know so that you don't find out through her or him. And I hope it's all right by you.' And I said, 'Jimmy, you do what you like.'

James: What do you mean, help out the redhead, darling?

Diana: With her publicity.

James: Oh, has he?

Diana: Sort her out. He said, 'you can't change a lame duck, but I've got to talk to her, cause that's the boss's orders and I've got to carry them out. But I want you to know that you're my number-one girl and I'm not ...'

James: Oh darling, that's not fair, you're *my* number-one girl.

Diana: [in the background] Harry, it might be in my bathroom [louder] What did you say? You didn't say anything about babies, did you?

James: No.

Diana: No.

James: Why darling?

Diana: [laughing] I thought you did.

James: Did you?

Diana: Yes.

James: Did you darling? You have got them on the brain.

Diana: Well, yeah, maybe I ... well, actually, I don't think I'm going to be able to for ages.

James: I think you've got bored with the idea, actually.

Diana: I'm going to ...

James: You are, aren't you? It was a sort of hot flush you went through.

Diana: A very hot flush.

James: Darling, when he says His Nibs rang him up, does he mean your other half of PA rang him up?

Diana: Eh? My other half.

James: Your other half.

Diana: Yes.

James: Does he get on well with him?

Diana: Sort of mentor. Talk in the mouthpiece – you moved away.

James: Sorry, darling. I'm resting it on my chin, on my chinless. Oh [sighs], I get so sort of possessive when I see all those pictures of you. I get so possessive, that's the least attractive aspect of me really. I just see them and think, 'Oh, God, if only ...'

Diana: There aren't that many pictures, are there? There haven't been that many.

James: Four or five today.

Diana: Oh.

James: Various magazines. So darling, I ...

Diana: I'm always smiling, aren't I?

James: Always.

Diana: I thought that today.

James: I always told you that. It's the old, what I call the PR package, isn't it? As soon as you sense a camera – I think you can sense a camera at a thousand yards.

Diana: Yes.

James: That smile comes on, and the charm comes out and it stays there all the time, and then it goes away again. But darling, how was your tea party?

Diana: It was all right. Nicholas was there and his girlfriend Charlotte Hambro. Do you know Charlotte?

James: Yes. She was there, was she? How was that?

Diana: It was all right. I went in terrific form.

James: Where are they staying then? Nicholas's?

Diana: They are all staying with her sister down the other side of Fakenham.

James: Oh, Jeremy?

Diana: Yes.

James: Was he there?

Diana: Yes. Difficult man.

James: Very difficult man. I saw him at the ballet the other night.

Diana: Oh, he's always there.

James: Yes, always. So quite a long drive, then?

Diana: Yes. But the great thing is, I went in and made a lot of noise and came out.

James: Were they all very chatty?

Diana: Yes. Very very very.

James: Very kowtowing?

Diana: Oh yes.

James: Were they?

Diana: Yes. All that.

James: Darling, you said all your yesses and no's, pleases and thank yous. You stared at the floor and there were moments of silence ...

Diana: No, no, no, no. I kept the conversation going.

James: Did you?

Diana: Yes.

James: What about?

Diana: Oh God, anything.

James: What's she like? His wife looks quite tough

Diana: Suzanne? I think she's quite tough. I think she's given quite a tough time.

James: Is she?

Diana: Yes.

James: So there with Charlotte and Willy Peel.

Diana: Yep.

James: I don't know him at all.

Diana: She's a very sexy number.

James: Quite. Bit worn out I reckon.

Diana: [laughs]

James: Bit worn out. I reckon, darling. I wish we were going to be together tonight.

Diana: I know. I want you to think of me after midnight. Are you staying up to see the New Year in?

James: You don't need to encourage me to think about you. I have done nothing else for the last three months. Hello.

Diana: Debbie says you are going to go through a transformation soon.

James: I am?

Diana: Yes. She says you are going to go through bits and pieces and I've got to help you through them. All Libra men, yeah. I said, 'Great, I can do something back for him. He's done so much for me.'

James: Are you Squidgy? Laugh some more. I love it when I hear you laughing. It makes me really happy when you laugh. Do you know I am happy when you are happy?

Diana: I know you are.

James: And I cry when you cry.

Diana: I know. So sweet. The rate we are going, we won't need any dinner on Tuesday.

James: No, I won't need any dinner actually. Just seeing you will be all I need. I can't wait for Ken to ring. And I will be thinking of you after twelve o'clock. I don't need any reasons to even think about you. Mark Davis kept saying to me yesterday, 'Of course you haven't had a girlfriend for ages. What's the transfer list looking like? What about the woman in Berkshire.'

Diana: Oh God.

James: And I said, 'No Mark, I haven't been there for months.' He said, 'Have you got any transferees in mind?' I said no. We then went off on a walk and we started talking about Guy Morrison. He was telling me how extraordinary Guy had behaved towards me at Julia's party. And he said, 'Oh well, the only reason he probably didn't want to speak to you was because you had been speaking to you-know-who for a long time.' And so I just didn't sort of say anything. And

I said, 'I suppose that is my fatal mistake.' And Mark said, 'You spend too much time with her' and that was that. Then he said, 'I wonder whom she's going to end up with?' And I said, 'What do you mean?' And he said, 'Well, she must be long overdue for an affair.' And I said, 'I've no idea. I don't talk to her about it. And I have only spoken to her twice since I saw her.' And that was it. I just kill every conversation stone dead now. It's much the best way.

Darling, how did I get on to that? Oh, the transfer list. So I said no, there was no list drawn up at the moment. And even less likely there was anybody on it. I tell you, darling. I couldn't. I was just think again about your going all jellybags, and you mustn't.

Diana: I haven't for a day.

James: You haven't?

Diana: For a day.

James: For a day. Why? Because you have no other people in the room. There were only three of us there last night. Four, actually, Mark, Antonia, their nanny and myself, and that was it. And I definitely didn't fancy the nanny, who was a twenty-three-year-old overweight German.

Diana: Did you just get my hint about Tuesday night? I think you just missed it. Think what I said.

James: No.

Diana: I think you have missed it.

James: No, you said, 'At this rate, we won't want anything to eat.'

Diana: Yes.

James: Yes I know. I got there.

Diana: Oh well, you didn't exactly put the flag out.

James: What, the surrender flag?

Diana: Oh.

James: Squidge, I was just going over it. I don't think I made too much reference to it.

Diana: Oh bugger.

James: I don't think I made too much reference to it. Because the more you think about it, the more you worry about it.

Diana: All right. I haven't been thinking a lot else.

James: Haven't you?

Diana: No.

James: Well I can tell you, that makes two ... I went to this agonizing tea party last night. You know all I want to do is get in my car and drive around the country talking to you.

Diana: Thanks. [laughter]

James: That's all I want to do, darling. I just want to see you and be with you. That's what's going to be such bliss, being back in London.

Diana: I know.

James: I mean, it can't be a regular future, darling, I understand that, but it would be nice if you are at least next door, within knocking distance.

Diana: Yes.

James: What's that noise?

Diana: The television, drowning my conversation.

James: Can you turn it down?

Diana: No.

James: Why?

Diana: Because it's covering my conversation.

James: All right ... I got there Tuesday night, don't worry. I got there. I can tell you the feeling's entirely mutual. Ummmm, Squidgy ... what else? It's just like unwinding now. I am just letting my heartbeat come down again now. I had the most amazing dream about us last night. Not physical, nothing to do with that.

Diana: That makes a change.

James: Darling, it's just that we were together an awful lot of time and we were having dinner with some people. It was the most extraordinary dream, because I woke up in the morning and I remembered all aspects of it. All bits of it. I remembered sort of what you were wearing and what you had said. It was so strange, very strange and very lovely, too.

Diana: [unclear]

James: [sighing] Squidgy ... kiss me [sounds of kisses by him and her]. Oh God, it's wonderful isn't it? This sort of feeling. Don't you like it?

Diana: I love it.

James: Um.

Diana: I love it.

James: Isn't it absolutely wonderful? I haven't had it for years. I feel about twenty-one again.

Diana: Well you're not. You're thirty-three.

James: I know.

Diana: Pushing up the daisies soon, right?

James: No more remarks like that. It was an agonizing tea yesterday with, er, do you know Simon Prior Palmer?

Diana: I know who you mean, yes.

James: And his wife Julia. Julia Lloyd-Jordan, you must remember her?

Diana: Yes, I dooooo.

James: Do you?

Diana: God, yes ... who was she after – Eddie?

James: I can't remember. She lived in that flat in Cadogan Gardens, didn't she, with Lucy Manners.

Diana: Yes, she did.

James: She lost weight. You lived there for a while, didn't you?

Diana: No, it's the wrong place [garbled]

James: Oh! But the ummm ... honestly, I loved going to [garbled] I mean, they've got quite a nice house and things. And there was quite a nice Australian/Polish friend of theirs who was staying. And God – Simon! He's thirty-eight years old, but

honestly, he behaves older than my father. I cannot believe
it. I find it so exhausting when there's people that age. They
behave as if they're fifty.

Diana: I know.

James: Anyway, we did time there. And that was it. We got back.
A very nice quiet dinner. Mark was sort of exhausted from
last night. And that was it really. He was talking about
hunting ... hunting gets you gripped, doesn't it?

Diana: It does.

James: I mean, he drove six hours yesterday.

Diana: [laughter] My drive was two and a half to three.

James: He's now talking about both ways. He drives three hours
from Hungerford. He was hunting with – can't remember
who he was hunting with – oh yes, the Belvoir yesterday.

Diana: The Belvoir, ummmm.

James: That was three hours there and three hours back.

Diana: God.

James: And he'd done the same on Wednesday to the Quorn.

Diana: How wonderful.

James: Ummm, tell me some more. How was your lunch?

Diana: It wasn't great.

James: Wasn't it? When are the Waterhouses turning up?

Diana: Next Thursday, I think.

James: Oh, I thought they were coming today.

Diana: No, Thursday.

James: To hold on to you, I've gone back to another point
about your mother-in-law, no, grandmother-in-law, no, your
grandmother-in-law. I think next time, you just want to
either out stare her and that's easy.

Diana: No, no.

James: It's not staring ...

Diana: No, no listen – wait a minute. It's affection, affection – it's
definitely affection. It's sort of ... it's not hostile, anyway.

James: Oh, isn't it?

Diana: No. She's sort of fascinated by me, but doesn't quite know how to unravel it, no.

James: How interesting. I'm sorry, I thought, darling, when you told me about her, you meant hostile.

Diana: No, I'm all right.

James: I miss you, Squidgy.

Diana: So do I.

James: I haven't spoken to you for twenty-eight hours. I've thought of nothing else.

Diana: I know, I know.

James: Oh, that's all right. If it's friendly, then it doesn't matter.

Diana: My stars said nothing about 1990 – it was all sort of terribly general.

James: Fine, but it's definitely him *within* the marriage.

Diana: Right.

James: It's not ...

Diana: [interrupting] Did you see the *News of the World*?

James: No. He's got to start loving you.

Diana: Yes, I saw that. Yeah. She ...

James: Did you? I thought, 'Well, there's not much chance of that.'

Diana: No. I know. I know. But, um, definitely she said I am doing nothing. I am just having a wonderful, successful well awaiting year.

James: A sort of matriarchal figure.

Diana: I know. She said, anything you want, you can get next year.

James: You should read *The People*, darling. There's a very good picture of you.

Diana: Arr.

James: Oh no, it's ... where is there a good picture? In the *Express*, was there? I think there's a ... wearing that pink, very smart pink top. That excellent pink top.

Diana: Oh, I know, I know.

James: Do you know the one I mean?

Diana: I know.

-253-

James: Very good. Shit hot, actually.

Diana: Shit hot. [laughs]

James: Shit hot.

Diana: Umm. Fergie said to me today that she had lunch with Nigel Havers the other day and all he could talk about was you. And I said, 'Fergie, oh how awful for you.' And she said, 'Don't worry, it's the admiration club.' A lot of people talk to her about me, which she can't help.

James: I tell you, darling, she is desperate to tag on to your coat tails.

Diana: Well, she can't.

James: No, she absolutely can't. Now you have to make that quite clear …

Diana: If you want to be like me, you have got to suffer.

James: Oh Squidgy!

Diana: Yeah. You have to. And then you get what you …

James: Get what you want.

Diana: No. Get what you deserve, perhaps.

James: Yes, such as a second-hand car dealer. [laughs]

Diana: Yes, I know. [laughs]

James: [laughs] Do you know, as we go into 1990, honey. I can't imagine, you know, what it was that brought us two together in that night.

Diana: No, I know.

James: And let's make full use of it.

Diana: I know.

James: Full use of it. Funnily enough, it doesn't hold any sort of terror, any fright for me at all.

Diana: [sound of knock on the door] Hang on. It's O.K. – come in, please. Yes, it's O.K. – come in. What is it? Ah, I'd love some salad, just some salad with yoghurt, like when I was ill in bed. That would be wonderful about eight o'clock. Then everybody can go, can't they?

Male voice: Bring it up on a tray?

Diana: That would be great. Edward will come down and get it.

Male voice: We'll bring it up.

Diana: All right, bring it up. That'll be great, Paul. No, just salad will be great, Paul. Thanks, Paul.

James: How much weight have you lost?

Diana: Why?

James: Darling, I'm sure lettuce leaves aren't going to keep you strong. You'll run out of energy driving to London.

Diana: I am nine-and-a-half.

James: Are you? Are you? Nine-and-a-half? So are you staying in tonight?

Diana: I am, because I am babysitting. I don't want to go out.

James: Oh, I see. So is he going?

Diana: Yes. He doesn't know that I'm not yet. I haven't told him that yet.

James: I was going to say, darling. That was shitty. You can't face another night like last Friday, absolutely right. But you are there, darling.

Diana: I know.

James: 1990 is going to be fine.

Diana: Yes, but isn't it exciting.

James: Really exciting.

Diana: Debbie said, I'm so excited for you. It's going to be lovely to watch …

James: I don't know, I've been feeling sick all day.

Diana: Why?

James: I don't know. I just feel sick about the whole thing. I mean wonderful. I mean straight-through real passion and love and all the good things.

Diana: Becky said it would all be O.K., didn't she? The most fulfilling year yet.

James: You don't need to worry, do you?

Diana: She's never questioned someone's mental state, or anything like that.

James: What, his?

Diana: Yes. Nobody has ever thought about his mind. They've always thought about other things.

James: [garbled] ... something very interesting which said that serious astrologers don't think that he will ever make it.

Diana: Yeah.

James: And becomes a [garbled]

Diana: And Becky also said this person is married to someone in great power who will never make the ultima ... or whatever the word is.

James: Absolutely. Oh Squidgy, I love you, love you, love you.

Diana: You are the nicest person in the whole wide world.

James: Pardon?

Diana: Nicest person in the whole wide world.

James: Well darling, you are to me, too. Sometimes.

Diana: [laughs] What do you mean, sometimes?

James: What?

Diana: I'm sorry.

James: No, I'm not actually.

Diana: I said, it's just like, it's just like ...

James: Playing with yourself.

Diana: Yes.

James: Nice quite as nice. Not quite as nice. No, I haven't played with myself actually. Not for a full forty-eight hours. Not for a full forty-eight hours.

James: It was very strange, very strange and very lovely too.

Diana: I watched Eastenders today.

James: It was very strange, very strange and very lovely too.

Diana: I don't want to get pregnant.

James: Darling, that's not going to happen. All right?

Diana: (Chuckle) Yeah.

James: Don't think like that. It's not going to happen, darling. You won't get pregnant.

Diana: I watched Eastenders today. One of the main characters had a baby. They thought it was by her husband. It was by another man. (laughs).

James: Squidgy, kiss me. [Kissing sound down telephone].

James: Ohhh G-o-d!

James: I got up quite late, went for a walk this morning and this afternoon. Had lunch. I only got angry because Mark gave the nanny too much wine and she was incapable of helping at lunch.

Diana: I love it.

James: He's a rogue, Mark David ... [garbled]

Diana: Oh, Wills is coming. Sorry.

James: Are you going?

Diana: No, no.

James: He's such a rogue, darling. He's the man you met.

Diana: I remember. But I didn't recognize him.

James: He's incorrigible.

Diana: Would I like him?

James: He's a sort of social gossiper in a way. He loves all that, Mark. He's got a very comfortable life, you know. He hunts a lot.

Diana: He's got the pennies?

James: He's got lots of pennies. He calls all the horses Business or The Office because when people ring him up and he's hunting midweek, his secretary says, 'I'm sorry, he's away on Business.'

Diana: [laughs] It's great to hear it.

James: But, ummm ... an incredible, sort of argument last night about subservient women in marriage.

Diana: Well, you're an expert.

James: I kept very quiet actually. I could think darling, of nothing but you. I thought, 'Well I should be talking to her now.' You know it's five past eleven.

Diana: I know.

James: You don't mind it, darling, when I want to talk to you so much?

Diana: No. I *love* it. Never had it before.

James: Darling, it's so nice being able to help you.

Diana: You do. You'll never know how much.

James: Oh, I will darling. I just feel so close to you, so wrapped up in you. I'm wrapping you up, protecting.

Diana: Yes please. Yes please. Do you know, that bloody Bishop, I said to him …

James: What's he called?

Diana: The Bishop of Norwich. He said, 'I want you to tell me how you talk to people who are ill or dying. How do you cope?'

James: He wanted to learn. He was so hopeless at it himself.

Diana: I began to wonder after I'd spoken to him. I said, I'm just myself.

James: They can't get to grips that, underneath, there is such a beautiful person in you. They can't think that it isn't cluttered up by this idea of untold riches.

Diana: I know. He kept wittering about one must never think how good one is at one's job. There's always something you can learn around the next corner. I said, 'Well, if people know me, they know I'm like that.'

James: Yes, absolutely right. So did you give him a hard time?

Diana: I did, actually. In the end I said, 'I know this sounds crazy, but I've lived before.' He said, 'How do you know?' I said, 'Because I'm a wise old thing.'

James: Oh, darling Squidge, did you? Very brave thing to say to him, actually. Very.

Diana: It was, wasn't it?

James: Very Full marks. Ninety-nine out of a hundred.

Diana: I said, 'Also, I'm aware that people I have loved and have died and are in the spirit world look after me.' He looked horrified. I thought, 'If he's the Bishop, He should say that sort of thing.'

James: One of those horoscopes referred to you – to Cancerians turning to less materialistic and more spiritual things. Did you see that?

Diana: No, I didn't. No.

James: That's rather sad, actually. Umm, I don't really like many of those Bishops especially.

Diana: Well, I felt very uncomfortable.

James: They are a funny old lot.

Diana: Well. I wore my heart on my sleeve.

James: They are the ones, when they've got a five-year-old sitting between the, their hands meet. Don't you remember that wonderful story?

Diana: Yes, yes.

James: Gosh, it made my father laugh so much. Go on, darling. When you wear your heart on sleeve ...

Diana: No, with the Bishop, I said, 'I understand people's suffering, people's pain, more than you will ever know.' And he said, 'That's obvious by what you are doing for the AIDS.' I said, 'It's not only AIDS, it's anyone who suffers. I can smell them a mile away.'

James: What did he say?

Diana: Nothing. He just went quiet. He changed the subject to toys. And I thought, 'Ah! Defeated you.'

James: Did you? Marvellous, darling. Did you chalk up a little victory?

Diana: Yes, I did.

James: Did you, darling? Waving a little flag in your head.

Diana: Yes.

James: How marvellous. You ought to do that more often. That flag ought to get bigger.

Diana: Yes, my surrender flag. [laughs]

James: You haven't got one, have you?

Diana: Yes.

James: What, a big one?

Diana: Well, medium.

James: Is it? Well, don't wave it too much.

Diana: No.

James: Squidge, in this lay-by, you know, people understand how frightened people feel when they break down in the dark.

Diana: I'm sure.

James: I suddenly thought someone could have a shot at me from the undergrowth. Or someone suddenly tried to get into the car. I always lock the door for that reason.

Diana: Gosh! That's very thoughtful. That's very good of you.

James: I know. Darling, how are the boys?

Diana: Very well.

James: Are they having a good time?

Diana: Yes, very happy. Yeah. Seem to be.

James: That's nice. Have you been looking after them today?

Diana: Well, I've been with them a lot, yes.

James: Has he been looking after them?

Diana: Oh no, not really. My God, you know ...

James: Have you seen him at all today, apart from lunch?

Diana: I have. We went out to tea. It's just so difficult, so complicated. He makes my life real, real torture, I've decided.

James: Tell me more.

Diana: But the distancing will be because I go out and – I hate the word – conquer the world. I don't mean that, I mean I'll go out and do my bit in the way I know how and I leave him behind. That's what I see happening.

James: Did you talk in the car?

Diana: Yes, but nothing in particular. He said he didn't want to go out tonight.

James: Did you have the kids with you?

Diana: No.

James: What, you just went by yourselves?

Diana: No, they were behind us.

James: Oh, were they? How did he enjoy it?

Diana: I don't know. He didn't really comment.

James: No. Oh, Squidgy.

Diana: Mmmmm.

James: Kiss me please [sound of kisses]. Do you know what I'm going to be imagining I'm doing tonight, at about twelve o'clock. Just holding you close to me. It'll have to be delayed action for forty-eight hours.

Diana: [laughs]

James: Fast forward.

Diana: Fast forward.

James: Gosh, I hope Ken doesn't say no.

Diana: I doubt he will.

James: Do you?

Diana: He's coming down on Tuesday and I'm going to tell him. I've got to go back on Tuesday night. And I've got to leave and be back for lunch on Wednesday. But I can do that.

James: You can?

Diana: And I shall tell people I'm going for acupuncture and my back being done.

James: [laughs] Squidge, cover them footsteps.

Diana: I jolly well do.

James: I think it's all right. I think those footsteps are doing all right.

Diana: Well, I've got to kiss my small ones.

James: Oh no, darling.

Diana: I've got to.

James: No, Squidgy, I don't want you to go. Can you bear with me for five minutes more?

Diana: Yes.

James: Just five.

Diana: What have you got on?

James: I've got the new jeans I bought yesterday.

Diana: Good.

James: Green socks. White and pink shirt.

Diana: How very nice.

James: A dark apple-green V-neck jersey.

Diana: Yes.

James: I'm afraid I'm going to let you down by the shoes.

Diana: Go on, then. [laughs]

James: You can guess.

Diana: Your brown ones [laughs]. No, those black ones.

James: No, I haven't got the black ones, darling. The black ones I would not be wearing. I only wear the black ones with my suit.

Diana: Good. Well, get rid of them.

James: I have got those brown suede ones on.

Diana: Brown suede ones?

James: Those brown suede Guccis. [laughs]

Diana: I know, I know.

James: The ones you hate.

Diana: I just don't like the fact it's so obvious where they came from.

James: Di, nobody wears them anymore. I like those ordinary Italian things that last a couple of years, then I chuck them out. It was sort of a devotion to duty. I was seeking an identity when I bought my first pair of Guccis twelve years ago.

Diana: Golly.

James: And I've still got them. Still doing me proud, like.

Diana: Good.

James: I'm going to take you up on that, darling. I will give you some money. You can go off and spend it for me.

Diana: I *will*, yeah.

James: Will you? [laughs]

Diana: I'm a connoisseur in that department.

James: Are you?

Diana: Yes.

James: Well, you think you are.

Diana: Well I've decked people out in my time.

James: Who did you deck out? Not too many, I hope.

Diana: James Hewitt. Entirely dressed him from head to foot, that man. Cost me quite a bit.

James: I bet he did. At your expense?

Diana: Yeah.

James: What, he didn't even pay you to do it?

Diana: No.

James: God. Very extravagant, darling.

Diana: Well, I am, aren't I? Anything that will make people happy.

James: No, you mustn't do it for that, darling, because *you* make people happy. It's what you give them ... [interruption in tape]

Diana: No, don't. You'll know, you'll know.

James: All right. But you always say that with an air of inevitability [laughs]. It will happen in six months' time. I'll suddenly get 'Yes, James Who?' [laughs]. I don't think we've spoken before.'

Diana: No.

James: I hope not. Well, darling, you can't imagine what pleasure I've got in store this evening.

Diana: It's a big house, is it?

James: It's a nice house. Thirty people for dinner or something.

Diana: God.

James: I know. Do you want me to leave the phone on?

Diana: No, better not.

James: Why not?

Diana: No, tomorrow morning.

James: I can't, I can't ... all right, tomorrow morning. Shall I give you a time to call?

Diana: Yes, I won't be around from nine-thirty to eleven.

James: Why not?

Diana: I'm going swimming with Fergie.

James: Are you? Are you taking the kiddies?

Diana: Might well do.

James: You should do. It's good for you. Get them out. It gives you enormous strength, doesn't it? Have the lovebugs around you.

Diana: I know, I know.

James: Beautiful things pampering their mother.

Diana: Quite right.

James: That's what she wants. I think you should take them darling. At least you are not breaking with the rest.

Diana: No, I'm not.

James: Are you ... [interruption in tape]

Diana: I'd better, I'd better. All the love in the world. I'll speak to you tomorrow.

James: All right. If you can't get me in the morning ... you're impatient to go now.

Diana: Well, I just feel guilty because I haven't done my other business.

James: Don't feel guilty. They'll be quite all ... [interruption in tape]

Just have to wait till Tuesday. All right.

Diana: All right.

James: I'll buzz off and simply behave. I'll approach the evening with such enormous confidence now.

Diana: Good.

James: And you, darling. Don't let it get you down.

Diana: I won't. I won't.

James: All right.